THE WOMEN AN

THE WOMEN AND MEN OF 1926

THE GENERAL STRIKE AND MINERS' LOCKOUT IN SOUTH WALES

SUE BRULEY

CARDIFF
UNIVERSITY OF WALES PRESS

www.uwp.co.uk

British Library Cataloguing-in-Publication Data.
A catalogue record for this book is available from the British Library.

ISBN 978-0-7083-2450-9
e-ISBN 978-0-7083-2451-6

Printed and bound by CPI Group (UK) Ltd, Croydon, CR0 4YY.

CONTENTS

ACKNOWLEDGEMENTS

I would like to take this opportunity to say a very big public thank you to everyone who has helped me on this project. My colleagues at the University of Portsmouth have been very supportive, particularly Brad Beaven, David Andress, James Thomas, June Purvis and Maureen Wright who expertly proofread the manuscript. Bill Johnson, map librarian, made the excellent illustration of the coalfield. Peter Sparkes gave me technical help with the photographs. The inter-library loan staff at the University of Portsmouth have always done their best to meet my many requests. I am very grateful to the anonymous reader from the University of Wales Press who proved to be of invaluable assistance in preparing the final manuscript.

During all my trips to Wales I was given unfailing assistance from the excellent library and archive staff at the South Wales Miners Library, local libraries in Treorchy, Aberdare, Pontypridd and Bridgend, Glamorgan and Gwent Record Offices and the National Library of Wales. Sue Thomas and Elisabeth Bennett were fantastically helpful in the archives of the South Wales Coal Collection at Swansea University. Many people in Wales helped me to meet elderly people to interview. Through personal contacts I met Ann Heathley and Ken Stone who set me on the road to Pontycymer and the wonderful Eileen Price (and her son Wyn) and from there I developed other contacts. I also quickly learnt that wardens in sheltered housing in south Wales are a wonderful breed of women who provide an endless flow of loving support for their residents, going well beyond the call of duty. In particular, I would like to thank Chris Hall and Karen Robbins. Most of all, I must thank all the people who agreed to tell me their stories. I enjoyed listening to every one of them. Lizzie Davies and Gladys Davies (and great niece Linda Williams) allowed me to use treasured family photographs. Friends in *Llafur* always responded to my many queries and requests for help, particularly Neil Evans, Angela V. John and Steven Thompson. I also owe a huge debt to the late Ursula Masson who is sorely missed. During my time in Swansea, Jane and Paul Elliot welcomed me into their home which made intensive research trips a great deal more enjoyable.

Paul Thompson inspired me to be an oral historian. The work of Hywel Francis was important to me in deciding to write this book. Alan Campbell's enthusiasm for my earlier work on women in south Wales set me out on this road, so I must thank him for reviving my interest in this research.

Research can be a lonely business and without the love and support of friends and family I could not have completed this project. I would like to thank in particular Meg Arnot, Valerie-Anne Baker, Sarah Booker, Martin Durham, Sue Harper, Brenda Kirsch, Sue Laurence, Jane Lewis, Siri Lowe, Fred Milsom, Mary Nixon, Mari Reynolds, John Shiers, Roger and Sally Thomas, Jeffrey Weeks and Paulene Wilkinson. Last, but not least I would like to thank my children Eric, Charlotte and Rowan for just being there for me.

FORMAL ACKNOWLEDGEMENTS

The University of Portsmouth gave me a sabbatical semester 2004–5 which enabled me to complete the research and begin writing up the book.

The Scouloudi Fund, University of London provided financial assistance with research trips to Wales. The National Museum of Wales supplied the image of coal miners at work (F74.372/94) and the image of Evan Jones bathing with wife assisting (96.702–3.60). Bridgend Library supplied the picture of Ffaldau Girls School, Pontycymer, from the Valley and Vale Collection. The photograph of Llwyncelyn Ladies v Gents Football Match is taken from Aldo Bachetta and Glyn Rudd's *Porth and Rhondda Fach* and is not in copyright.

The South Wales Coal Collection at Swansea University supplied the following photographs, all of which are believed to have been taken in 1926: Banwen Staff Canteen PHO/DIS/43; Penybont Colliery PHO/COL/79; Dulais Colliery miners eating PHO/DIS/49; Salem staff canteen committee PHO/DIS/45; St Athan summer camp

PHOT/REC/63; Tredegar Jazz Band PHO/REC/2/47; Treorchy Zulu Jazz Band PHO/REC/2/49; Gwendraeth Valley poachers PHOT/TOP/1/38; Miners Singing in Piccadilly Circus, London PHO/DIS/41.

Thanks to John Batstone for permission to reproduce the Treorchy Zulu picture and the miners singing in London.

Thanks to Lowri Newman for allowing me to use two images from her PowerPoint presentation on Women and Labour Politics 1918–39. These contemporary images were originally published in *Labour Woman*.

There are instances where we have been unable to trace or contact the copyright holder. If notified, the publisher will be pleased to rectify any errors or omissions at the earliest opportunity.

Some photographs are understood to be taken in 1926 but cannot be verified as such, in which case I have put '*c.*1926'.

ABBREVIATIONS

CLC	Central Labour College
CPGB	Communist Party of Great Britain
CWM	Colliery Workers Magazine
GRO	Glamorgan Record Office
ILP	Independent Labour Party
JP	Justice of the Peace
LMU	London Metropolitan University
MFGB	Mineworkers' Federation of Great Britain
NLW	National Library of Wales
NUM	National Union of Mineworkers
NUWSS	National Union of Women's Suffrage Societies
RUDC	Rhondda Urban District Council
SWCC	South Wales Coal Collection
SWMF	South Wales Miners' Federation
SWML	South Wales Miners' Library
TNA	The National Archive
TUC	Trades Union Congress
UAB	Unemployment Assistance Board
UDC	Urban District Council
WCRMWC	Women's Committee for the Relief of Miners' Wives and Children
WGE	Women's Guild of Empire

Map of the South Wales coalfield showing places mentioned in the text

1

INTRODUCTION

The British economy before 1914 was heavily dependent on exports. One third of all manufactured goods were for export, with coal, shipbuilding and cotton being the leading export industries. There were over a million miners in Britain in 1914. The rise of overseas competition and increasing use of oil as an alternative fuel was, however, gradually eroding the pre-eminent position of coal. During the First World War the declining fortunes of the coal industry were masked by government protection. After the war the Mineworkers' Federation of Great Britain (MFGB) pressed for the industry to be taken into public ownership and reorganised. The government was only prepared to countenance temporary subsidies rather than wholesale nationalisation. After the speculative boom of 1919–20 collapsed, the export price of coal slumped and the industry was in serious trouble. Government and mineowners sought to restore profitability by imposing wage cuts. The pre-war trade union movement had begun to make alliances across industrial sectors to form the Triple Alliance of miners, railwaymen and transport workers, but when it came to the crunch in 1921, the alliance disintegrated. After Black Friday, as 15 April became known, the miners were left to fight alone. After eleven weeks of lockout, the miners were forced to give in and accept wage cuts. During 1923–4 the coal industry made a brief recovery, largely due to the artificial stimulus to production created by the French occupation of the Ruhr cutting off the flow of German exports. There was much unease at this time about the influence of revolutionary socialist ideas. The famous Zinoviev letter in late 1924, purporting to show Bolshevik influence on the British labour movement,was proved to be a forgery, but the damage was done and the Red Scare brought about the downfall of MacDonald's minority Labour government in October and created an atmosphere of increased suspicion of trade union power and fear of communist activity.[1]

By 1925, the industry was again in crisis and to make matters worse the government announced in April a return to the pre-war gold standard, rendering British exports overvalued and hence even more unprofitable. There was at this time an upsurge in industrial militancy. It was perhaps the last hurrah of really assertive labour power which had its roots in pre-war industrial syndicalism, war time militancy buoyed up by full employment, and the Russian Revolution of 1917. Mine-owners and many in government felt that the deflation (and hence the deliberate creation of unemployment) caused by a return to the normalcy of the pre-war gold standard would be a good method of curbing the growing power of the unions.[2] In June 1925, with the industry losing over a million pounds a month, coalowners posted notices announcing wage cuts of 10–25 per cent. Industrial action was averted by government intervention in the form of a subsidy for nine months and a Royal Commission. The Samuel Commission of March 1926 did not (and could not) solve the industry's problems given the government's rigid approach to economic policy and the determination of both coalowners and government to make the miners pay for the decision to return to the gold standard. New notices of wage cuts, longer hours and an end to national agreements were posted on 30 April.

This time no offers of government subsidies were forth-coming and the Strike, or Lockout as the labour movement referred to it, began from 3 May. Unlike in 1921, the Triple Alliance stood firm and the first line of transport workers and railwaymen came out with the miners, involving just under two million workers.[3] A second line of engineers and shipbuilders was held back, ready to be called out when required. This deci-sion by the Trades Union Congress (TUC) General Council to divide the movement at such a crucial time was criticised by the left wing for undermining the overall effectiveness of the strike. The General Council, unenthusiastic about the strike and carried along only by the Triple Alliance, undertook no preparation whatsoever. Even if the TUC had the will to prepare, there was little in the way of institutional apparatus to draw upon. The General Council had only had had a full-time secretary since 1923.[4] The government, on the other hand, had been preparing for nine months. The Organisation for the Maintenance of Supplies was a regional network of volunteers recruited to break the strike. University students and other volunteers ran trams, buses and trains, often causing serious accidents and damage to the transport infrastructure in the process due to lack of training and expert knowledge. Debutantes and other upper-class women were recruited to run canteens and keep up morale for the strikebreakers. Prime Minister Stanley Baldwin and other members of the Cabinet emphasised that sympathetic strikes were a 'threat to constitutional government'.[5]

Around the country trades councils took over the implementation of the strike in their own localities. There were over 400 trades councils and they varied enormously in their activities during the dispute. In many areas, the main emphasis remained with the individual unions and that was TUC policy, but in others such as the north-east and south Wales the trades councils evolved into councils of action and virtually took over the running of the district, preventing all movement of goods without its authority.[6] By the eighth day it was clear that the progress of the strike was very uneven. There were some signs of disintegration, for example in parts of Birmingham, but in the most militant areas a momentum had been established which led the most left wing elements to refer to a situation of dual power and revolutionary leadership. In reality, it was always an entirely defensive action which the TUC General Council had no interest in fighting. On the ninth day, with the flimsiest of excuses and with no concessions to the miners, the strike was called off by the General Council, leading to shock, bewilderment and cries of betrayal from the most militant sections of the rank and file.[7]

The miners refused to accept defeat and fought on alone. The mineowners became more entrenched and insisted on an eight-hour day, district settlements and wage cuts.

The dispute developed into a war of attrition with both sides possessing a siege mentality.[8] With stockpiles of coal and no effective method of preventing imports, the dice were heavily loaded against the miners, but they were amazingly resilient and determined to hold out. The first cracks began to appear in August with a drift back to work, particularly in the more prosperous coalfields where in the early stages of the dispute coalowners had been much more modest in their demands. One such area was the Midlands where a breakaway 'non-political' union sprang up as a rival to the MFGB. Although Winston Churchill, as Minister of the Board of Trade, made some effort with the mine owners on the whole, the government did little to try and effect a compromise. Finally, in September, Baldwin offered a faint hope of preserving national agreements if the miners accepted longer hours and wage cuts.[9] The miners responded by calling out the pit safety men whose duties were vital to keeping the mines open for work. Numbers of men returning to work drifted steadily upwards during September and October, and in November what began as a trickle became a flood so that by 29 November, the MFGB had no choice but to tell local federations to accept whatever terms they could get for a return to work. Early in December the miners resumed work on the mine owners' terms, defeated and demoralised.

The General Strike and the epic struggle of the miners which followed have long been regarded as seminal events in the history of the twentieth-century labour movement. It is remembered as perhaps the greatest episode in working-class solidarity in British history. Historians writing from a left wing perspective have also been drawn to the leap in class consciousness which occurred in some local areas, transforming the Strike/Lockout from a struggle to defend wages and living standards to the exercise of real workers' power.[10] The vast specialist historiography on this topic, much of which emanates from the 1970s and earlier, focuses very much on the politics of industrial conflict as played out at both national and local levels.[11] Writing in 1990, Keith Laybourn summarised the historiography of the General Strike by reducing it to three debates: first the causes of the dispute; secondly the overall effectiveness of the strike and the notion of a 'betrayal' by the General Council; thirdly the consequences of the failure of the General Strike for the labour movement.[12] This emphasis on traditional labour history left women either invisible or on the margins of the conflict, although attempts were made from a women's history approach by Sarah Boston and Shiela Lewenhak to include women in the General Strike in their more general narratives.[13] Despite the advent of gender history from the late 1980s, there have been no major studies of the social and gender impact of the 1926 dispute, although recently both Ian Haywood and Maroula Joannou have addressed gender aspects of the General Strike through the literature of the period.[14] Ellen Wilkinson's novel *Clash* is perhaps unique in that it develops a socialist-feminist perspective through her heroine, labour activist Joan Craig, who is committed to preserving her independence within marriage.[15] A recent journalistic account by Anne Perkins reflects the decline in labour history since the 1970s by focusing on personal narrative and the absence of violence and serious public disorder during the nine days of the dispute.[16] She underplays class conflict and makes much of good-humoured incidents such as the football match in Plymouth between strikers and police which was watched by a crowd of 10,000.[17] Tapping into recent debates about national identity, she attributes the failure of the strike to the idea that in Britain there is a notion of 'Englishness' which overrides class conflict.[18]

Virtually all the studies of this topic focus heavily on the nine days of the General Strike with little consideration of the seven month Lockout which followed the collapse of the General Strike on 12 May 1926. Until recently the only specialist work on the Lockout was Gerard Noel's forgotten text *The Great Lockout of 1926*.[19] This impressionistic account attempts to incorporate social aspects of the dispute, although even here women make only a fleeting appearance and there is no serious attempt to examine the position of women in the coal field communities. More recently McIlroy, Campbell and Gildart have provided the most serious academic work on the Lockout to date.[20] This edited work brings together an analysis of the conflict and up-to-date scholarship on the various regional struggles in 1926, and breaks new ground in examining other aspects of the dispute, such as the role of women which is the origin of the present book. It was writing the chapter on women and gender in 1926 in the above book that convinced me this topic deserved a more detailed study.

The fundamental aim of this book is to provide a gendered history of the General Strike and Miners' Lockout of 1926.

This topic necessitates a detailed account of gender relations before, during and after the Lockout and this must necessarily be grounded in the more general social history of the dispute. Upon embarking on this research it was immediately obvious that mining communities in Britain were enormously varied in socio-economic composition and cultural practices. It made sense, therefore to make a detailed case study of one particular coalfield. South Wales was chosen as it was the largest and most militant coalfield at this time and has developed a rich historiography.[21] Due to its near mono-industrial base the south Wales coalfield was also the most cohesive. By 1926 it was in decline, which meant that class confrontation was more pronounced than elsewhere. I set out to explore the prevalent notions of masculinity and femininity in south Wales mining communities before the Lockout and to find out if the experience of the Lockout altered these perceptions. To explore this topic I have used a wide variety of sources. I have made use of official records such as Rhondda Urban Council minutes held in the Glamorgan Record Office in Cardiff. I was also fortunate in having access to the South Wales Coalfield Collection held at Swansea University with its invaluable collection of miners' archives. Extensive use has also been made of the contemporary press and autobiographical accounts. The problem for the gender historian is that these written sources very much reflect the male-dominated society of the time. Gender history and particularly the experiences of women cannot be easily accessed from written documents. Women's lives in coalfield communities dominated by heavy domestic labour and patriarchal cultural practices were to a large extent submerged, making the task of uncovering their lives challenging for historians. For this reason, doubts were expressed to me as to whether this project could make a book.[22] What has made this book possible is oral testimony. Hywel Francis has written of the 'secret world of the south Wales miner' revealed by the use of oral testimony.[23] Dai Smith has also written of the exciting potential of oral history in creating an 'imaginative repossession of the past'. This form of integrated history would go beyond narrow institutional-based labour history and depict life for the whole community, capturing

what it was like to stand in drizzling rain in Kenfig Hill in 1928, waiting
amongst bankrupt boarded up shops for an infrequent stuttering bus;
how peeling, green-distempered Institute walls smelled; what it meant
to buy spectacles from a job-lot in a penny Bazaar by a squinting process
of trial and error, and how good a day out at the vulgar, gimcrack
seaside was after years of being hemmed in by the brown-varnished
houses and black tar-papered sheds.[24]

The creation of a history from below or total history as advocated by Hywel Francis, Dai Smith and others, owes something
to the Annales school in France as well as Antonio Gramsci's
theoretical concept of 'hegemony'. It is a powerful concept in
researching gender and social aspects of the Lockout.
Fortunately, a great deal of oral testimony was available for this
project. The South Wales Coalfield History Project headed by
Hywel Francis and R. Merfyn Jones conducted a large number
of interviews in the 1970s and early 1980s, as well as salvaging
miners' written archives. This priceless collection is focused
on the world of men and particularly the miners' lodge but
Francis and Smith went beyond the boundaries of traditional
labour history in an attempt to embrace the whole community. They were particularly keen to document the experience
of women and this is evident in their book, *The Fed: A History of
the South Wales Miners in the Twentieth Century* which contains
much valuable information for the gender historian.[25] Where
possible, I have also accessed other oral history collections
such as the Valley and Vale project in the 1990s which
produced a publication based on people's recollections of life
in the Llynfi, Ogmore and Garw valleys.[26] Sadly, the women
and men of 1926 are no longer with us, but many of the children and young adults of 1926 are still alive. With this in mind,
I conducted my own small-scale oral history project in 2004.
Working through personal contacts and wardens of sheltered
accommodation, I interviewed 23 people.[27] Amazingly, I
discovered that two of my respondents had significant family
backgrounds; Nancy Wood is the daughter of Mark
Harcombe, leading Rhondda councillor in the 1920s and
Lizzie Davies, now sadly passed away, was the daughter of Sam
Davies, secretary of both the Maerdy Miners' Lodge (approximately 2000 members) and the Distress Committee in the
1920s. Again, doubts were expressed to me about the useful-

ness of material gathered from elderly people who were children in 1926. It is certainly true that in conducting this research I felt I was working at the limits of viable oral history. It is evident however from reading this book that it has been greatly enhanced by the addition of this new testimony.

Dai Smith made a passionate case for the use of oral testimony. He also recognised that the mediating influence of the historian was crucial and that oral history could become a form of 'human antiquarianism' if oral testimony was treated with 'exaggerated respect'.[28] Since Smith made this pioneering statement in 1975, oral history methodology has developed and we now have a greater understanding of the complexities of using oral testimony.[29] Alessandro Portelli has indicated that debates about the reliability of oral testimony can be misguided, as oral history 'tells us less about events as such than about their meaning . . . there are no false oral sources . . . untrue statements are still psychologically "true" . . . these previous "errors" sometimes reveal more than factually accurate accounts'.[30] A useful illustration of this point is the weather in 1926. Oral history accounts frequently mention the summer of 1926 as being unusually hot and sunny. In fact, as Steven Thompson has shown, meteorological records indicate that the weather in 1926 was not exceptional at all.[31] This does not mean that the oral testimony is unreliable. More likely is that locked-out miners whose lives were no longer dominated by work underground in the dark regardless of weather, would notice the sunshine when it appeared and make the most of it. This would in turn make them more likely to remember the warm weather when asked to recall events of 1926. The important point is not what the meteorological records say but what miners and their families believed about the weather. In essence, oral history is based on subjective accounts and it is this very subjectivity which makes it fascinating for the historian.

The south Wales coalfield covers a large area from Pontypool in Monmouthshire to eastern Carmarthenshire.[32] Between the 1870s and 1914 steam coal and anthracite mining transformed the predominantly rural landscape into a vast industry employing over a quarter of a million men which, together with families, constituted a population of over half a million.[33] The unusual physical geography of the region, with its many narrow, steep-sided valleys, combined with very heavy dependence on deep coalmining produced a unique pattern of settlement. A large number of settlements sprang across the coalfield from semi-rural large villages to small townships, always centred around the pit. Despite the growth of primary industry, manufacturing failed to develop and a mass urban society did not come into being as it did in many other regions of Britain at this time.[34] There were important variations within the coalfield. The population was predominantly in the mining valleys of east Glamorgan and Monmouthshire, where steam coal was already more costly to produce than in other British coalfields in the 1920s. The upper western valley of Monmouthshire, where the coal seams were relatively shallow, was in crisis before the Lockout, as pits in Nantyglo and Brynmawr had become uneconomic. Blaina and Abertillery were also very badly affected.[35] Heads of the valleys communities such as Merthyr and Blaenavon, where coal mining was linked to the near-defunct iron and steel trades, were already in serious decline by 1926. On the other hand, on the western side of the coalfield, where anthracite coal was mined, many

Penybont Colliery, Abertillery, with miners' housing behind.

mines remained profitable into the 1930s. Here mines tended to be smaller and sparser, giving the coalfield a more rural appearance. It was not unusual for a miner in the Swansea or Neath valley to retain a foothold in the land or some other rural pursuit.[36]

Relative isolation, poor communications and the fact that the overwhelming majority of people lived near where they worked produced an intensely localised society. Gilbert, in his study of Ynysybwl (between mid-Rhondda and Aberdare), has pointed to the strong sense of local identity and separateness.[37] Almost all social contacts were face-to-face. In small settlements this would encompass the entire community, in small towns most people operated almost entirely within the close-knit network of streets around their home. Information which was not gained through informal networks of neighbours, kin and workmates was received through the town crier whose bell-ringing was a feature of local society before the days of mass communication.

Before 1900, the coalfield was populated predominantly by migration from the surrounding rural counties of Wales. Men gave up agricultural work in favour of more highly-paid employment in the pits. Initially Welsh was the dominant language, but from the 1880s bilingualism became more usual, with non-Welsh speakers having to learn some basic Welsh to get by.[38] With the mass influx of rural English labour, mainly from the western English counties from the 1900 to 1914 the situation was reversed. By 1914, English was in command and was essential for any role in public life, although Welsh was still spoken in many households whose older members were monoglot Welsh speakers.[39] With high birth rates and rapid migration into the area, a serious housing shortage soon developed, with most houses in multi-occupation and many families taking in single male lodgers in already overcrowded homes. Social life was centred around the Nonconformist chapels, whose leaders acted as 'village elders', making them powerful figures in the community.[40] By the 1920s, the union lodge had largely replaced the chapel as the central social institution, although chapels remained very important organisations.[41] Medical aid was one of the many ways in which community solidarity was expressed, as numerous medical aid societies provided access to health care well beyond the employed men who subscribed to the schemes.[42] Strong localism and social cohesion also produced an amazing flowering of cultural activity as the valleys resounded with the sounds of choirs, brass bands, plays, operas, cantatas and 'penny readings'. Organised sport, particularly rugby, also played an important role. A thirst for knowledge was also evident. Through evening classes a significant number of Rhondda miners became acquainted with writers such as Marx, Einstein, Balzac and Dietzgen. This, combined with the revivalism which swept the coalfield in 1904–5, seems to indicate a determination among valley people to make some sense of their new world.

For many the answer lay in socialist ideology. From the mid-1890s, the voice of independent labour gradually superseded 'Lib-Labism'. The miners also made great strides in collective organisation at this time, culminating in the formation of the South Wales Miners' Federation (SWMF) in 1898. The 'Fed', as it rapidly became known, had a federal structure of semi-autonomous branches or lodges. Despite difficulties with a small minority of non-unionists and high levels of arrears at times, the Fed went from strength to strength and its influence spread far beyond industrial relations into health, education, recreation, housing, transport and poor relief. An impressive network of physically imposing miners' institutes and welfare halls also sprang up at this time. In 1908, the SWMF voted to affiliate to the Labour Representation Committee. This came at a time of hardening class conflict. Rationalisation in the industry, creating giant companies such at the Cambrian Combine, which controlled two thirds of the coal production in the Rhondda in 1914, produced a remote and unyielding management, indifferent to safety issues despite the alarming accident rate in the mines.[43] Increasing bitterness and disillusionment with the management resulted in a series of disputes between 1910 and 1912. The Tonypandy Riots of 1910 produced a head-on clash between rioting demonstrators and police baton charges. According to Dai Smith we should not see this large-scale public disorder, in which the centre of Tonypandy was destroyed, as merely a by-product of an industrial dispute. More importantly, it was a symptom of a social crisis, 'a deliberate assault on the civil order of a world which had been made for them'.[44] Henceforth, a much more assertive and self-conscious working class was evident in south Wales. The syndicalist tract *The Miners' Next Step* (1912), which advocated class conflict and workers' control of the mining industry, did not win official approval but was undoubtedly very popular amongst activists.

By the early 1920s, the miners' lodges had become hegemonic institutions, whose democratically-elected officers wielded considerable power in their communities.[45]

Lizzie Davies's father Sam Davies was the secretary of the Maerdy SWMF miners' lodge. She described to me how important her father was in the Maerdy community; 'I think everybody in Maerdy used to come to our house.'[46] Arthur Horner, another key local activist, who went on to become President of the SWMF and later General Secretary of the NUM was a frequent and popular visitor. During the 1926 dispute, Sam Davies became secretary of the local distress committee. Lodges attached to the larger pits in the more urban areas such as Merthyr were very large and often linked up into inter-lodge combines to match the ownership structure amongst the employers. The Cambrian Combine in the mid-Rhondda was perhaps the best example of this. Religious observance was very important and the chapels were an essential component of community cohesion, but by the mid-1920s social leadership had passed to the miners. The lodges, acting under popular control, involved themselves in all aspects of life and often acted as a sort of unofficial court adjudicating in local disputes. Many social activities were organised from the miners' institutes, as was the weekly cinema.[47] This near mono-

Sam Davies, Secretary of the Maerdy Distress Committee, 1926, and father of Lizzie Davies.

industrial society, whose male workforce was heavily dependent on a single industry, was overwhelmingly proletarian. Coalowners had retreated from mining communities and the middle classes were too small to assert an independent voice. Conservatism did not disappear altogether but remained very much a minority force. Liberalism collapsed to minor party status and Labour, dominated by the miners, took command both in parliamentary representation and in local government institutions. A government enquiry into industrial unrest in 1917 noted the fact that the scattered nature of mining communities had inhibited the growth of municipal buildings and a sense of civic pride and community solidarity.[48] In fact, mining communities possessed intense pride in their own local institutions and nowhere was this more the case than in the Rhondda.[49] The miners and their families had created their own kind of communities. Smith and Francis have referred to the 'alternative' nature of coalfield society, with its rejection of consensus, emphasis on class solidarity and desire for grass-roots democracy.[50] Williams argues that we should not overplay this, citing the many conventional aspects of coalfield society in the 1920s, such as the popularity of romantic novels and commercial cinema, and support for the First World War.[51] Mike Lieven has also emphasised that only a minority of miners were politically active and that the Conservatives were active in some miners' lodges.[52] This study takes the view that in some respects coalfield society at this time did possess significant 'alternative' features and that these were further developed during the temporary period of the Lockout.

The work of Dai Smith and Hywel Francis described above was an important part of the new social history of the 1960s and 1970s which challenged traditional history based on ruling elites and sought to bring into the historical mainstream the lives of previously neglected groups, particularly the working class. Integral to this movement for history from below was the explosion of women's history and feminist history which came on the back of the second wave of feminism. The women's liberation movement of the 1970s produced new women's historians such as Sheila Rowbotham whose popular appeal was largely outside of mainstream academic history.[53] Rowbotham and her contemporaries rose to the challenge to make women visible. Much of this new history was focused on the lives of working-class women which was partly a reflection of the fact that the women's movement in Britain was heavily orientated towards socialist-feminism. Political activists from the past such as Sylvia Pankhurst and Alexandra Kollontai were rapidly adopted as socialist-feminist icons by women's liberation activists. But by the 1980s it was realised that, valuable though it was, at best women's history was merely being tacked on to the existing corpus of historical writing. Women had become marginal rather than invisible; what was necessary was to acknowledge that all history has a gendered aspect and so break down the notion that it was based on a vague concept of 'universal' human experience and recognise both men and women as gendered historical subjects to be studied in relation to each other, rather than in isolation. The growth of gender history in the 1980s and 1990s gave rise to important new works on masculinity, with John Tosh and Michael Roper leading the field.[54] History had always been about men but not *as* men. Now, for the first time, men became gendered historical subjects *as men*. The study of gender history, which in Britain has centred on the journal *Gender and History*, has been entirely academic rather than rooted in mass activity as women's/feminist history was and has owed much to post- structuralist theory.[55] Language and discourse acquired a new importance and men and women are seen not as fixed biological entities but as the socially constructed identities of masculinity and femininity. These identities, although still in binary opposition, are not singular but multiple and problematic. They are dynamic and fluid, unstable and contested.

In Wales, women's history has developed in parallel to developments elsewhere. As a result of the work of historians such as Deirdre Beddoe, Angela V. John, Neil Evans, Siân R. Williams, Dot Jones and Rosemary Crook we have a critical mass of work on the lives of women in south Wales over the last two centuries.[56] It has been pointed out, however, that these writings have largely been marginal to mainstream coalfield historiography, which has emphasised the militant miners and the homogenous nature of coalfield communities and played down elements of opposition and conflict other than class conflict.[57] The challenge of gender history is to revisit coalfield history and analyse changing gender identities and relationships in mining communities.[58] This approach is based on the idea that gender has been a central organising principle of modern society and must be present in every aspect of social history. This book will focus on a critical period in the history of the south Wales coalfield, the General Strike and Miners' Lockout of 1926. It is not intended to be a 'celebratory' history of the Lockout. It does not accept uncritically the idea of the 'heroic' militant miner as the centrepiece in the narrative. Similarly miners' wives are not seen as one-dimensional, passive victims of the Lockout but as historical agents in their own right, capable of creating historical change.[59] Recognition is given to the multiple and contested nature of both masculine and feminine identities during this period of crisis. Gender relations in the General Strike and Lockout are studied in the context of families, neighbourhoods and communities, without privileging the organised labour movement and its internal politics.

Chapter 2 is an account of gender, family and neighbourhood in the south Wales mining community before 1926. This is vital background to the dispute itself. The heart of the book is an examination of communal eating and its gender aspects in the valleys during the Lockout. This includes an account of relations between miners and public authorities. This third chapter reveals that there was a significant shift in gender relations around communal eating at this time. By focusing on a local context, it has also been possible to examine how the dispute affected the local economy, particularly family budgets. I wanted to know how families survived without any waged income for almost seven months. The neglected area of the cultural aspects of the dispute has also been explored, including the huge range of sporting and musical events which took place in 1926. All these aspects come within the remit of the fourth chapter. An essential aspect of this study is an analysis of the role of women in local politics in 1926. This fifth chapter brings to light the outstanding women who provided leadership for miners' wives at this very difficult time and the extensive involvement of women in street protests against blacklegging. These three thematic chapters tell the story of the Lockout from three different perspectives, providing for the first time a truly comprehensive social history of the 1926 dispute in south Wales. Inevitably, this thematic approach does involve a small amount of repetition, for which I ask the reader's understanding, as the alternative would be a chronological approach which would be much less appropriate for this study. The sixth chapter provides a detailed account of the aftermath of the dispute and the legacy that lives on in collective and individual memory, including a comparison with the role of women in the 1984–5 mining dispute. The final threads are drawn together in the short conclusion.

2

GENDER AND FAMILY

The social and economic upheaval generated by the First World War witnessed an unprecedented unsettling of established gender distinctions. Dominant conservative forces within society found these trends deeply disturbing. Integral to the post-war settlement was the notion that a return to normality meant a resurgence of separate spheres ideology and a reconstruction of domesticity ideology for women.[1] As collectivist ideology retreated in the 1920s, women sought fulfilment in privatised domestic spaces in which their identity was inextricably bound up with being a full-time wife and mother. Women longed to escape from shabby rented rooms with a shared toilet and outside tap, to occupy one of the newly built flats and houses. These new dwellings which characterised the interwar period came with the unheard of luxury of a private bathroom, kitchen and garden. As labour saving devices such as electric irons and modern cookers appeared on the market, women emerged as an important consumer.[2] The new market for women's periodicals promoted the idea that a housewife was no longer a drudge but a technician in charge of an advanced scientific workshop. According to Judy Giles, women were ready to accept the new 'discourse of housewifery' as it gave them respectability and self-definition.[3] Men also underwent significant changes in this period, noticeably the retreat from the 'heroic' man of the age of Empire, to the more domestic and family-centred man of the interwar years.[4] Adrian Bingham has pointed to the way in which male sporting heroes were given prominence in the popular press at this time and regarded as models of masculinity.[5] As birth rates within the working class plummeted and family size shrunk to two or even less children more emphasis was put on quality of life and the nurturing of children.[6] The rise of the companionate marriage meant that husbands and wives spent more time together and men increasingly felt it was their duty to consider their wives' sexual needs as well as their own.[7] An important feature of this new, privatised family life was distance, physical and psychological. The rise of modern methods of transport made it more likely that men worked away from home. Front gardens now separated women from their neighbours. The new housing developments did not have the vibrant street and community life of the old inner city tenements. Being respectable now meant being reserved and 'keeping to one's self.'

This representation of gender in the interwar years has considerable resonance in the areas of Britain experiencing economic growth and prosperity, but for the areas of depression and high unemployment this is much less so. Hit by the post-war slump, families in Britain's former industrial heartlands of the north of England and south Wales were struggling to maintain living standards at pre-war levels. Here labour movement activism remained an important force, and the notion of the male worker as a heroic class warrior was still very much alive. Women in these communities were expected to be hard-working, stoical, subordinate and sacrificial and to keep to the domestic realm. Poverty meant that, unlike the women described above, these women still relied on each other for mutual support, which usually meant neighbours or female kin living nearby. Just how bad the lives of working-class women were was revealed in the Women's Health Enquiry. Based on research in 1933 on 1,250 women and apparently weighted towards depressed families, it depicts a picture of chronic malnourishment and poor health, with less than a third of the women in the survey in good health.[8] This widespread problem of maternal morbidity (the chronic ill health of poor mothers) was scarcely even recognised at the time. In addition, although death rates had fallen, particularly infant mortality, maternal mortality remained high and actually worsened during the depression years. Given the harsh lives and expectations of poor working-class women, it is hardly surprising that they had little time to be sentimental towards their children, seeing their first duty as providing sustenance and maintaining a home environment rather than emotional support. In fact, this 'emotional thrift' of mothers towards their children was observed across the working class, not just affecting the most disadvantaged women.[9] The intense focus on housework, complete identification with the home as a set of physical commodities and managing the household, however adverse the circumstances, involved a retreat from emotional engagement which we will refer to again below.

Before examining masculine and feminine identities in the south Wales coalfield at this time, it is necessary to place men and women's lives within the family context.

As the oral history respondents reveal, families were rarely small, privatised nuclear structures, but complex and fluid entities, continuously adapting to new circumstances and contingencies. Two thirds of the sample came from families of five or more children. Mining families were late to reduce family size compared to other occupational groups, so it was not unusual for families to have ten or even twelve children. The long spread of women's fertility meant that it was often the case that women had adult children and babies in the household at the same time. Despite the fact that over-crowding was endemic, it was common for women to take in paying lodgers, reflecting both women's relative lack of earning power and men's need for women's services.[10] These 'Welsh uncles', as they became known, were very much part of the family.[11] Lilian Roberts told me how her mother took in two lodgers in 1921, 'out of necessity'. One stayed for five years and was married from Lilian's house.[12] The death of a parent with dependent children was not a rare occurrence. Six of the respondents – including two sisters – out of 23, lost a parent before the age of twelve, only one of whom remarried. Martha Jones lost her mother at the age of three from bronchitis, leaving four dependent children and older siblings. She was brought up by her sister Hilda and her father.[13] Nancy Lewis's mother was already a widow with children from her first marriage when she was widowed for a second time in 1918 when her husband died of pneumonia, leaving her with Nancy who was only eight months, a ten-year-old and older working children.[14] The father of Blod Davies and her sister Sally Poulton also died of pneumonia, in 1927. The family of seven children lived with their mother and maternal grandparents and an unmarried uncle. Blod and Sally regarded their grand-mother as more of a mother to them, as their mother was totally consumed by meeting the needs of such a large family.[15] It was often the practice for a child to be reared with grandparents living elsewhere. Ethel Roberts had a sister who 'passed for county' and was sent to live with her grandmother in Mountain Ash as she had a good army widow's pension and could afford all the extra costs of grammar school.[16] 'Lil' told me that one of her sisters stayed with her grandmother as 'the children came so close'.[17] This was also the case with Lilian Lawrence whose mother had four children in quick succession. Lilian never lived with her parents except for the occasional week in the school holidays. Lilian spent her childhood in Nelson with her grandmother, step-grandfather, to whom she was devoted, and her grandmother's two youngest children who were still at home.[18]

Grandparents, aunts, uncles and cousins often lived nearby, so that neighbours were also often kin. Both Gwyneth Evans and Lilian Roberts had grandparents living next door.[19] Children appear to have moved in and out of families with ease. Blod and Sally had a cousin living next door who stayed with them for long periods, despite the fact that their small house already contained eleven people. Neighbours and extended family were in and out of each other's houses constantly. Doors were rarely locked and I was told by more than one respondent that it was a regular practice for an insur-

South Wales miners at work c.1910.

ance book to be left with money on a sideboard with the expectation that the insurance man would walk in, sign the book and take the money. With such cramped conditions inside, street life was very important, particularly in fine weather. Elsie Pritchard told me that 'the women used to sit out here on the doorsteps and have a natter ... all hours.'[20] Jean Ellis came from a musical family in which her father would give impromtu ukulele sessions on the doorstep.[21] If a misfortune occurred, neighbours would close in, usually bringing *cawl* (broth) or Welsh cakes. They would take home washing, look after children and take turns to nurse the sick or injured. Oral history respondents were keen to tell me how strong the bonds of community were. As Lizzie Davies put it, 'we were all as one, lovely'.[22] In reality, poverty meant that families were locked into an interdependent network of neighbours and wider kin. This mutual support was an essential component of daily life.

The work of miners working at the coalface was both hugely physically demanding and dangerous. Men usually faced a lengthy walk underground, which might be several miles uphill, in the dark before they even started work. Coal seams varied in height and could be as little as two feet high forcing men to work lying down as they hacked away at the coal. Sometimes they worked in soaking wet clothes with their feet in water for the entire shift. The meal break was usually accompanied by rats and cockroaches scuttling about. The most detailed and eloquent descriptions of the work of the south Wales miner come from Bert Coombes, whose autobiographical work *These Poor Hands*, was published in 1939. Born in 1893 and working as a miner in Resolven in the Vale of Neath from before the First World War, he began writing in the early 1930s. Fired by a need to 'tell the world what really happens underground' and what has been described as 'a strong sense of righteous masculinity' he wrote about his life.[23] His first day at the coalface was traumatic.

> My legs became cramped, my arms ached, and the back of my hands had the skin rubbed off by pressing my knee against them to force the shovel under the coal. The dust compelled me to cough and sneeze, while it collected inside my eyes and made them burn and feel sore. My skin was smarting because of the dust and flying bits of coal.[24]

Miners depended on each other for safety underground which led to a very strong form of male bonding. This cohesive workforce produced a highly developed sense of collectivism and class consciousness, as manifested in the South Wales Miners' Federation (SWMF) formed in 1898.[25] By 1914, the south Wales coalfield was the most militant in Britain. In many areas, it was very difficult for a man to work in deep coal mining in south Wales and not be a member of the SWMF. In Maerdy, non-unionists were driven out of their lodging and forced to leave the area.[26] Masculine identity was inextricably bound up with the miner at work and assertive and combative unionism. Equally important to masculine identity was the breadwinner ethos and the notion of separate spheres which went with it. The south Wales coalfield was a deeply patriarchal society, based on the idea of the miner as a breadwinner supporting a full-time housewife and dependent children.[27] In return, the wife serviced the husband's needs, which were very great.[28] The foundation of marriage was a labour contract. This was made possible by the expulsion of women from deep coalmining in the late nineteenth century, the relative absence of alternative forms of employment and the growth of domestic ideology for women. As Wyn Price has written, 'it was generally accepted that it was a personal affront to the head of the household if his wife needed to work as this suggested that he was incapable of providing for the needs of his family'.[29] The notion that a woman's primary role in life was to be the wife or mother of a miner led to exaggerated and oppressive sex roles in which women were vulnerable to the exercise of male power and largely excluded from public life. It was always the needs of men who claimed priority.[30] Domestic violence and wife desertion, although not common, were a constant threat to women.[31]

Outside work, men tended to seek the company of other men.[32] There were some mixed sex events such as the occasional dance at the miners' institutes, but these activities appear to have been dominated by younger men and women 'of courting age'. Union participation and recreational activities such as darts, skittles and library use at the local miners' institute were usually for men only. Men joined male voice choirs, brass bands and were active in local chapels. They also kept allotments which were a welcome supplement to the family's food supply. All these activities were represented in the oral history respondents by fathers, grandfathers or uncles. In *The Valleys Autobiography*, David Rees writes of his father, 'He was proud of the fact that he was able to sustain his family by producing his own vegetables. He also kept a pig and a few chickens.'[33] In Blaengarw, Grafton Radcliffe's uncle Jack came from an agricultural background. His garden, which provided all the family's fresh vegetables was 'a work of art'.[34] Miners were also known to be heavy drinkers and south Wales was no exception to this.[35] Elsie Pritchard, whose father was a butcher, told me that, 'my father liked his pint . . . I expect he was going up there every night as far as I can remember. In those days you got used to it. See, that was the norm with most of them wasn't it?'[36] Edith Davies was born in Ynsybwl in 1907. Her autobiographical work, *The Innocent Years* tells the story of her childhood. She describes the common sight of 'drunken men staggering home "without a leg to stand on.". . .occasionally a drunk would lie senseless in the gutter for hours.'[37] A study of inter-war Bedlinog also indicated serious drinking, particularly on Saturday nights after men had been paid.[38] Walter Davies, who grew up in Bedlinog has written of drunkenness as a 'deeply ingrained and widespread habit'. He draws the link with domestic violence describing how drunken miners 'terrorized wives and families'.[39] The tendency of miners not to be at home is well documented, but when they were at home they were likely only take on roles which were thought of as being gender appropriate. Generally, any household chores associated with 'women's work', particularly cleaning, were to be avoided.[40] Husbands and wives sought out their own domestic spaces. Men kept pigeon lofts and garden sheds where they could repair the family boots (known as tapping), fashion things from wood and generally potter about away from female interference.[41]

What has been described above is the image of hegemonic masculinity; the strong, muscular, heroically militant miner with the stoical, almost invisible wife to service him. Beneath this constructed identity there were other 'submerged' masculinities. Michael Lieven hints at occasional physical relationships which miners formed. This is not surprising given the close physical proximity underground and the high degree of male bonding that took place. Few details have emerged, however, as Lieven writes 'such things are taboo and not to be spoken about; they leave no evidence behind'.[42]

Also, the public or recognised representation of the miner described above was in fact only accurate for miners during their peak years of earning, usually from early twenties to forties. The realities of the miner's life were hidden from this public image. Despite the fact that mining was a very dangerous occupation, employers were callous in their disregard for safety, a factor which contributed to workplace solidarity and union militancy. The appalling accident rate led to large numbers of disabled miners as well as amputees, for example, or those who went blind or who had broken spines.[43] Sally Poulton's uncle Arthur broke his back in a pit accident when he was twenty five 'and died a cabbage at thirty five'.[44] Grafton Radcliffe's *Back to Blaengarw* describes how when a miner took his jacket off a cloud of dust appeared.[45] The constant inhalation of coal dust inevitably took its toll on the lungs. According to Ferdynand Zweig, silicosis, or 'the dust' as it was known, was particularly prevalent in south Wales.[46] This lung disease, once it had taken hold, led to a lingering, painful death. Most miners could no longer retain their physical strength by the time they were in their forties. Bert Coombes was concerned for the aging miner,

> I sympathise with the older men, and watch their struggle to keep up. I listen to the labour of their dust-clogged chests when they climb the drift to go out. They climb a few steps, pause to regain their breath and watch the younger ones hurry past . . . I watch how the few men who are old come to work; how weary they look . . . how desperate they are that the officials shall not think they are slower at their work than the younger men.[47]

Eventually, these men were withdrawn from coalface work and either dispensed with altogether or offered lighter jobs elsewhere in the pit with the appropriate loss of earnings and status. Miners (and their wives) beyond working age who were without wage-earning children living at home, usually had little option but to claim parish relief, with the associated stigma of pauperism.

Avoidance of almost all domestic work was seen by miners as necessary to uphold their masculine identity and status, but this was difficult to enforce once 'breadwinning' status was lost. Walter H. Davies's fictionalised account of life in a mining village humorously depicts an elderly miner being awarded an 'MA', Mangle Assistant, by his wife on her washday. This is a role he is keen to avoid so he escapes on a fishing trip.[48] It was understood that if a wife was poorly or even absent entirely sheer necessity would dictate a loosening-up of gender roles without subsequent loss of public face for the man involved. In the case of Martha Jones, whose mother died when she was three years old, her father shared childcare with older sister Hilda who was seventeen at the time of her mother's death.

> We had a good father. My father used to work nights to put us to school in the mornings . . . He was going to work then in the pits and he would come home in the mornings and then he would call us up to go to school. There were me and Enid and Phyllis, Linda and Mary and he put us all to school . . . I used to love porridge, so my father used to make me porridge . . . My father used to bath in front of the fire, in the back, after we went to school . . . my father would wash his hands and things . . . for breakfast . . . he used to go to bed and then he'd be down about half past three to four. When we'd come home from school we'd all have the dinner, my father would be there then.[49]

White and Williams suggest that men might have been more involved in domestic labour than they were willing to admit.[50] The elderly people interviewed for this project produced a range of responses when asked about their fathers. The father of Nancy Wood was Mark Harcombe, probably the most influential man on the Rhondda Urban District Council during the interwar years. Unsurprisingly, Nancy was extremely proud of her father's achievements, but did not recall anything particularly significant about him in the domestic context, which would indicate that he was not at home very much.[51] Lizzie Davies's father was secretary of the Miners' Federation in Maerdy, which meant that he had a pivotal role in the community. Similarly to Nancy, Lizzie's memories of her father stressed his public role, rather than his life at home.[52] On the other hand, there is evidence of men cooking and taking an active role in childcare. Phyllis Lewis recalled that her father was fond of making pancakes and rabbit stew and was generally thought to be 'a good cook'.[53] Blod Davies told me that, before his untimely death in 1927, it was her father who would get the children ready for bed,

> He would wash us in the corner of the table by the sink . . . He would be washing us, give us a good wash down and while he would be doing that my mother would be making a big jug of cocoa. And then he'd set us all around the fire. Then we'd have a cup of cocoa before we went to bed.[54]

This bedtime ritual was also recalled by Blod's sister Sally Poulton in a separate interview. She said that she had a 'wonderful father. . .my father was like a woman in the house'.[55] It is not being suggested here that Blod and Sally's father was typical, but it does appear to be the case that away from the public gaze, gender roles could be a good deal less rigid than many imagined. It is also evident that, whether they were home much or not, south Wales miners loved their children.[56] Phyllis Lewis told me that her father would play jigsaws and other games with them at home. At Christmas, the children would ask him to play the piano, presenting him with a prepared list of numbers. He would feign resistance, 'So what we did (laughs), he didn't mind, four of us, each would have one leg, one arm . . . carry him into the front room as we called it, 'cos that's where our piano was'.[57] Gladys Davies recalled an incident that took place at Christmas when she was 'ten or eleven' (in about 1926) when there was no money for presents. Her father won on a sweepstake in a local working men's club where they were living in Pontycymer. Although it was evening and the shops were closed he knocked up the owner of a local toyshop in order to buy toys for his six children.[58]

Turning now to femininity, and beginning with work, the separate spheres ideology meant that effectively men and women operated in different labour markets. Gender, acting in conjunction with class and other social divisions, defined work opportunities. Work for women in mining areas was primarily viewed as relevant only for the period between leaving school and marriage. Consequently the overall participation rates for women in the labour force was very low. In the 1921 census only 12.5 per cent of women in the Rhondda were recorded as economically active, compared to a figure for England and Wales as a whole of 32.3 per cent.[59] It was a similar

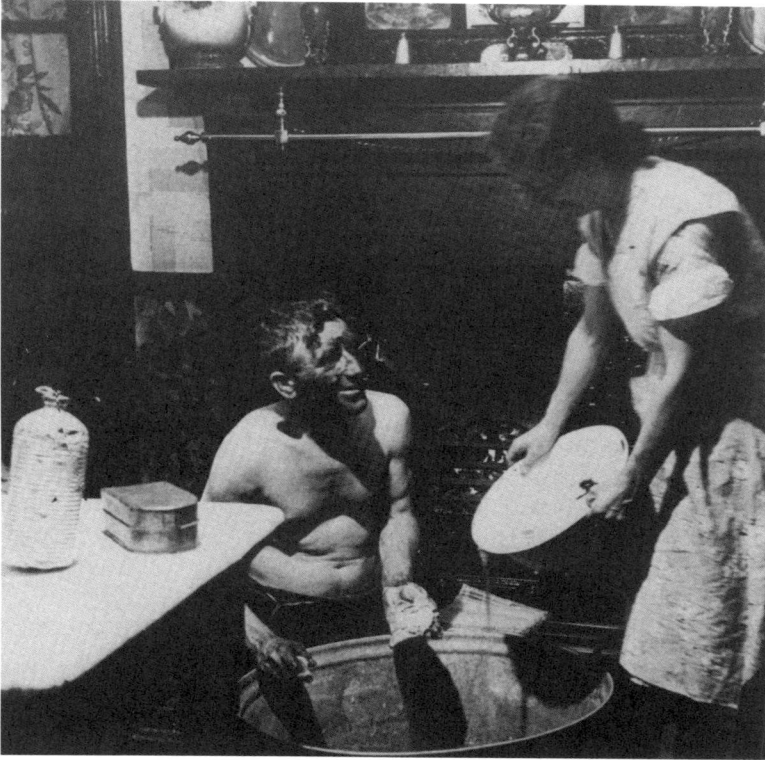

Evan Jones, Penrhos, bathing, with wife assisting, 1920s.

picture elsewhere in the coalfield. The most common form of work for these overwhelmingly young women was domestic service, which was viewed as an excellent preparation for a future miners' wife. (More on domestic service below.) Women were also represented in shop and secretarial work, laundries, dress making and as cinema usherettes. The only industrial form of employment for women was in the tinplate industry in the Swansea, Neath and Afan valleys. According to Chris Williams over 3,000 women, almost entirely unmarried, were employed in the early 1920s in tinplate.[60]

Public disapproval of wives and mothers working did not extend to households without a wage earner. Economic necessity forced widows and the wives of disabled miners into the workforce, but very little work was available. Nancy Lewis's widowed mother cleaned the local Ocean Colliery offices in Blaengarw, a position she held for 24 years.[61] Jobs such as these, which were much sought after, were usually reserved for widows or wives of disabled colliers. Widows were known for selling faggots and nettle beer on Sunday mornings. Even more enterprising unsupported mothers set up shops, often in their front rooms. Gwen Ratcliffe's father died in 1925 leaving her mother with eight children. Gwen, was the second youngest. Her mother rented a shop in Blaenllechau (near Ferndale) and had to work very long hours to make a living. Gwen told me that at times her mother would keep the shop open until midnight as she was 'desperate' for the takings.[62] Despite outward appearances, not all wage-earning men could live up to the 'breadwinner ideal', particularly in large families where earnings were poor, forcing already overworked mothers into largely invisible low-status, poorly-paid casual work. As we have seen, taking in lodgers was a common practice, the usual rate being 7s 6d per week for full board and washing. It was, of course, a disguised form of employment.[63] Women commonly took in one or two lodgers, but it could be as high as four (sometimes lodgers shared beds if working different shift patterns). Poor women also undertook the kinds of work which they traditionally have done in all communities; taking in sewing, washing and ironing. Jean Ellis told me that her mother did 12 shirts with stiff white collars for 2s 6d.[64] It also appears to have been a tradition for south Wales women to do wallpapering. Two respondents, Phyllis Lewis and Helena Charles, told me that their mothers did papering and that this was an established practice.[65] Phyllis's mother also went out to do washing for other families.

A small proportion of the female workforce in south Wales was in professional employment, primarily teachers, nurses, midwives and health visitors. Women professionals were expected to resign on marriage, but not all did so. In the early 1920s, as part of the post-war 'backlash', local authorities formalised these arrangements into official 'marriage bars', so that professional women were forced to resign on marriage. In addition, women such as Elizabeth Price of Cwmclydach Infants School who had been teaching since 1897 were sacked.

Price led a legal challenge by married women teachers against Rhondda Education Authority over their actions.[66] Although unsuccessful, the legal dispute cost the local council £3,320 in legal costs to fight, at a time when finances were very hard pressed, which must provide an indication of just how seriously the council took the marriage bar.[67] Some couples were forced to keep their relationships secret. Beatrice Davies (née Phippen), born in 1901 in Aberdare into a mining family, trained as a nurse and then became a health visitor. She told me her story in an interview in 1977. Through involvement in the socialist movement she met Dai Davies who worked on the trams. In 1925, when Mrs Davies was working in Herefordshire, but soon to take up a new appointment in Aberdare, they decided to get married:

> The thing was to get married without anybody knowing. So we discussed this and I went to the registry office . . . and I told them that I wanted to get married and was there a way of getting married without people knowing. And he said 'well the only way was by a special licence'. By having that nobody could look at the books to see, you know . . . So we got married. He came up one morning to Herefordshire and we went to Ledbury together . . . We decided not to dress up or do anything . . . The daughter and son-in-law of the registrar came in to act as witnesses . . . So we went back to Aberdare and I had my room (rented) and he stayed with his parents. My mother lived here so we were able to spend weekends in my mother's home. Not that my mother was a happy woman that we had married in that way . . . I told her and his parents and neither of them were happy about it, no . . . But we just said we were going to do it and we did.[68]

Despite the fact that Mrs Davies's mother was 'terrified' that they would be found out these arrangements continued for five years until 1930 when she left work to have her daughter. Henceforth, Mrs Davies was a full-time wife and mother which was the fate of the great majority of women in the south Wales coalfield. If life was hard for working-class women at this time, it was doubly so for miners' wives. Often there were several working miners in a household, including sons, fathers, unmarried brothers and lodgers as well as husbands. Each man expected a cooked breakfast before leaving and a substantial meal on return. In addition, lunch boxes had to be made up for the men to take with them. Huge tubs of hot water had to be prepared for baths. Pit clothes had to be washed and patched. The three shift system, including the night shift, meant that women could be working a seventeen-hour day. Disabled or sick miners had to be nursed at home, which was often a round-the-clock process. After the needs of the men had been met, children were the next priority. Although fertility was declining, large families were still common in the 1920s. With tight budgets and hungry mouths to feed, women considered their own needs last with consequent detrimental effects to their health. In addition, the almost complete absence of hospital provision for maternity to deal with obstetric complications meant that the south Wales coalfield had female death rates far higher than the national average. Between 1924 and 1933 deaths related to childbirth in Wales were 35 per cent higher than the figure for England, leaving many young children to grow up without a mother.[69]

Miners' wives worked in the most adverse of circumstances, without the aid of any modern labour saving devices. Few miners' homes had electricity until the late 1920s. The only form of lighting was gas mantles and candles. The water supply was usually only an outside tap. Modern sanitation did not exist. Toilet seats and other surfaces were made of wood which needed regular and vigorous scrubbing. On wet days, clothes had to be hung up to dry in already overcrowded rooms. There was a constant struggle against dust and cockroaches, which were brought in by the men on their pit clothes.[70] The Royal Commission of 1919 into the coal industry heard evidence from three miners' wives, including the Labour activist Mrs Andrews of Ton Pentre. All the women spoke of the 'very great strain' of keeping the house clean on account of the dust brought in by the men.[71] Every six weeks, concessionary coal was delivered, but it did not come in convenient bags, but was merely dumped loose on the doorstep. Gladys Davies had to help her mother bring in the coal. She told me that carrying the coal through to the back in buckets was only the start of the process:

> Then came the cleaning part ... You'd be carrying these buckets of water to wash the pavement's outside. Often it would be quite dark before you got in. Then you'd have to clean right through. Start outside, wash the window sill, the door step, right through, every six weeks you did that.[72]

South Wales miners' wives were known to be extremely conscientious about housework. Edith Davies recalled that this sometimes led to competition, with women 'vying with each other in keeping their homes like little palaces'.[73] Keeping the house clean, neat and tidy earned respectability. The most important symbol of this respectability was the front parlour, which was mam's domain. Mam kept her precious china and best furniture in the parlour which was only used on Sundays and special occasions, when best clothes would be worn. Of course, in poorer households where houses were divided into what were called 'apartments', the symbolic status of a parlour could not be acquired. Usually there was a set routine with a major task being allocated to each day. Oral respondents spoke of their mothers being 'regimental' or 'methodical' in their routines. 'Sarah' told me that 'we knew what meal we were go'ner have each week . . . it was all automatic'.[74] Monday was usually reserved for washing. The mother of Blod Davies and sister Sally Poulton had to wash for a household of twelve, including three miners. It took her three days:

> She would do all the whites on a Monday. Then she would do all the flannels as they call it my grandpa used to wear, long flannels. Those on a Tuesday and all the coloureds on a Wednesday, on the rubbing board. Three days to do the washing.[75]

At least once a week baking was undertaken. With such big families the quantities involved had to be large. In an interview recorded in 1973, Mrs W. R. Jones said that three times a week her mother would bake 14 1lbs (or 5.6 kg) flour for bread. At the weekend, twelve plates of tarts would be baked. When her mother made Welsh cakes, she would use 7lbs of flour at a time.[76] According to Rosemary Crook rigid routines were adopted by housewives as a way of coping with their hard lives:

> When women had no choice but to work at home they elevated the status of that work by adding ritual to it. This then became the norm, a standard to live up to, and gradually acquired the status of a moral principle.[77]

In popular mythology, the Welsh 'Mam' is a powerful matriarchal figure. It needs to be stressed however, that Mam's sphere of influence was entirely domestic within what was a fiercely patriarchal society.[78] And as Chris Williams has pointed out, power and control should not be confused with responsibility.[79] When the miner handed over his pay packet to his wife and she gave him back his 'beer and baccy' money (pocket money) it was not the act of a subordinate.[80] He was merely recognising her responsibility to manage the household. Above all, miners' wives had to be good managers. The household depended on her ability to manage on very limited resources. Miners' earnings fluctuated a good deal, but the wife still had to produce daily meals however little she had coming in. Miners' wives had to be thrifty. Nothing was bought for cash unless it was strictly unavoidable and nothing was wasted which could be turned to some other use. Most women's and children's clothing was made at home from cloth bought in the market. Worn collars were 'turned' and worn sheets were cut up with the best ends made into pillow cases. Old shirts were made into aprons. Old dresses were converted into petticoats. Families were fed on potatoes and vegetables from family allotments and cheap meat such as breasts of lamb or stuffed hearts. A handful of bacon pieces could be made into a filling bacon pudding or pie. Sometimes Mam would have to 'make something out of nothing'. Phyllis Lewis remembers her mother's desperation to buy auctioned meat:

> she used to go down Porth and there was a Mr Williams and a meat shop. And you had to go down there at nine o'clock in the night and he'd auction meat and you'd have enough for the week, one and six, my mother would go down there and kill . . . to get meat to last all the week.[81]

Grafton Radcliffe had to accompany his mother on shopping trips to Maesteg from Pontycymer as food was a little cheaper in the Maesteg market, 'we trudged over the mountain and carried heavy bags of groceries home the same way'.[82]

Unlike their husbands, miners' wives had very little opportunities for formal leisure pursuits. Evenings were often devoted to ironing or sewing. Women would interact with each other on an informal basis whilst hanging out washing or scrubbing front steps. Severe public disapproval meant that women could not smoke and neither could they drink in pubs, although so-called dubious characters were known to 'slink along the back lanes' to the side entrance of the pub with jugs for supplies to take home. According to Edith Davies, such behaviour was regarded as 'scandalous'. [83] Outside the home, the most important social centre for women was the chapel.[84] Women who rarely left the house would make time to attend a weekly evening prayer meeting. Cultural life centred around the chapel, particularly the *cymanfaoedd canu* (singing festivals). All weekend baking, cooking and housework had to be completed by Saturday night, as Sundays were devoted to multiple chapel attendances. On the whole, men do not appear to have been so dedicated to the chapel as their wives. Ethel Roberts told me her father would join the rest of the family for an evening walk after chapel:

> He'd come down to meet us in the evening and then it used to be a nice long walk down along Pentre and along home ... All the men that didn't go used to come and meet the mothers and children.[85]

Sundays were also a time for visiting grandparents and other relations. These occasions were probably the only times when husbands and wives did anything together outside the home. A minority of women were in the Labour Party women's sections which grew rapidly during these years.[86] Three of the oral history respondents told me that their mothers were in 'Labour sections' as they were referred to. Also significant were the local groups of the Women's Co-operative Guild which was an important voice for working class women in the valleys. Beatrice Davies told me that when her children had grown up, her mother joined a local Guild in Tonypandy and became a fervent supporter. When the family expressed surprise at her taking up an activity outside the home she replied, 'I'm not so dumb as I used to be.'[87]

Reviewing the oral evidence it is clear that what respondents were most keen to tell me about their mothers is how hard they worked. Gladys Davies said, 'my mother had a terrible hard life.'[88] Nancy Wood's mother had eleven children. The family was affluent enough for her mother to have help on washdays, but she was still very busy. I asked Nancy if her mother was always doing housework. The reply was 'Did she ever stop?'[89] Blod Davies told me, 'all I can remember of my mother was washing and ironing, scrubbing, bluestoning ...

all I can remember of my mother was work, work, work'.[90] Her sister, Sally Poulton, said their mother worked, 'very, very, very hard.'[91] This oral evidence is reinforced from other sources. Walter Davies described the life of women in the mining community as 'by and large one of child bearing, cooking and home management, which amounted to slavery, drudgery and bondage.'[92] Bert Coombes commented on the effect that their hard lives had on women, 'The women work very hard – too hard – trying to cheat the greyness that is outside by a clean and cheerful show within. They age themselves before they should because of their cleaning and polishing.'[93]

It was also noticeable from the oral evidence that whilst several women became emotional or spoke with obvious affection when talking about their fathers or grandfathers, this was much less likely when they talked about their mothers. There were few stories of mothers being kind or engaging in playful behaviour with their children. As we shall see below, it was more likely to be the case that children recalled a stern and distant relationship with their mothers, based not least on the fact that their mothers had to extract labour from them in order to meet the very high standards of housework required. In large families rearing the younger children was often left to an older daughter as Mam was overwhelmed by domestic duties. The 'emotional thrift' referred to early on in this chapter, and recognised by gender historians as a national phenomenon amongst working-class women between the wars, seems to have had special resonance for women in south Wales. Rosemary Crook mentions that women's lives were 'hard emotionally' as well as physically.[94] It is important, however to appreciate the complex identity of these women. As Angela V. John has argued, we need to view miners' wives as neither helpless victims nor free agents able to determine their own destiny.[95] We also need to be careful not to see them as primarily subjects of gender oppression in circumstances where their husbands were brutally exploited by the colliery owners. Coalfield society was both capitalist and patriarchal.

Finally, this chapter briefly examines the lives of children and adolescents within the mining community. Poor housing and large families made bed spaces scarce. It was the usual practice for the newest arrival in the family and a toddler to

Ffaldau Girls School, Pontycymer, 1925.

sleep with parents. There were, however, reported cases of children up to sixteen still sleeping with their parents.[96] Live-in grandparents would also often sleep with a child. The remaining children would almost always share beds, often sleeping 'top and tail' to squeeze in as many as possible into one bed. When Sylvia Pankhurst came to Bettws (near Bridgend) for a speaking engagement on her recent trip to Russia, she objected strongly when she was told that she would be sharing a bed with a young girl whose bed had enough room for two. Consequently, whilst the meeting was in progress a scout had to be sent round the town to find a room which would be free for Pankhurst's sole use.[97] Clearly the gulf between living standards in comfortable middle-class London and this working-class mining community was a very wide one.

Childhood diseases such as diphtheria and scarlet fever were common. Tuberculosis was also rife. Several of the oral respondents mentioned the death of a sibling. Nancy Lewis, for example, lost a sister at the age of eleven from 'rapid consumption'.[98]Accidents with water were also a common occurrence, which sometimes resulted in the death of a toddler. Helena Charles was very badly scalded at the age of nine when she disobeyed her mother and ran into the kitchen when she was at a critical point in the washing, 'as she was coming with a saucepan full of boiling water with soda and powder in it, I went and ran under her arm and it tipped all over me'.[99] No hospital bed was available, so she had to be nursed at home for six months before being well enough to return to school. Toys were rare although children had stockings at Christmas with a few nuts, sweets and perhaps a colouring book.

Similarly, a birthday might be marked by a special tea, but it was not usual to have a present. With little road traffic, except for the occasional delivery, the street provided a welcome escape from the confines of home. Oral respondents spoke of the many street games played at this time: skipping, marbles, hopscotch, 'whip and top', 'cattie and dog' and football with an old tin can. Older children also explored the mountains and would set up camps in the holidays. Jean Ellis from Pontycymer told me that she 'spent holidays up the mountain, took jam sandwiches and a bottle of water and stayed all night. Then run down and get a refill and wash and go back.'[100] Sunday attendance at chapel was obligatory, with special clothes reserved for this purpose. For better off children, this was a chance to show off, but poor families had difficulties if they could not provide their children with Sunday best clothes. The annual Sunday school outing, to Porthcawl or Barry, funds permitting (otherwise it was a country picnic) was the highlight of the year. These events involved hundreds of children, with each child carefully labelled or ribboned for identification. Edith Davies recalled that 'nothing else was talked of for weeks beforehand and its delights were enhanced in retrospect'.[101]

Sooner or later, children had to face up to the fact that at some point they would be expected to take on jobs within the household. This mainly affected girls but older school-age boys were also sometimes given weekly tasks to perform. Lizzie Davies had to clean the brass; Ethel Roberts had to clean and blacklead the grate before her mother started baking; Helena Charles had to scrub the toilet seat and outside steps on Saturday morning.[102] I asked Gwyneth Evans from what age she had to start helping, 'oh golly school days. I should say to my mum on Saturday, "Can I go with my friends in the village?"

"No, you can scrub the kitchen, scrub the toilet, the yard", all that, yeah.'[103] Phyllis Lewis's mother would be waiting at the door for Phyllis and her sister when they arrived home from school; 'she'd say, "right Phyllis you one bedroom, Jessie, you the other". And we would fight because one was bigger than the other. Not fight, but we'd argue . . . but we had to do it.'[104] From the age of ten or eleven Phyllis was also sent out on cleaning jobs on Saturdays for a shilling which she had to give her mother. Mothers exerted firm discipline and this was also applied outside the home. Grafton Radcliffe remembers a twelve-year-old girl with a sick mother who had to provide breakfast for her younger sisters and get them off to school. Despite these responsibilities, the girl was caned if she arrived late for school herself.[105] The *Glamorgan Gazette* cites the case of a boy of thirteen who was given six strokes of the birch for stealing rubber to mend boots in July 1926.[106]

Despite the harsh discipline and endemic poverty, the oral history respondents almost all described their childhood as a happy time. This could be the nostalgia of old age seeking to reconstruct a romanticised childhood, but it also seems to be the case that the strong sense of social cohesion in mining areas gave them a sense of community and belonging which is largely lost in today's world. At the age of eleven, pupils could be entered for grammar school selection, where they would be expected to stay on until at least sixteen. The remainder would continue with elementary education and leave at fourteen. Nancy Lewis was made to stay on at school until sixteen as her mother continued to receive five shillings widow's pension for her if she remained at school.[107] On the other hand, a girl who could read and write fairly well could leave school at twelve if there was a large family with an ailing mother.[108] Lilian Roberts, Gladys Davies and Jean Ellis went to grammar school. Gwyneth Evans and 'Sarah' both passed the 'eleven plus' but did not go. Gwyneth's mother told her that as she would have to leave at fourteen anyway, there was little point.[109] 'Sarah' passed for the Porth County higher grade grammar school, an indication that she had excellent academic potential. Her parents wanted her to go but, 'You had to have your own pencils, your own pens, everything had to be bought. And the uniform and things for sport . . . couldn't afford it . . . Mum

and Dad were most upset to think that they couldn't . . . but no
way, they didn't have the money.'[110]

For boys, the rite of passage to manhood was firmly linked
with leaving school to enter the local pit. Once they had left
school, boys acquired a new status within the household. In
The Valleys Autobiography, Kitty Bishop said this about her
brother Freddie, 'I could tell a tale about our Freddie, when
he started working. They thought they were keeping us girls,
you know. He was having fifteen bob a week, and expecting us
to wait on him hand and foot . . . "Don't forget, I'm keeping
you", and he was only about that high.'[111] Walter Davies
describes the prestige of wearing 'man's clothes' and carrying
the miner's lamp, the symbolic trappings of masculinity.[112]
Schoolboys were entranced by the prestige of earning a wage
and exaggerated stories of life underground from the boys
who had already entered the workforce. For Davies, the reality
was a grim awakening:

> By the end of the day I could hardly walk home. There, I bathed and
> went straight to bed, but not to sleep, for the smell of the oil had given
> me a severe bilious attack. I arose the following morning sick at heart,
> and I would have given anything to have remained at home rather than
> go to the colliery.[113]

Boys at St Athan summer camp *c.*1926.

A similar account can be found in the Lewis Jones's fiction-alised account of life in a Welsh mining village between the wars, *Cwmardy*:

> Big Jim's son Len longed to join his father in the pit. When the day finally came he worked alongside his father, who tried to ensure that Len was not overtaxed but even so the effect of the first day was a terrible ordeal, The lad dragged his weary, painful limbs back into the roadway, where he stretched himself full length in the dust. He saw his heart pumping against the bones of his naked chest, and felt pins and needles run through his flesh in spasms of excruciating agony.[114]

For the girls, it was a very different story. Two of the grammar school girls 'went into business', meaning that they did some sort of office work. Gladys Davies, however, did not use her grammar school education but left at sixteen to enter domestic service.[115] Three did shop work, two did dressmaking and one became a hairdresser. Several stayed at home to help their mothers, although these women are not always easy to categorise. 'Sarah', for example, stayed at home, but gradually built up an income by taking in sewing.[116] Over half the women interviewed for this project entered domestic service. According to Mari Williams, in some areas of the south Wales coalfield such as Mountain Ash and Merthyr Tydfil the numbers of girls entering domestic service was as high as eighty per cent.[117] The oral history respondents did not necessarily enter domestic service immediately after leaving school. Lizzie Davies, for example, stayed at home for several years and then went into service.[118] Phyllis Lewis was sent to live-in as a domestic servant in a house in Penygraig at the age of thirteen for five shillings a week. She was overworked, underfed and home sick.[119] Blod Davies told me that she 'worked like a dog' when she was in service, from 7 am until 8 pm with two half days a week.[120] In an interview with Rosemary Scadden 'May' talked about her time in service: 'we are talking about homesickness and it was cruel ... all we knew was once we came to fourteen, we had to go away from home, because there was not a penny coming in to feed us.'[121] On the other hand, some girls were aware that their poor clothing carried the stigma of poverty and longed for some money of their own. Echoing the new-found consumerism among women in the 1920s, Gladys Davies told me, 'Well, when you reach the age of sixteen you wanted nice things didn't you and you didn't have them'.[122] In fact, it was expected that girls would send most of their wages (usually between four and ten shillings a week) home, keeping only a small proportion for themselves.[123] Concerns were raised in the local press about the fact that girls were often sent off on the train to London or other large cities with no money for emergencies and little idea of where they were going or what was to be expected of them.[124] Welsh churches with links in London took an interest in Welsh girls in the capital as they were felt to be at risk from immoral influences, particularly if they lost contact with home.[125]

In conclusion, it is clear that life was very hard for both men and women in the mining valleys of south Wales in the 1920s. The domination of deep coalmining influenced almost every aspect of social life. For men, the close working relationships developed underground spilt over into social life where male bonding was often practised through a drinking culture. The notion of a miner as a breadwinner and his wife as servicing his needs meant that the separate spheres ideology was regarded as a very significant organising principle for this society. The lives of miners' wives were governed by back-breaking domestic toil. Older daughters were reared with the expectation that they would take on domestic responsibilities, particularly childcare, from early adolescence. In addition lack of employment for women meant that large numbers of girls were sent away into domestic service when they left school. Poverty, large families and very cramped living conditions meant that families were intermeshed with wider kin and neighbours into cohesive communities by the pressures of mutual dependence. Within these communities there were, however, a significant number of female teachers and other professional women, but their careers were cut short by the marriage bar and the expectation that married life for women was incompatible with employment.

3

COLLECTIVE EATING AND PUBLIC AUTHORITIES[1]

After the collapse of the General Strike on 12 May 1926, it was evident that the miners would be in for the long haul. The question then arose – what was the legal position and government policy (via the Ministry of Health) regarding relief for striking miners and their families? It had long been established as a principle of Poor Law administration that no relief would be provided for the able-bodied as they were deemed to be destitute through their own moral failings. In the post-First World War climate of slump and civil unrest, the workhouse system was considered to be politically unacceptable and the principle of out-relief was conceded for the unemployed. The position of strikers (and those locked out, as in this case) was governed by the Merthyr Tydfil judgement of 1900 which prohibited relief to strikers, but allowed relief for their dependents.[2] Strikers who became ill and were deemed by a Medical Officer to be unfit for work could also be relieved until they resumed fitness. Assistance would only be provided to relieve actual destitution and should be in kind wherever possible.

The government was far from happy with the Merthyr Tydfil ruling. It contradicted a cardinal rule of Poor Law administration that the household should be regarded as an indivisible unit, and was 'practically impossible to put into operation'.[3] It was recognised that within the household, relief for wives and children would be shared with the locked-out men. The government was faced with a dilemma on this question. It did not want to be seen to be supporting industrial disputes from public funds. On the other hand, with over a million miners locked out across the country, the possibility of serious and widespread unrest if no poor relief was allowed was a major concern and appears to have been the deciding factor in upholding the Merthyr Tydfil ruling and allowing relief for dependents.[4] This left single men, particularly if they had been solitary migrants from other areas of Britain, as the most vulnerable component of the workforce as they were thrown back entirely on their own resources.

Fear of unrest was also a factor on the question of meals for schoolchildren. The Education Act 1921, which incorporated the Provisions of Meals Acts 1906 and 1914, empowered local authorities to provide meals for children in public elementary schools if they were deemed to be 'unable by reason of lack of food to take full advantage of the education provided for them'.[5] A Ministry memorandum written before the strike stated, 'it seems fairly clear that there will be serious trouble if there is a strike in the mining area and if no meals are forthcoming'.[6] Local authorities could recoup funds for school meals from the Poor Law authorities. Assistance could also be provided for expectant and nursing mothers and infants in need through the supply of free milk at Maternity and Infant Welfare Clinics. Parents could choose not to allow their children to be fed at school if they preferred to keep the maximum relief allowances. The Ministry favoured centralised feeding of children as it enabled Poor Law authorities to keep relief to adults to a minimum.[7] It appears to have been the expectation that with practically no cash income, families would soon become demoralised and lose the will to continue the dispute.

The need to keep expenditure on assistance to striking families to an absolute minimum was a major feature of the ministry's stance. Mindful of the fact that many local councillors and Poor Law guardians were either miners or had close connections with mining families, it was felt that there was a serious danger of over-generous provision. If this resulted in excessively high rates and ratepayers refused to pay, it could result in the breakdown of the entire Poor Law system. As mining was a highly localised industry, the burden of the strike fell entirely on public authorities within the mining districts, most of which were already in a weak financial state. It was apparent from the start that some local authorities would need substantial loans in order to meet their commitments. These needs went beyond the capacity of the private banking system and ultimately could only be met from centralised funds. In stipulating conditions for loans, the government was therefore in a prime position to dictate terms to local authorities and thereby curb 'excessive' spending. The main weapon which the Ministry used was the infamous Circular 703, issued early May 1926, which dictated maximum relief scales for striking families of twelve shillings for a wife and four shillings per child.[8] In fact, some Welsh Boards of Guardians, particularly in rural areas, were paying less than this maximum scale.[9] It was expected that where school meals were provided, allowances for children would be cut. This was fiercely opposed by the labour movement.[10] It was also clear that school feeding should not be a blanket provision and that only those children who met stipulated criteria were catered for.[11]

Resistance to the Ministry scales in south Wales, particularly the refusal to allow relief for single men, was vigorous, but ultimately futile. The SWMF failed in its attempt to secure collective unemployment benefit on the grounds that the dispute was a lockout rather than a strike.[12] Federation rules allowed for strike pay of a pound a week, plus two shillings for each dependent child. In practice, funds were totally inadequate for such payments and grants to lodges proved to be poor and intermittent. Following an international appeal for aid, Russian trade unionists voted to impose a small levy on their membership which resulted in donations totalling £1,161,459 during the dispute.[13] Within Britain, fund raising for the miners was centrally coordinated in London by the Women's Committee for the Relief of Miners' Wives and Children (WCRMWC) organised by Labour Party women and headed by Marion Phillips and Ellen Wilkinson.[14] The committee made a non-political humanitarian appeal based on relief (in kind, not cash) for wives and children only. It proved to be an effective body for mobilising funds averaging about £6,000 a week during the lockout.[15] These donations, although welcome, could not match the scale of the problem. Essentially, except for very basic poor relief and small sums of money coming from outside, mining communities had to make their own arrangements for survival. In south Wales they were disadvantaged from the start, by debts still outstanding from the 1921 dispute and the very poor economic conditions prevailing before the start of the Lockout. On the other hand, South Walian mining communities were extremely resourceful and resilient and had been coping with long disputes since the

1870s. From early on, collective strategies had been developed which enabled the miners to hold out when many other occupational groups would have caved in. Communal eating, in the form of soup kitchens, was an important part of this. Not all mining communities voted to organise communal eating. In order to fund soup kitchens, almost all grants from the SWMF had to be directed for this purpose. A minority of lodges voted to distribute food vouchers to individual miners instead. In most cases, however, some attempt was made to organise communal eating. The soup kitchen, referred to by Paul Jeremy as 'the most characteristic institution' in south Wales in 1926, became the symbol of the Lockout.[16]

MINERS' CANTEENS

In the larger towns, quite sophisticated structures to manage the Lockout at a local level were established during the period of the General Strike. These usually revolved around the local trades council. In Merthyr, for instance, the Trades Council was a very large body with fifty two miners' lodges and three unemployed organisations affiliated, plus many members from other occupations such as railwaymen. Merthyr Trades Council organised a central strike committee which had four tiers of organisation and six sub-committees including one dealing with food. Beneath this structure were four district committees.[17] In smaller communities, simpler structures were established, usually emanating from the local miners' institute. As the Lockout wore on, strike committees evolved into distress committees and these were the driving force behind the soup kitchens. In larger towns, such as Pontypridd, central distress committees were formed with broad representation from across the community. In some instances councils of action, based on the local trades councils, were constituted for the General Strike and spontaneously formed themselves into distress committees after 12 May. This appears to have been the case in Aberdare. In most cases, the distress committee was based on the miners' lodges with extra representation provided for local businesses and professionals, such as teachers and doctors, who could assist in the securing of funds. Chapels and political parties were also represented. In

Miners' canteen, Dulais Colliery. The men are dressed for a special occasion.

Maerdy, where the lodge was both dominant and strongly influenced by Communists, conflict occurred when serious pressure was applied on local trades and businessmen for funds.[18] An article in the *South Wales Echo* on 25 May complained about the power exerted by the Strike and Distress Committee and referred to Maerdy as a 'Little Moscow'. Complaints also surfaced in Tredegar, where, according to his biographer, Aneurin Bevan was the 'uncrowned king'.[19] Bevan was criticised by some local councillors for presiding over a relief committee which was 'too sectional' and 'representing only one section of the community'.[20]

By late May, a network of soup kitchens had been opened across the valleys. The *Colliery Guardian*, a publication representing the employers, noted that 'soup kitchens were being opened in every direction' in the south Wales coalfield.[21] By early June, Merthyr, where the Mayor had instituted a central

distress fund, had opened 27 communal kitchens which operated from district headquarters at Hope Chapel, Merthyr.[22]
Aberdare had eleven canteens for locked-out miners, where
unemployed men could also be fed if they surrendered part of
their unemployment benefit.[23] Numbers involved in communal feeding were often very large. The Merthyr district
committee organised meals for four to six thousand men a day
both in the town and at Dowlais and Penydarren.[24] In
Pontypridd, 7,357 men were registered with the Central
Distress Committee by the second week of June. The
Committee promised that 'every man and boy in want without
visible means of support would be provided for.'[25] Abertillery
was reported to be feeding over 1,600 a day in communal
kitchens.[26] According to the *Colliery Guardian*, 9,000 men were
being fed daily in the Rhymney Valley in mid-June. According
to Michael Foot, Tredegar in the Sirhowy Valley was feeding
1,500 a day.[27] Even quite small settlements were engaged in
large-scale communal feeding. In mid-July there were eight
canteens in the Garw valley comprising three at Blaengarw,
three at Pontycymer, one at Pontyrhyl and one at Llangeinor
feeding a total of 2,000 men a day.[28]

The soup kitchens were usually organised from the miners'
institutes or local vestries and chapels. Management was
democratically controlled by the membership. As funding was
always tight and numbers large, appeals were made for those
who could find sustenance elsewhere, through relatives and so
on, to stay away. It was necessary to create a register, to make
sure that only those entitled to eat could do so. Miners who
were unemployed before the Lockout and therefore in receipt
of unemployment benefit were not entitled to eat (unless
paying as in the case of Aberdare above) and occasionally
problems arose when a diner was found to be fraudulently
using the canteen. In Maerdy, any miner who was in arrears
with union dues (the possibility of non-members was not even
recognised) was not allowed to register, but this rule was not
universally applied.[29] Communal kitchens were a serious business from the start. Capital equipment such as tea urns was
purchased and buildings modified and outbuildings erected.
Lizzie Davies's father, Sam Davies, became secretary of the
Maerdy Distress Committee in the Lockout. Lizzie describes

her father as 'in charge of the soup kitchens as far as the ordering of the food and all that.'[30] Usually some kind of 'pantry' sub-committee was elected to make bulk purchases from local grocers who tendered for orders. Although the Co-op was widely used, efforts were made to rotate suppliers. In the more rural, western parts of the coalfield farmers donated lambs as they knew that it was likely they would be stolen otherwise.[31] Miners were fed either once or twice a day. Menus were worked out, costed and food ordered a week in advance. Simple, filling food was supplied, which by today's standards was possibly lacking in some vitamins and minerals. In some cases, all that could be provided was broth and bread, or bread and cheese or corn beef, with perhaps a mug of cocoa or tea, but many canteens produced hot dinners. The most favoured hot meal, funds permitting, was either boiled or roast beef and potatoes. In Maerdy, vegetables were supplied on Sundays, and occasionally rice pudding.[32] Pea soup, stew, hotpot, shepherd's pie and meat pies also appear on menus in Tylorstown.[33] Tea, where supplied, as in Maerdy, was usually sandwiches or bread and cheese, sometimes supplemented with cake or fruit. A memoir from Chris Evans gives us some insight into the miners' canteen at Seven Sisters in the Dulais valley:

> The soup kitchen was held at the Reading Room, and what a sight it was to see the men and boys wending their way each day to the reading room, carrying their cups and plates or basins, as determined by the menu of the day. What a welcome sound the voice of Charley Burt – one of the cooks in charge of the soup kitchen – became. You could hear his voice shout 'Come and get it' long before one came near the Reading Room. There was not a great variety of food, but it was good, wholesome and clean. Some days it would be pea soup, other days sausage and mash.[34]

Apart from the very occasional petty squabbling among the cooks or unruly behaviour among the diners, communal eating proceeded with impressive order and dignity. Huge efforts were made to make the canteens pleasant and attractive places to eat and to avoid the humiliating stigma associated with 'relief'. Gerard Noel has pointed to the huge difference between charitable soup kitchens as traditionally known in London's East End and elsewhere and the communal kitchens of the Lockout, 'being run by the people themselves for each other'.[35] In Aberdare, the local paper gave enthusiastic reports on both its visits to local canteens, commenting on the hygienic methods used and the quality of the food, writing that a visit to the canteen was 'a pleasure' with tables 'beautifully laid' and 'artistically decorated'.[36] At the Blaengarw canteen, diners were entertained by music relayed from gramophones and singing from local talent amongst the guests.[37] Mavis Llewellyn, a young woman about to embark on a teaching career in 1926, speaking in 1977, remembered the Nantymoel kitchen with pride and affection:

> They prepared proper meals . . . they cooked the most excellent meals. I had some photographs of the tables being laid in the local canteen. It was summer time. There were flowers on the tables. There were table-cloths. The waiters wouldn't dare go in without a clean apron every day. And one of the local fellows that got married, they had the wedding breakfast there . . . they organised everything properly. At that time, there was a Minister at every church here in Nantymoel, and they had to take it in turns week by week to go to the canteen to say Grace.[38]

As many of the soup kitchens were located in or near the miners' institute, the men were able to socialise and engage in recreation as well as eat. The Institute usually had a games room for billiards, dominoes, skittles, cards and other indoor games. Lodge meetings were also held around meal times as good attendance was assured. Communal eating, therefore, played an important role in overcoming isolation and demoralisation. Adult communal eating in 1926 was a male experience, although there appear to have been attempts in both Bedlinog and Maerdy, both with strong revolutionary socialist elements, to include women in the canteens. In Bedlinog, it was suggested that parish relief food tickets for miners' dependents should be pooled with lodge funds to provide canteens for whole families.[39] This proposal does not appear to have got anywhere. In Maerdy, the Labour Party Women's Section proposed that miners' wives be fed, but this was not taken up, due to the 'financial situation'.[40] To succeed this would also have necessitated surrendering individual food tickets for the collective effort. This implied a fundamental challenge to the existing sexual division of labour, removing meal preparation almost entirely from the home. This was too radical a step even for Maerdy and Bedlinog. There are examples, however, in small communities where schoolchildren and miners were fed together. According to the *Glamorgan Gazette* 1800 adults and children were fed daily at Memorial Hall in Nantymoel (which must be the soup kitchen described by Mavis Llewellyn above).[41] Ethel Brown grew up in Cwmgwrach, a small village in the Vale of Neath. She recalled in detail her daily visits to the miners' welfare hall where about a hundred men and children were fed. According to Ethel, there were only about five children in the village whose fathers were not connected with mining, so almost all the men and school-age children were fed.[42] This was apparently all organised by the miners' lodge and the local Labour Party, although it is likely that the local education committee contributed towards the cost of the children's meals.

Closer examination behind the scenes in the soup kitchens is revealing from a gender point of view. Miners freed from the gruelling routines of underground life were enthusiastic volunteers. Miners' wives and mothers were temporarily released from the daily grind of servicing the miner for work, and the constant drive to keep on top of the coal dust. This was a potentially liberating situation, enabling childless wives and women with school-age and above children to volunteer for the communal kitchens. In this situation, men and women worked together in public life as never before. Will Paynter, ex-general secretary of the National Union of Mineworkers, recalls in his autobiography that both his parents worked in the soup kitchen in Trebanog.[43] Some gender distinctions appear to have been drawn. Men took responsibility for supplying coal from outcrops, stoking boilers and making sure that the fires were lit for the cooking. In Pantygog, in the Garw valley, two brothers Herbert Jones, aged 26, and Cyril Jones, aged 19, were killed when ninety tons of rock fell on them whilst with a party of nine men collecting coal for a local canteen.[44] High-ranking colliery officials helped in the rescue party. In this society where 'stealing became a morally acceptable act of survival', sheep rustling was sometimes expected of men for the communal good.[45]

Len Jeffreys described such an episode in the Rhymney valley in 1926. When it was his turn to kill a sheep, he followed instructions laid down by the local council of action for a humane dispatch under cover of darkness, but due to his inexperience the sheep emerged apparently unscathed. He let the animal free, 'then I got a row from the members of the site committee and the Council of Action that I hadn't done my job.'[46] Other 'legal thefts' included a cask of butter and 561lbs of cheese which mysteriously 'disappeared' from the goods yard at Merthyr station.[47] As far as cooking went, however, no hard and fast rules applied. In Maerdy, according to Lizzie Davies, men and women shared the cooking.[48] It appears from the lodge minutes, however, that women took responsibility for the cooking, with a woman in charge, but it is likely that men peeled potatoes and performed other menial kitchen tasks.[49] In other kitchens it was men, particularly if they had experience as army cooks in the First World War, who took main responsibility for the food. As Mavis Llewellyn put it, 'they wanted a cook and who'd had experience of cooking on that scale. The army cooks who had been in the 1914–18 war came back into their own.'[50] An article in the *Glamorgan Gazette* gives the names of the cooks in the Nantymoel soup kitchen as William John and Frank James.[51] The Christ Church canteen in Aberdare also had male cooks: F. Liddiard was cook, Aeron Thomas, assistant cook with Len Flook providing back up.[52] Lilian Roberts, from Porth, told me that her father 'helped the men' with the cooking in their local canteen.[53]

Contemporary visual images of soup kitchens usually show proud displays of men and women together. The image below of the Salem Chapel canteen in Nantyffyllon in the Llynfi valley in 1926 shows a large group, including 36 women, 28 men and numerous children. Some of the men were smartly turned out, with ties and floral buttonholes. These were the waiters. Men usually appear to have taken on this role. There are numerous signs of affection among those present, including three men who have their arms draped affectionately over nearby women, almost certainly wives or sisters. There are numerous other similar photographs depicting canteen staff in 1926. These images reveal not just determination and hard work by soup kitchen volunteers, but also men

Salem canteen staff, Nantyffyllon.

and women who are happy and relaxed working with each other. Ethel Roberts ate in the Cwmgwrach soup kitchen, where her father helped. She told me that 'he worked as hard during the strike as when he was at work'[54] She went on to explain that both men and women worked together in what sounds like quite a pressurised atmosphere:

> The men had to carry the water didn't they, chop the wood and pick the coal, bring the coal back to the miners' welfare 'cos they had these great big boilers. Well, it was coal fires. Maybe there was two or three only stoking the tiny fire underneath to keep that going. Well, others then was helping the women cleaning potatoes, fetching and carrying. There one's job was only carrying water. So when it come to clear up, everybody had to muck in, because you had to boil water again, get started then.[55]

This increased gender alignment made it possible for women to begin to encroach on male space in the public domain. Susan Demont's study of Tredegar and Aneurin Bevan notes that the soup kitchens in Tredegar brought women more into public life.[56] Although groups such as the Labour Party Women's Sections could book rooms for their meetings at the miners' institutes (or welfare halls), they were still very much male institutions, with men and boys making extensive use of the leisure side of the institutes. In North's Workmen's Institute (Maesteg), a Mrs Mospan, speaking for the local Labour Party women's section asked the committee if a room could be set aside for the women's recreational use, with periodicals supplied.[57] The committee agreed to allocate 'the old billiard room' to the women, but told them to supply their own periodicals, thus refusing to allocate any of the library budget to women's publications.[58] The question of women's direct access to the library (they had to ask male family members to borrow material for them) was not raised.[59] In Maerdy, women spread from the canteen to other areas of the lodge. During entertainments they began to act as stewards, policing doors and stairs at busy times, which would have given them authority over men.[60] By November, Mrs Bowen and Mrs Feltham were acting as chairwomen for concerts at Maerdy, an indication that women were becoming a serious force in the Institute.[61]

SCHOOL FEEDING

School feeding also developed on a large scale, with head-teachers taking responsibility for identifying children in need, recruiting voluntary labour and generally overseeing the preparation of the meals.[62] The *Colliery Guardian* reported in July that over a hundred schools in Glamorgan were providing meals.[63] In late May, over 6,000 Merthyr children a day were being fed a breakfast of bread, jam, cocoa and porridge, with corn beef sandwiches and soup at lunchtime.[64] Many local authorities continued school feeding throughout the dispute. In Aberdare, in September 1926, the average number being fed was 3,300.[65] Rhondda UDC, the most densely populated authority, was feeding nearly 18,000 children a day in September.[66] In her 1976 article on the 'Poor Law in 1926' Patricia Ryan stated that 'school meals were not generally provided' in Wales.[67] Clearly, this was not the case. Arrangements for funding school meals created many problems. The Ministry of Health expected the cost of meals to be deducted from poor relief. Anything less was regarded as a subsidy to the miners. The picture appears to be fairly diverse. When a shilling poor relief deduction was made in Monmouthshire, so many children were withdrawn that school feeding was discontinued in some areas.[68] The Pontypridd Union deducted the full four shillings, whilst in the Rhondda the Guardians paid two shillings a week to the council for each child on school meals. For this it was expected that three meals a day would be provided, but two meals was usually the case.[69] The Board of Education, alarmed at the costs of school meals, pressured local authorities to make more enquiries into means.[70]

Controversy has raged over the nutritional status of children during the 1926 Lockout. A report from the Rhondda Medical Officer noted in September that childrens' health had been maintained, if not actually improved.[71] This very much fitted in with the government's desire to cut off support for the miners by giving credence to the view that miners' families were not starving or suffering appreciably as a result of the Lockout. Charles Webster has noted the 'egregious displays of loyalty' to the government shown by interwar medical officers, so this evidence has to be treated with caution.[72] The Rhondda Medical Officer's controversial standpoint was strongly challenged by the labour movement at the time, especially the Women's Committee for the Relief of Miners' Wives and Children. Particular objection was raised to the fact that the report asserts that improved children's health was due to school feeding instead of the 'feckless' mothering that existed previously.[73] Recent research has shown, however, that the weight of evidence for south Wales is that the Lockout did not have a detrimental effect on children's health.[74] This is not to say that children were not in distressing poverty but that unemployment, low incomes and large families meant that miners' families were already suffering before May 1926, and school feeding is likely to have given them a better diet than could have been provided by parents at home. When I asked Gladys Davies if she remembered ragged women and children during the Lockout she replied, 'well, they were ragged when the men were working . . . because . . . we didn't have much money to live on'.[75]

Memories from this period reveal a variety of responses to collective feeding. Martha Jones from Ynyshir, Rhondda, was impressed by the soup kitchen in a nearby church hall with its clean scrubbed tables and waiters with white aprons. When asked about the food she was enthusiastic, 'Lovely, oh I think it was great, butter and jam. I thought it was great having that for tea, and sandwiches. I used to love to go to the soup kitchen and then have a good basin of, or a dinner, whatever they'd have.' [76] Martha told me that her sister Enid, who was at the Porth County Grammar School, was 'too snobbish' to go to the soup kitchen. In fact, she would not have been allowed to attend as school feeding was only intended for elementary school children. In his autobiographical memoir, Vernon Chilcott describes his time at the Ffaldau Boys School in Pontycymer, Garw valley. During the Lockout, he attended the school soup kitchen which was set up in a nearby ambulance hall, where the local blacksmith, Towyn Jones, had become cook. At the end of the Lockout the grateful boys gave Towyn and his helpers such a rousing vote of thanks that they were 'almost overwhelmed.' [77] Gladys Davies also came from Pontycymer, but her reaction to the soup kitchen in the local chapel was rather different. Although her brothers were happy to attend, she disliked it intensely:

> When I think of it now I feel very ashamed of myself because I hated going there, because I used to feel physically sick. I couldn't stand the smell of the cocoa . . . And they used to make this soup and they used to burn it. It used to catch in the saucepan . . . I didn't want to go and I should have gone because I was taking food out of my parent's mouths, wasn't I? I always felt sorry that I did that . . . I didn't go all the time, I couldn't. I just felt sick when I went through the door. [78]

As with the miners' soup kitchens, there is evidence of increased fellowship between men and women in the school canteens. There does appear, however to be less fluidity in arrangements over the cooking, with this being seen as a male responsibility. Although information is sparse, there is evidence that male school cooks were paid. [79] This was certainly the case in Mountain Ash, with cooks being paid two guineas a week, so it is likely to have been the same elsewhere. [80] As with the miners' canteens, many of the school cooks were ex-army cooks. The *Merthyr Express* lists a fifty-strong staff at a canteen in Bargoed which includes men in the positions of head cook, assistant cooks (six), and storekeeper. There were, however, many women listed as helpers. Men also acted as waiters for children. A photograph of small children seated at tiny tables and being waited on by two large white-coated men at the Nantgarw Junior School shows a poignant image of male nurturing which is very distinct from the hard, conventionally 'masculine' image of the miner.[81] It certainly was unusual to see men in mining areas performing such 'maternal' roles in public. Parents were an essential component of the volunteer labour in the childrens' canteens. Both men and women had time on their hands and were happy to be doing something positive and appeared to have enjoyed the enhanced sense of community spirit which came about with collective feeding. The *Aberdare Leader* described the picture behind the scenes at the Park School in September, with men and women busily occupied with apparently little distinction of gender.[82] A similar story was told in *The Miner*: whilst children ate soup and rice pudding at tables adorned with wild flowers, 'willing men and women were washing up in a corner of the playground'.[83] Teachers were also closely involved with the school feeding, which was conducted on a seven-day basis. The teachers' employers, local councils, made it clear that their attendance was required to assist with school feeding whenever it took place. Teachers therefore gave up both their weekends and their Whitsun holiday to be in the canteens. This does not seem to have created much resentment, as many teachers in south Wales were from mining families. Unease was expressed, however, about the prospect of continuing throughout the summer.[84] These difficulties were overcome with the introduction of rotas for teachers' summer duty and the promise of an extended break after the dispute.[85]

Although children's canteens were mainly supported by public funding, this was not the case with adult feeding, which depended on huge fund-raising efforts.[86] Most miners' institutes decided that all competitions, tournaments and entertainments would only be permitted if they were in aid of the distress fund. This resulted in a massive output of musical and sporting activity. Some fund-raising took place outside south Wales, for instance by male voice choirs which toured for the Women's Committee for the Relief of Miners' Wives and Children. In the main, however, it was what remained of the local working population who were most pressured for support: colliery office staff, local businesses, police, postmen, railwaymen, teachers, council workers and hospital staff. There were dances, plays, concerts, boxing competitions and whist drives. Assisted by fine summer weather in June and July and people who were determined to enjoy themselves, a blossoming of carnivals and sports competitions took place. From the lists of winners and prizes printed in the local press, it is clear that there were a large number of events and entries including egg and spoon races, sack races, running races for all ages and the tug of war.[87] Such activities involved both men and women as participants and spectators and again there is evidence of increased gender alignment. This theme is developed further in the following chapter.

Despite all these fund-raising events, many miners' canteens were in financial difficulties by August. The Cambrian Combine Lodge which supervised mid-Rhondda canteens, was only able to provide bread and corn beef due to lack of funds.[88] Even in Maerdy, cheese and cake had to be cut from the meals.[89] All efforts were focused on keeping the soup kitchens going. In an interview recorded in 1975, Pencoed ex-miners' leader Merfyn Payne recalled, 'we spent every penny we had in maintaining the canteens.'[90] As the situation became increasingly desperate and overdraft facilities were exhausted, institutes sold assets to raise funds and even tried to mortgage their buildings. The Caerphilly District Miners' Hospital Fund voted to pay out a five shilling 'refundment' to subscribers. A second payment was organised, but legal action prevented it.[91] Some canteens closed, but usually this was only temporary as they managed to engage in another round of frantic fund-raising and re-open. Despite the precarious funding, most of the soup kitchens remained open until the end of the dispute and even beyond it. Maerdy was open for Christmas and did not close until well into January 1927. [92]Even with the soup kitchens, however, mining families had to develop strategies to get by with very little income and these are dealt with in the next chapter.

It is worth reflecting here on the role that communal eating might have had in sustaining community solidarity. Francis and Smith have asserted that areas of the coalfield which opted for food vouchers to individuals rather than pooling resources for communal feeding, 'tended to be the very areas which suffered the most serious blacklegging'.[93] This can be supported by oral evidence such as that of retired miner Will Arthur, speaking in 1973, who claimed that there was no drift back to work in his village near Merthyr because 'our canteens were always full, you see'.[94] Francis and Smith cite James Griffiths, then a miners' agent from the anthracite district as saying, 'We went through the seven months in our area without a single breakaway . . . due . . . to the fellowship engendered by that one meal a day'.[95] The only example which Francis and Smith themselves offer to link lack of communal feeding with breakaway factions is the Lady Windsor Lodge in Ynysybwl, where there was no communal kitchen.[96] Ynysybwl did not have school feeding either as parents opted for the full amount of poor relief.[97] Although Lady Windsor ran a successful soup kitchen in 1921, in 1926 the Lodge resolved to negotiate with local tradesmen who had no real option but to offer discounts to those redeeming food vouchers.[98] A breakaway occurred in August and all available pressure, including physical, was exerted to persuade the blacklegs to cease work but in vain. The breakaway group remained limited to a small proportion of the workforce; only about forty men out of a Lodge of over 600.[99] The discipline of the Lodge was solid to the end, with the names of the blacklegs publicly recorded and shamed at the Lodge.[100] According to David Gilbert, the breakaway group were not from the village of Ynysybwl itself but the 'old village' some way away or even as far away as Pontypridd.[101] The recent introduction of bus routes and other transport improvements in the valleys, meant that by the mid-1920s there were miners who no longer lived within walking distance of the pit.[102] As we have seen, the 'alternative society' of the coalfield was essentially a local society. The pressures of locally-based morality and codes of behaviour could not be applied nearly so effectively on men who were not resident in the community. On the other hand, it has to be recognised that Ynysybwl was already a community which had experienced an unusually high degree of conflict. Michael Lieven has recently reminded us that the Conservatives retained a presence in the valleys in the 1920s and they were particularly active in Ynysybwl so possibly the conflict was generated as much from within as from outside.[103]

Regrettably, with the notable exception of Maerdy, there is little surviving SWMF documentation on soup kitchens, so it is very difficult to make an overall judgement on this issue. Extensive research on lodge archives which have survived and a search of all other available evidence reveal only one other possible connection between an early return to work and the absence of communal feeding. In mid-June, the *Glamorgan Gazette* reported that miners working in the Pencoed and Llanharan districts were opposed to Federation grants being used for soup kitchens.[104] About one hundred miners working in the Meiros Colliery petitioned the Miners' Federation to this effect, on the grounds that they lived too far from the colliery to be able to enjoy the benefits of communal feeding. It appears very unlikely, therefore, that these districts established communal feeding schemes. On 13 August, the paper reported that over a hundred miners in Llanharan had returned to work. Ted Williams, miners' agent for the Garw valley, called for the men concerned to be 'socially ostracised' and their names 'blacklisted', which apparently had no effect.[105] Clearly this is a complex issue. Communal kitchens obviously played an important role in maintaining community solidarity. There were, however, other activities which kept people occupied, promoted social cohesion and kept up morale. Lady Windsor, for example operated a collective boot repair scheme (a common activity at this time) and brought in fish from the coast to be sold at discount prices.[106] Lodges also organised barber shops, sewing circles, voluntary building work schemes and many sports activities. Barber shops and boot 'hospitals' were also often associated with school canteens.

The drift back to work, particularly from late October, meant that the miners' canteens gradually became unsustainable. Closures became frequent from late November and by the end of December most canteens had closed. School kitchens also wound down after the return to work in early December, although efforts continued to keep the most needy children fed. Further details can be found in chapter 6. Information is sparse on the total numbers fed in miners' canteens over the period of the Lockout, but it must run into millions of meals. In the Garw valley, for example 67,445 meals had been provided in the adult canteens by mid-July.[107]

We have more details of total numbers of schoolchildren fed over this period. In Merthyr, for instance, 1,604,743 meals were provided over a 28-week period. The average number of children fed was 5,489 at an average cost of 2.7d per meal.[108] The Bargoed kitchen alone provided more than 250,000 meals over a 30-week period, organised by headteacher Mr D. Davies BA. Total numbers of schoolchildren fed in the Rhondda during the Lockout are staggering: 5,986,257 meals supplied at an average cost of 2.31d per meal.[109] Even though school feeding was widespread in the mining communities, overall numbers fed did not exceed half the school population at any time.[110] Numbers fed in Monmouthshire were substantially lower than in Glamorgan, even bearing in mind that Monmouthshire contained fewer miners' children, with a total 646,567 meals provided for about 8,000 children at an average cost per meal of 2.8d.[111] As we have seen, many Monmouthshire parents preferred to take the full amount of poor relief when faced with a choice between reduced relief and school feeding. It may also have been the case that the required 'inquiry into means' was tighter in Monmouthshire than in other areas of the coalfield.

For seven months in 1926, the objective circumstances of people's lives in the south Wales coalfield had a different framework. The General Strike and Miners' Lockout had set them against the employers in a situation of brutal class confrontation and as a result the feeling of separation from mainstream society grew stronger. The mining community drew into itself, thus intensifying the characteristics of an 'alternative society'. Gerard Noel has drawn attention to the degree of co-operative living that sprang up in mining communities during the Lockout, asserting that the 'community' became a 'commune'.[112] Communal eating was the key component of this co-operative approach to life which was developed as a strategy for survival in a time of crisis. Although not adopted in every mining community, it was widespread and quite unprecedented in its scale. To feed so many for so long entirely on their own resources was an incredible achievement for the people of the south Wales coalfield.

4

HAVING FUN, GETTING BY AND OUTSIDE HELP

A great deal of what has been written about the Lockout of 1926 centres around the political struggle, particularly picketing and the descent into violence towards the end of the dispute. Much less has been written on day-to-day life in the seven long months of the Lockout.[1] The purpose of this chapter is to focus on how the south Wales mining communities survived during this period. The constant need to raise funds for the distress committees which ran the soup kitchens created a tremendous flowering of sporting and cultural activity which is documented. On the level of individual households, strategies to manage on extremely small incomes are examined. The picture is completed by an account of the role of voluntary organisations in the dispute. Nationally, the labour movement mobilised in support of the miners. These efforts were brought together most forcefully in the Women's Committee for the Relief of Miners' Wives and Children. The work of the Society of Friends (Quakers) was also significant in south Wales in this period.

Autobiographical accounts from the Lockout often refer to the exceptionally good weather in the summer of 1926. In fact meteorological evidence indicates that 1926 was not significantly different from the previous or subsequent summers.[2] What was different about 1926 was that men who had been working underground since the age of fourteen were suddenly free to enjoy the fine summer weather. As Arthur Horner put it, 'it's a thought that probably did not occur to anyone outside the coalfields, that hundreds of thousands of miners spent their first summer in the sunshine.'[3] Men bathed in local rivers and streams, rambled over the mountains and generally enjoyed their new sense of freedom. Cycling was also a popular hobby among men who toured the valleys and visited coastal resorts such as Porthcawl or Southerndown. Leonard Smith recalled the atmosphere:

We were out on strike, all of us. We couldn't have what we wanted, mun,
but we carried it through and it was a lovely bit of weather. We could get
out and about and we used to go on picnics to different places of the
valley. It was grand.[4]

Women, on the whole, had rather less time to indulge in these
recreational pursuits, but they were still able to appreciate the
sense of release and relaxation created by the Lockout. Idris
Davies's poem *Gwalia Deserta* refers to the 'laughter and the
cursing in the moonlit streets' and it certainly seems to have
been the case that there were late-night street parties.[5] In
Mountain Ash, there were street concerts which did not start
until 10 pm and went on until one or two in the morning.[6] Mr
Rogers of Blaenavon recalled the 'Glorious weather, sure to
have been about ninety degrees. And in the nights, you know,
you were dancing on the corners, dancing on the streets.'[7] An
outside observer also noticed the great sense of social cohesion in the mining areas in 1926; 'there were concerts in every
street, and the sense of fellowship in the community was more
marked than at any other time'.[8]

On a more formal level, carnivals were organised in every
district, usually with all proceeds dedicated to the local distress
committee. On the day of the carnival, the streets were decorated with flags and bunting. Usually the carnival, headed by
the local brass band, processed through the streets making
collections from the crowds lining the route before retiring to
a local field for judging and sports events. The *Merthyr Express*
of 4 September reported the success of a local carnival where
over 3,000 spectators gathered to watch when the procession
reached the athletic ground in Treharris. The bigger carnivals
were over a mile long, took over an hour to pass and attracted
a huge number of entrants. There was a bewildering number
of costume-based events; adult fancy dress, children's fancy
dress, best film star impersonator, best ornamented bicycle,
best mounted entry, best comic couple and so on. There were
reported to be 150 competitors for the fancy dress events
alone in the Cwmbach carnival.[9] 'Chinaman', 'Zulu' and 'Stone
Age Man' appear to be among the most popular characters
portrayed for the 'best national character' category. There was
often also a baby competition. Part of the attraction was

usually the cash prizes offered to the winners. This was also the case for the sporting activities, where again there were a large number of events. There were running races in all categories from children to 'old men', sack, egg and spoon, relay, skipping and three-legged races and also musical chairs. There were usually men's and women's events for each race type and strong evidence that all joined in. Carnivals were carefree, celebratory events in which the whole community participated. Pram racing, held in the Garw valley, was an event only for women. The tug of war generated great excitement. The Saunder's Fairy tug team from Tymeinor Avenue in Pontycymer developed a great reputation after defeating teams from Aberkenfig and Porthcawl at the Ffaldau Colliery sports ground. Through the *Glamorgan Gazette* they offered to take on any ladies team in the Ogmore, Garw or Llynfi valleys.[10] Apparently this six-woman team had a combined weight of 90 stone. Fetes and galas were also held and appear to have been similar to carnivals, such as the one in Ynysangharad Park, Pontypridd, in July which included a flower, fruit and vegetable show, maypole and country dancing and a bowls tournament as well as the usual carnival sports and fancy dress events.[11]

Clearly the desire to find some escape from the humiliation of grinding poverty was a significant factor behind the surge in carnivals and jazz bands in the Lockout but, in reality, desperate poverty was never far away. Articles in the press criticised carnival organisers for making small, ill-dressed children participate in carnival processions. A carnival in Hirwaun in July in wretched weather prompted an extended critical comment from the *Aberdare Leader*:

> It is bad form and bad taste . . . to introduce small children into these processions. Very young children formed part of some of the competing groups last Monday, and they were obliged to walk wearily for about two hours through the wet and dreary streets until they were drenched to skin . . . there was one small child . . . who had but one small article of clothing on. From the waist up it was naked, while its feet were bare. And this little chap (or little girl, I know not which) walked the rough roads – through Merthyr Road, Station Road, High Street and up Brecon Road – until it must have been on the point of collapsing. Such an exhibition as this is nothing short of sheer cruelty and the attention

of the Society for the Prevention of Cruelty to Children ought to be called to it.[12]

The determination to raise funds to support the soup kitchens drove men, women and children into miserable and distressing circumstances such as these. The Maerdy carnival in July raised £12 8s 3½d after an awful lot of work, which cannot have gone very far in supporting a soup kitchen feeding several hundred men.[13] This small example illustrates just how difficult it was to keep the Lockout going in those hard times.

Jazz music was an important influence on popular culture in the 1926 Lockout, which is sometimes referred to locally as 'the jazz band strike' or 'the gazooka strike'. Jazz bands, or 'character' bands as they were sometimes called, proliferated throughout the coalfield. The music was more 'jazz influenced' than jazz and the bands possessed very few instruments except gazookas (which was the cheapest sound available), but even so their colourful costumes and intricate military-style marching added hugely to the spectacle of the carnival.[14] The Cilfynydd carnival in August brought together 81 bands, each with a force of about 40–60 members. The jazz band festival held in Quakers Yard, Treforest, for the local distress

Tredegar Jazz Band c.1926.

Treorchy Zulus *c.*1926. Winners of the South Wales Jazz Band Tableau Championship.

committee attracted 50 bands at the end of September.[15] Although carnivals were mainly a feature of the summer months, there was still some carnival activity into the autumn, as witnessed by the event in Taff Vale Park in Treharris in late October in which over 2,500 competitors took part, including 27 bands.[16] By this time, a South Wales and Monmouthshire Carnival Bands Association had been formed, with over 75 bands involved. A major factor behind the formation of the Association appears to be disquiet concerning the conditions under which some bands had to perform, expecting members to march ten or eleven miles on carnival parades, for example.[17]

Each small town or village had its own jazz band such as the Toreadors of Aberdare who won first prize at the Treorchy carnival.[18] There were the Ystrad Zulus, the Cwmparc Gondoliers, Blaenllechau Long Row Spuds Jazz Band and many others. Mountain Ash had a large number of bands, including the Dyffryn 'Jocks' (dressed as Scottish

Highlanders), and others which were associated with particular streets, such as the Napier Street Convicts, the 'Chinks' of Dover Street (dressed as Chinese mandarins), the 'Coons' of Victoria Street (dressed as black and white minstrels) and the 'Stone Age men' from Newtown.[19] Trecenydd had a 'Nigger Nogger Coon Troupe'.[20] The image above reproduces a picture of the prize winning Treorchy Zulu Jazz band. Zulu 'warriors' are posing attacking a pensive-looking male missionary and child who are standing very close together in a large cooking pot. Although obviously light-hearted and humorous the costumes and mannerisms reflect crude racist stereotypes which were common to British society at this time. There is no evidence, even from the revolutionary left in the south Wales coalfield, of any challenge to this racist ideology. In this respect the 'alternative society' of south Wales did not differ from the mainstream.

The jazz bands appealed particularly to youth and became the central focus of life for many young people during the Lockout. Reg Fine belonged to a 'Sheik Band' in Maerdy. He told an interviewer in 1973:

> Well I myself was in the character band, what you call a Sheik Band . . . Harem Band, they were all dressed up as Harem Ladies, veils on their faces and the beads etc. And we had the slaves in front, of course the sheik first and slaves, stripped to the half and all black, and behind them was the slave driver and he was cracking the whip . . . as you were going along.[21]

'Mary K' was also in a band in Treorchy: 'I was "a lady with a veil" and we used to be in this band with kazooks. Remember the kazooks? We'd go in for competitions.'[22] 'Sarah' did not dress up but was a supporter of a Sheik Band in Dinas, helping and travelling with the band. She told me that 'they used to make the clothes out of anything, out of anything . . . everything was made out of nothing, everything'.[23] According to 'Sarah', the cash prizes were a major inducement to participate:

> The thing was, because there was no money, the money prize was for the best one. And we walked miles with them, you know, we used to march by the side and we walked miles. We had marvellous times, you know, as kids, we did.

A cash prize of two guineas would only mean a few pence for each band member, but in an economy with very little cash was a significant sum. 'Sarah' was keen to emphasize the point that, strange though it might seem, her memories of 1926 were positive: 'instead of being a miserable time for teenagers, it was a happy time'.

The jazz bands were not without their critics, as a series of articles in the *Aberdare Leader* revealed. As we have seen, the 1920s witnessed a decline in the hold of the chapels on coalfield communities and this became more apparent during the Lockout. Religious leaders, whose authority was draining away, lashed out against the jazz bands for being 'immoral and blasphemous' and encouraging drunkenness and gambling.[24] Besides encouraging vice, it was felt that more sinister forces were at work: Communism, spiritualism and modernism were named specifically in the press. There are also indications that the lure of jazz bands and carnivals was seen as a threat to the established gender order. The Rector of Dowlais wrote that:

> the women of today thought more of jazz bands, jazzing and dancing than they did of their domestic duties. They were not cooking for their children and too lazy to make a drop of broth for them . . . some of these women ought to have six months.[25]

No evidence was produced to support this allegation in what appears to be an attack on the school soup kitchens for taking responsibility for feeding school-aged children away from mothers, as well as on the jazz bands. Hywel Francis and Dai Smith have argued that the 'alternative society' of the coalfield can be seen most clearly in the jazz bands.[26] As we have seen, racial stereotypes were accepted within coalfield society. Moreover the drinking, dancing, gambling and escapism associated with carnivals and jazz bands were activities very much present in mainstream British society of the 1920s, rather than being an alternative to it. On the other hand, the collective resistance, resilience and sheer determination to support the Lockout clearly evident within the carnivals and jazz band culture uphold the view that this was a unique group of people with their own values which were pitted against the dominant elements in society. As Idris Davies, the Welsh poet put it, 'Do you remember 1926 . . . the bravery of the simple, faithful folk'.[27]

Many other sporting and recreational activities were held in and around the miners' institutes which were the chief focus of community life. All tournaments were in aid of the distress fund. Boxing was a favourite, the cash prizes being a major attraction. Such was the boxing boom in the Rhymney valley in 1926 that a local championship was set up. A crowd of 2,000 attended the tournament held at the 'Empire' in Bargoed, Caerphilly.[28] Outdoor games were also pursued with enthusiasm. The *Glamorgan Gazette* for 28 May reported that in Nantymoel football, rounders and cricket were played every day in the park with spectators. In the Garw valley, weekly cricket matches were held between different teams from Pontycymer and Blaengarw. The matches had to be held in Llangeinor where the only area of flat ground could be found, causing both players and spectators to trek up and down the valley every week to participate.[29] In August, there were disturbances in Blaengarw after the safety men were withdrawn and one refused to vacate his post. Eighty police were drafted into the area, but by the evening police and miners were playing a game of cricket. The *Glamorgan Gazette* reported that the game created a 'friendly feeling to take the place of the previous suspicion'.[30] In Aberdare, a fund-raising comic cricket match was held. The 'England v Australia' match was said to be very entertaining. Rugby, rounders, hockey, quoits and tennis were also played. The *Rhondda Gazette* in early June reported on the good spirit prevailing during the stoppage, 'splendid behaviour characterises the whole of our area' with men and boys engaged in a whole range of sporting activities, cricket apparently being the most popular.[31] Some institutes were fortunate enough to possess playing fields and possibly even a sports pavilion. Nixons Workmen's Hall in Mountain Ash could proudly boast both tennis and bowling greens and a pavilion. During 1926, a tennis club was established.[32] The Cambrian Welfare Association also had playing fields and a pavilion, regularly used by rugby, football, cricket and quoit teams.

An interesting feature of the dispute was a revival of the game 'cattie and dog'. Bearing similarities to both rounders and cricket, and requiring only two sticks, there was a resurgence of interest in the game during the Lockout. Three of my respondents told me that they played 'cattie and dog': two of them, Gladys Davies and Jean Ellis, were from Pontycymer. Gladys remembers playing outside her garden gate and was particularly keen to tell me about it as she said that nobody today believes that it was a real game.[33] Lilian Roberts played with her cousin Colin in Porth.[34] In the Garw valley when the 'Pantygog Mud-slashers' took on challengers at 'cattie and dog' there were over 300 spectators.[35] According to Wyn Price other 'cattie and dog' teams in the Garw valley included the 'Herbert Street Slashers', the 'Pwllcarn Russians' and the 'Railway Rippers'.[36] Such was the interest in the game that the Rhondda valley held a 'cattie and dog' tournament which went on over several days and attracted 954 entries. The *Rhondda Gazette* reported that the event 'took the valley by storm ... thousands of people attended daily ... excitement was intense'.[37]

There is also evidence that 'cattie and dog' teams involved women. Early mentions of tournaments refer to men's teams but this appears to have changed rapidly. The 'gossip' section of the *Glamorgan Gazette* made some revealing comments about women's participation in 'cattie and dog' matches:

> A local 'hubby' was recently heard saying that it was all right to see the little 'wifie' enjoying herself with a game of 'cat-and-dog', but he did not consider it fair that he should have to do all the housework. Poor old chap. But it seems that 'everybody's doing it now!'[38]

It is difficult to make an overall assessment regarding gender in these sporting and carnival activities, as documentary evidence is sparse and it is too late to acquire oral testimony of any range or depth. It must be remembered that the backdrop for almost all these activities was usually the miners' institute which was a very male space. Whilst women did participate in sporting events at carnivals, organised games were usually for boys and men. In Nantymoel, it was the organiser of the boys club, Captain Glyn Edwards, who took over the arrangements for the daily games of cricket, rounders and football in the park.[39] There is no mention of any activities for women and girls. As we know, during the Lockout women were released from some elements of their domestic responsibilities such as servicing the miner at work, but they continued to bear a domestic burden, and this was particularly so for women with

Llwyncelyn Ladies v Gents football match, 1926. The men played with one hand tied behind their backs.

children and infants below school age. A rare glimpse of life for women during the Lockout can be seen in the film *Women of the Rhondda*, made in the early 1970s in which four elderly women look back on their lives.[40] One of these women says that she could not follow a jazz band as she had children to look after. Another woman states that 'my brothers ended up very, very sunburnt, whereas my mother was worn out'. As we have seen, in the soup kitchens there were some signs of increased fellowship between men and women. Although overall sporting, carnival and jazz band activity appeared to be male-dominated, there are certainly many indications of joint activity between men and women. The fact that so many sporting events at carnivals were for women – women's tug of war, sack, egg and spoon, pram races and so on – at least brought women out more into the public domain. A fascinating photograph, reproduced above, survives of a match played in 1926 between the Llwyncelyn Ladies football team from Porth and a local men's team, with the men apparently playing with one hand tied behind their backs. Two of the players are wearing outlandish costumes. The captains of each team are seated in the centre of the group, arm in arm and men and women seem to be thoroughly at ease with each other and enjoying the event.[41] It is hard to imagine that this match could have taken place before the Lockout, except possibly in the 1921 Lockout where the circumstances were equally exceptional. Other 'comedy' football matches involving mixed teams took place, such as the one organised by the Aberfan and Merthyr Vale Strike Committee at the end of May when single and married teams competed for a faggots and peas supper.[42]

> Mixed bathing is not in it with the present 'cat-and-dog matches' between the sexes. A wife who had taken part in a recent match returned home to find that hubby had not prepared her tea, and cat-and-dog started over again, hubby on this occasion being a good second.[43]

Although the above is obviously written tongue-in-cheek, if we take all this evidence together it does seem to be the case that men and women during the Lockout were engaging together in sporting activities much more than previously. Gender mixing had become much more common.

There were also many other non-sporting events to raise funds to support the miners. Whist drives were popular, such as the one held in September by Pontyrhyl Labour Women's section to provide boots and shoes for miners' children, with prizes donated by local trades people and friends.[44] The NUT in Pontypridd organised a whist drive in support of the local distress fund which attracted 300 competitors and raised £2 16s.[45] Again, there is evidence that people felt satisfied when they were doing something positive. Henry John, who was in Abercraf, Swansea valley, during the Lockout, put it this way:

> Now the '26 strike everybody was happy . . . because we were utilizing our time, we had carnivals, we had sports, we had concerts, we had whist drives . . . I was the sec. of the entertainment committee at that time and we organised all these things . . . the whist drives that we had . . . the first prize would be a tin of corn beef and, mind you, think of that as a wonderful prize, a tin of corn beef or a parcel of food that some sympathetic grocer was prepared to give us, or a pound of butter from somebody else . . . you would have 24 tables playing whist.[46]

Concerts of all kinds were held in aid of the miners. Dramas, operettas, oratorios, brass and silver band concerts were held all over the coalfield. Variety concerts were very popular, especially the comic acts and impersonators. Most mining communities had several choirs: men's, women's and children's. Many of the oral history respondents had connections with bands or choirs. Martha Jones, whose father was a single parent, told me that his only activity outside the home, except for work, was his male voice choir.[47] The father of Mary Lowrie was in the Hibernia band. According to Mary some band members could only afford a whistle, but 'as long as you could make music' you were welcome.[48] As is well known, male voice choirs, particularly the Treorchy Male Voice Choir, were particularly strong in the valleys and many choirs travelled beyond south Wales to raise funds. The Ystrad Mynach choir toured Devon and Cornwall and the Bargoed Glee Party visited the Bournemouth area. Travelling choirs would often bring back bundles of much needed clothes and boots. Choirs also visited Russia and Germany to raise funds. The Rhondda First Miners' Choir, which toured Germany, was headed by pipers from a Fifeshire miners' band.[49] According to Marion

South Wales miners singing in Piccadilly Circus, London, c.1926.

Phillips, there were about 65 bands and choirs fund-raising for the miners.[50] Inevitably, there were accusations in the press that money collected by bands and choirs was being spent in pubs.[51] Sometimes men set off on these trips on a casual basis and found themselves stranded as no arrangements had been made for them.[52] Of course, not all the miner's newly found leisure time was spent on collective pursuits. B. L. Coombes became seriously interested in music in 1926 and began violin lessons. In later years he helped to form an orchestra in his home village of Resolven.[53] The reading rooms of the miners' institutes were well used during 1926, even though sometimes reduced funds meant that subscriptions to newspapers and journals had to be cut back. Many miners were eager to keep up with current affairs and had a keen appreciation of the progress of the Lockout and the overall political situation. Women had no direct access to these libaries, but could ask a male family member to take books out on their behalf.[54] By the mid-1920s, an extensive network of adult education had developed in south Wales, through the Workers Education Association (WEA) and the Central Labour College (CLC). Classes were held in history, literature, philosophy, psychology and music as well as vocational courses in various aspects of mining. Regrettably, no figures are available on the gender breakdown of adult education classes. Although miners had more time on their hands in the Lockout, the effect of the dispute on adult education appears to have been adverse. A WEA psychology class in Clydach Vale is reported to have suffered with some members 'so disheartened by the prevailing conditions that it was impossible to revive their interest'.[55] The CLC classes suffered as these politically motivated students were too busy with more practical matters, such as organising soup kitchens and other relief activities.[56]

Locked-out miners and their wives engaged in all kinds of voluntary work during the dispute. The *Rhondda Gazette* reported in 'Ystrad and Llwynpia Notes' that 'men and women of Bodringallt Church have been busily cleaning and renovating different parts of the building'.[57] Emma Noble, who toured south Wales in June 1926, reported that in several towns miners were painting and decorating their chapels.[58] In the little village of Penywaun near Aberdare between 60 and

Unemployed men on work relief building a road from Llangeinor to Ogmore, 1926. Gladys Davies's father, William Price is in the back row, far right.

70 volunteers laboured for over three months to level and drain some land near the local school so that the children could benefit from outdoor playing fields. According to the *Aberdare Leader* the men were happy to give their labour and a 'loyal and harmonious spirit had prevailed during the whole time'.[59] The booklet *Mountain Ash Remembered* recounts a relief project during the Lockout to fill in an old canal, thus creating what is described as 'one of the finest by-pass roads in the whole of the South Wales valleys'.[60] Miners in Ferndale built a culvert during the Lockout. Oral respondents from the Pontycymer area told me about the relief project for the unemployed in 1926 to build a road over the mountain from Llangeinor to Ogmore. Gladys Davies has kindly supplied a photograph of her father, William Price, working on the construction of what is still referred to as 'the new road' in 1926, which is reproduced above. Blod Davies told me that what is now Garth Park, Trealaw, was begun in 1926, when miners built a swimming pool and bathing huts.[61] Of course, many miners were also involved in voluntary work through

their local miners' institute; soup kitchen labour, boot repairing and barber shops. Eventually Poor Law authorities and other organisations such as local Labour Parties were persuaded to cover the cost of shoe leather for the volunteer boot depots as so many children were barefoot or poorly shod, with many not attending school on account of this.

'MAKING DO'

The south Wales miners, with their long history of militant activity stretching from the 1880s to the anthracite strikes of 1925, were accustomed to managing during long disputes. Resort to the humiliating system of Poor Law relief was inevitable for many families.[62] Such was the scale of Poor Law relief in the more densely populated areas that extra relieving stations had to be opened in parish vestries. Lockout miners were not eligible for poor relief, but wives were granted about ten shillings a week and dependent children between two and four shillings, depending on whether they were school fed. Infants were given milk. Surviving records from Monmouthshire indicate that attendance at infant welfare clinics increased when milk and free or reduced price food was on offer.[63] After the resumption of work, there was a sudden drop in attendance.

Communal eating, although very important was not universal. Not all miners' children were eligible for school meals. Miners' communal kitchens were extremely hard to keep going and miners were discouraged from using these facilities if they could obtain food elsewhere. Most miners' kitchens could only provide one meal a day, so additional food would have to be found from elsewhere. Households were, therefore faced with the problem of getting by on a drastically reduced income. How did they cope over such a long time? Very few miners had savings to fall back on, especially as the industry had been in a poor state since 1921, so the impact of the Lockout was felt almost immediately. Outgoings were reduced wherever possible. Rent was an obvious example and it was a long-established practice for miners to withhold rent for the duration of disputes.[64] This meant, of course, a backlog of crippling arrears upon resumption of work. Credit was another well-used strategy for grocery items such as flour, sugar and tea. Customers would have to have a good record before shopkeepers would grant credit, particularly since many bad debts from the three-month strike during 1921 were still not paid off.[65] The Co-op in particular was much more cautious about granting credit in 1926 than it had been in 1921. On the other hand, many shopkeepers felt that they had no option but to grant credit if they wanted to retain their customers after the dispute. Nancy Lewis lived with her family in Blaengarw thoughout her life. Her mother shopped at the Royal Stores in nearby Pontycymer, even after much closer shops were established in Blaengarw. As an adult, Nancy asked her mother, '"why are you coming down here in all winds and weathers to shop?" She said, "My dear, it kept us going during the strikes, the '21 strike, the '26 strike, yes".'[66]

As much food as possible was produced at home, in both back gardens and allotments. Most families grew some food and many also kept chickens. Pigs were also fairly common and, more rarely, goats, ducks and geese were reared. During the Lockout allotments were worked much more intensively than usual. Although all kinds of vegetables, fruit and salads were grown on allotments, potatoes were particularly valued for their input to the family diet. Gladys Davies remembered that with addition of a tin of corn beef the family could enjoy a tasty meal. 'You grew stuff in the garden, it was a basic meal . . . my father had an allotment. We had corn beef and new potatoes, God, it was great . . . Kidney (runner) beans.'[67] Many other respondents spoke of the family's use of allotments, such as Helena Charles whose stepfather and older brothers worked continuously to produce food for the family during the Lockout: 'we had all our vegetables there. It was only buying the meat really.'[68] Turnips, sometimes gained from raids on local farms, could be made into paste and substituted for margarine. Many communities were prized for their gardening. In Ynysybwl, for example, the miners were very keen gardeners and in addition to supplying their families with vegetables, eggs, pork and bacon, they competed with each other for prizes at the annual flower and vegetable show.[69]

Community cohesion meant that if a surplus of something

Gwendraeth valley poachers c.1926.

was available, it was shared and favours were returned, so
much informal bartering took place. Family and neighbourly
solidarity was very evident from the oral history respondents.
When I asked Jean Ellis how people managed during the
Lockout she said, 'everybody clung together and shared'.[70]
Surplus produce was distributed to wider family and neighbours and in return the occasional cup of sugar or other item
might be offered as a mark of gratitude. In addition, food was
collected from the surrounding hillsides. Blackberries and
whinberries were gathered and made into pies and tarts.
Mushrooms were also collected for cooking. Nettles could be
made into nettle beer which women sold along with home-
made faggots. This could also extend into scrumping, as
Edwin Greening did in dawn raids on the large houses in
Aberdare during the Lockout where he gathered strawberries,
cherries, blackcurrants, redcurrants, raspberries, loganberries
and gooseberries and even tasted the rare and acclaimed
mulberry fruit.[71] Men also fished for trout, salmon and other
catch, sometimes illegally and shot rabbits for food. The image

reproduced above, believed to be from 1926, shows two poachers and their catch in the Gwendraeth valley, a westerly rural location in the coalfield. The services of rabbit catchers were much in demand in 1926. Blod Davies laughed mischievously after saying to me, 'there was no poaching in the valley'.[72] Sheep disappeared from the hillsides. Two men from Cwmbach, W. H. Jones and John Davies, were arrested after being caught with a lamb carcase near to a field where a sheep's head and skin had been left.[73] After being cautioned, Jones is reported to have said, 'I am sorry it has happened: I was never in a position like this before.'

In the absence of the usual concessionary coal from the colliery, men, and to a lesser extent women and children, worked for outcrop coal for fuel. It was expected that this would be carried out for domestic use and for soup kitchens, but in many areas outcropping went beyond this and developed into a commercial undertaking which undermined the Lockout.[74] In a case reported by the *Colliery Guardian*, eleven miners were fined ten shillings each at Bridgend Police Court for damaging land belonging to the Earl of Dunraven. They had sunk a 25ft hole and were being paid £1 a bag for coal which was being sold on for £1 15s.[75] Miners' lodges were aware of the problem but proved unable to control it effectively. Neath miners' communal kitchens took action against miners found to be selling outcrop coal and barred them from communal eating.[76] Outcropping operations were highly dangerous and there were numerous examples of fatal accidents.[77]

Mining men and women were extremely resourceful and would not engage in cash transactions if it could possibly be avoided. Fred Williams (born 1910) from Porth told me that his father was 'very careful what he spent, wouldn't waste a ha'penny, well they had to didn't they, more or less, in those days'.[78] Fathers could often tap (mend) boots and men would cut each other's hair. Common ailments were treated with traditional remedies, often plants gathered from the surrounding countryside. Miners' wives were used to 'making something out of nothing'. According to Mary Lowrie, milk which had turned sour was turned into cheese.[79] Scraps of bacon from the bacon slicer bought for a couple of coppers

would be made into a pie or pudding and lambs' hearts
bought for twopence each were stuffed and turned into a
nourishing meal. Children learned quickly that nothing was
wasted. As Ethel Roberts put it, when food was put in front of
her 'you ate it and didn't argue'.[80] Similarly with Lilian
Lawrence:

> I was brought up to know that if I didn't eat my dinner, I had it for my
> tea, she (Lilian was raised by her grandmother) would never waste
> nothing . . . no arguments. You either ate it or you went without. But if
> you went without, you had to have it at the next meal . . . oh yes, very
> strict in that respect.[81]

Extended family also helped out. Here the testimony of Lilian
Lawrence is useful again as she told me that her uncle kept
pigs and would keep the family well supplied:

> we always had half a side of bacon and half a side of pork hanging up in
> the kitchen, in the pantry . . . they had a marble slab in the pantry . . .
> when we wanted bacon all we had to do was go in and cut it. So we used
> to have bacon for breakfast . . . royal fry, sliced potatoes, bits of bacon . . .
> there was always some of that going in our house.[82]

According to David Davies, of the 15,000 or so miners in the
more rural western part of the coalfield only a minority actually claimed poor relief during the Lockout.[83] Humiliating
treatment, poor relief scales and the ability to find sustenance
from the land appears to have deterred these miners from
claiming it. Even families which had long migrated from rural
districts reached back into these rural roots during the
Lockout. Sally Poulton's grandfather came from a farming
family in mid-Wales who sent Sally's family tubs of butter and
sides of bacon so, like Lilian Lawrence, they never went short
of food.[84] Gwyneth Evans's father was from Pembrokeshire.
During both the 1921 and the 1926 Lockouts, he went home
and worked as an agricultural labourer, sending money to
support his family in Pontycymer.[85] There were also cases of
families relocating to Hereford for two weeks hop-picking.[86]
Helena Charles told me that her father's sister, who lived in
north Wales and was 'pretty good off', sent money to help
out.[87] Older married siblings, or aunts and uncles working
outside of mining, for example on the railways or in teaching,
might also help out. Betty Bowen had an uncle who worked at

Tonypandy station who helped her family out.[88] Older sisters working in service earned very small wages but were expected to send most of their wages home and keep on 'pocket money'. Both Martha Jones and Phyllis Lewis had older sisters in service who made financial contributions to the household. It was also common for these older working sisters in service to send home presents at Christmas time.

Even with such help, several families among the oral respondents came close to destitution during the Lockout. When I asked Gladys Davies if she ever went hungry during the 1926 Lockout, she replied 'Yes, during the strike there were times when my mother didn't know where the next meal was coming from, but something seemed to turn up'.[89] Phyllis Lewis also remembers it as a very difficult time: 'I can remember my mother very worried about food . . . terrible, terrible time then. I can remember my mother didn't know where to turn.'[90] The phrase 'didn't know where to turn' cropped up in other interviews. Oral evidence is inconclusive, however, as some respondents did not feel that the Lockout was significantly worse than at other times. With poor relief, communal eating and mutual support from extended kin and neighbours most families managed to get by. This may be partly attributed to the fact that mothers went without to feed their children. Also, arguably, low wages meant that families on poor relief and withholding rent were not markedly worse off than those in employment.

Single men, on the other hand, being ineligible for poor relief, were extremely vulnerable and in the last resort sought admission to the workhouse.[91] There is evidence of mass demonstrations of single men demanding admission to the workhouse. A Ministry of Health report was particularly concerned about Monmouthshire, where it refers to an 'invasion of single men' on the workhouse at Pontypool.[92] A deputation from the Merthyr Tydfil Trades Council and Labour Party and the Fochriw Strike Committee demanding admission for single men was reported at the Merthyr Tydfil Poor Law Union in late May.[93] Official ruling from the Ministry of Health was that single men could not be legally admitted unless certified unfit for work. In practice, there are examples of single men being admitted. The Merthyr Tydfil Poor Law

Union admitted eleven destitute men to the workhouse between 21 May and 18 June 1926, including William Cooper, an Englishman who had probably been evicted from his lodgings as he could no longer pay for his keep.[94] Emigration was a last resort. Poor Law records show that guardians occasionally helped families on poor relief to emigrate, usually either to Canada or Australia. It was very difficult for families to migrate to more prosperous areas of Britain, as without jobs to go to they had no funds to rent accommodation, but many single men and women did leave the area in search of work during the Lockout. Miners Robert Thomas and William Thomas were remanded in London for begging in September. The press report states that they had walked from Llanelli with very little food and had become disorderly whilst singing in Fenchurch Street because they were hungry.[95]

The miners were not alone in their struggle and received a great deal of aid both from inside and outside the mining community. Railway workers, teachers, hospital staff and many business people made regular subscriptions to distress committees and boot funds. At a meeting of Rhondda Urban District Council in September, a vote of thanks was given to council employees who had contributed from their salaries towards a boot fund for necessitous children.[96] In some pits colliery staff gave tea parties for miners' children such as the one in Abernant in July where 500 children enjoyed sports, a free tea and a packet of sweets each.[97] Ethel Roberts was at school in Cwmgwrach in the Neath valley during the Lockout. She remembers that the headmaster, Mr Nicholas used to arrange for two older boys to meet him from the station on Monday morning:

> to carry all the stuff he was bringing . . . he had connections down in Neath where they were a bit more affluent . . . well then the stuff that used to come . . . boxes of great big marrow bones . . . for the stew for the soup kitchens . . . plenty of veg that was going.[98]

Theoretically, members of the MFGB were entitled to strike pay but in practice the Federation was ill-equipped to cope with such a long dispute and very small sums were paid out. Other sums which came through the SWMF were of more significance, notably the grant of £1,161,459 after a vote by

Russian trade unionists to donate 1 per cent of wages to the British miners' relief fund.[99] Such was the gratitude of British miners that when Michael Tomsky, who had acted as a vital link between the MFGB and Russian trade unions, died the following year a minute's silence was held at the MFGB Congress. In some SWMF branches, such as Nine Mile Point, financial payments to members were openly referred to as 'Russian money'.[100] Other donations were also received from mine workers and other trade unionists abroad and many Co-op, Labour Party, trades councils and trade union branches in Britain paid regular subscriptions to the MFGB relief fund. In some areas, support was coordinated through a relief fund committee, such as the one in Tottenham, London, which raised £2,375.[101]

Labour and Quaker Women

The most outstanding contribution towards the miners' cause came from the Women's Committee for the Relief of the Miners' Wives and Children (WCRMWC). This organisation came about when the miners' leader, A. J. Cook, asked Marion Phillips, Labour Party National Woman's Officer, if Labour women could help with fund-raising. An office was rapidly established at the Parliamentary Labour Club in London and a committee formed with Ellen Wilkinson MP as chairman and Marion Phillips and Lilian Dawson as joint-secretaries.[102] By 31 January 1927, the WCRMWC had raised £313,874.[103] Such was the success of the Women's Committee that Cook decided that it was the only relief organisation that the MFGB would work with. Apart from the usual fund-raising methods, such as tapping wealthy sympathisers and making collections at cinemas and music halls, the Committee trailblazed new methods of raising money such as the sale of specially inscribed pens, pencils, calendars, Christmas cards, miniature and real miners' lamps.[104] It is interesting to note that the annual BBC Children's Appeal, now the BBC Children in Need Appeal, dates from 1927.[105] It appears to be the work of the Women's Committee which prompted the BBC to take up the cause of disadvantaged children. Meetings were also held to rally support. The Women's Section of the National Union of General Workers held a very successful rally in central London, chaired by Margaret Bondfield, at which the actress Sybil Thorndike and five miners' wives spoke. [106] Miners' wives also accompanied some of the travelling choirs to explain to audiences the hardship which the Lockout was causing.

The ideas that miners' families were in dire need was not universally accepted. Following a controversial report from the National Society for the Prevention of Cruelty to Children (NSPCC) arguing that Poor Law provision and school meals meant that miners' children were no worse off during the Lockout, the *Times* came out in support of the NSPCC, stating that 'children are being better fed than they were before the dispute began'.[107] This prompted prime minister Stanley Baldwin, in an obvious attempt to undermine the miners, to announce on the eve of a fund-raising tour of the US by Ellen Wilkinson, that miners' children were not in need.[108] In fact, the WCRMWC publicity material was somewhat alarmist, implying that miners' families were in imminent danger of starvation.[109] Marion Phillips's subsequent report on the work of the Women's Committee quoted cases of destitution where babies were born into homes with no food in the house and no provision had been made for mother and baby.[110] The report also asserted that babies had been stillborn as a result of the Lockout and this theme of acute deprivation was picked up by Hywel Francis, although he quotes only two cases of deaths which were attributed to the Lockout by oral respondents.[111] In general, there has been little evidence to back up these claims, although a report from Monmouthshire stated that 'the health and stamina of a great many mothers depreciated considerably.'[112] It went on to state that 'breast milk failed entirely or turned very poor quality' in many cases and argued that it was only the provision of free milk which averted a crisis. Evidence from Caerau Miners' Lodge shows that there were many more women sent to the lodge convalescent home in Porthcawl in 1926 than usual, an indication perhaps of the ill health which women experienced in the Lockout.[113] Statistical evidence, however, shows, as we have seen, that the Lockout had little effect on death rates; if anything they declined, although men's death rates fell more than women's.[114] This certainly does not mean that there was not desperate poverty, hardship, tragic deaths and exhausted mothers in the seven months of the Lockout. Large families, very poor living conditions and the parlous state of the coal industry meant that mining communities were suffering from 1921. In this sense, the 1926 Lockout may not be quite as significant a landmark as was previously thought.

Despite this controversy, it is undoubtedly the case that the Women's Committee for the Relief of Miners' Wives and Children did a tremendous amount of very valuable work during the Lockout. The Committee operated on certain basic principles. Funds were limited, so assistance was only rendered to the most needy cases where no other help was available. In an effort to be non-controversial the WCRMWC provided relief for miners' wives and children only, with nothing going directly to 'striking' miners. No cash was handed over as all payments were in kind: food vouchers, blankets, clothing, boots etc. Donors could earmark their contributions to particular categories of need, such as maternity cases or boot funds. The maternity fund was officially the Lady Slesser Fund, Mothers and Babies Scheme, named after the Treasurer of the Women's Committee. In these cases, a local representative acting for the Women's Committee ensured that the mother in need had food and warmth for two weeks and that the baby was adequately supplied with infant clothing.

After the first few weeks of the Lockout, by which time it was obvious that the dispute would be protracted, the idea was raised of temporary fostering for miners' children. Altogether the WCRMWC organised the fostering of over two thousand miners' children, 829 of whom came from Wales.[115] Many offers of help were received from sympathetic families and it appears that the first children were dispatched in August. Motherless and delicate children were given preference, along with children from large families as poor relief was usually limited to six children per family. The scheme worked well with Mrs Andrews, Welsh Labour Party Women's Organiser and Mrs Green, from Abertillery, helping to transport the children to their new temporary homes.[116] When the *Merthyr Express* reported in late September that a second group of local children had been sent to London it was reported that the first batch were said to be 'well and happy'.[117] Some foster parents extended help to the entire family and sent clothing, food parcels and presents. Almost all the children returned to Wales at the end of the dispute. In January 1927, the Rhondda Urban District Council publicly thanked the Women's Committee for the Relief of Miners' Wives and Children for the 'invaluable service rendered by them in arranging for the care and maintenance of many hundreds of children from this district whose parents were unable to provide for them during the period of the coal stoppage'.[118]

The Society of Friends (Quakers) also made a significant contribution to relief in South Wales. This involvement began after Emma Noble, a leading Quaker, was moved by what she heard about the Lockout at the Quakers' yearly meeting.[119] As a result she spent a week in south Wales, focusing on the Rhondda, Aberdare and Barry. She wrote a report outlining the case for 'material help and loving sympathy'.[120] According to Noble, although she found good fellowship and strong spirits, many were struggling to hide their poverty. After a second visit, when Noble stayed with a family in Tonypandy and shared their life, she began to develop the idea of self-help schemes. Raising the money for shoe leather through influential friends (later other groups contributed to this cost) Noble began a scheme of 'self-improvement' by launching a series of boot-repairing depots. Eventually, 520 miners were involved in 52 different centres, mainly in the Rhondda.[121] Twenty women's sewing groups were also developed, each with between ten and twenty women meeting regularly to cut up and remake donated unwanted clothing into useful garments. Both of these activities did much to reduce isolation and raise morale, as well as providing a valuable service. The Quakers were particularly active in Tonypandy and two of the oral respondents from this area commented favourably on their work. Blod Davies told me, 'oh the Quakers was wonderful during the miners' strike'.[122] The *Rhondda Gazette* was also impressed by the work of the Quakers, particularly the tolerant and interdenominational culture prevailing in the boot-repairing workshops, ending one report with the words, 'let us raise our hats to the Quaker Society of Friends'.[123]

The Quakers were also involved in casework and tried to help individual families where they were in particular need.

This work, especially the maternity cases, took them into the same territory as the Women's Committee for the Relief of Miners' Wives and Children. There is evidence of friction between the two groups over methods of working. Emma Noble was in constant touch with central offices of the Society of Friends in London. In a letter from this office to Emma Noble, Edith Pye mentioned her concerns about the Women's Committee: 'they have a ridiculous system by which every individual case has to be passed by a committee in London. Of course, for maternity cases this is quite absurd.'[124] It is clear from the letter that the Quakers were in touch with Marion Phillips, possibly in an attempt to provide a consistent working practice. Pye argued for the most urgent cases to be decided on the spot by caseworkers but it appears there was little agreement: 'I am afraid that their system is not really going to work. Dr Phillips would not hear of any doubts upon the matter.'[125]

At the end of the Lockout, further expressions of gratitude were made to the work of the Society of Friends. In Ynysybwl, a presentation was made to Mrs Noble of an elegant pair of shoes hand-crafted by George Dobson, master cobbler, together with a framed photograph of the workers in the Ynysybwl boot depot.[126] The Quakers felt strongly that their work in south Wales should continue and this story is developed further in chapter 6.

5

WOMEN, POLITICS AND PICKETS

This chapter focuses on women in politics in the south Wales coalfield during the 1926 dispute. 'Politics' is here broadly defined as not just the interaction of women with the local political apparatus but also women playing out roles in public with the aim of influencing events. By examining women in active, assertive roles we resist the tendency to view working-class women in the south Wales coalfield as victims. Lynn Sinclair has also argued that we should not see working-class women in Britain in depressed regions as 'quiescent, passive victims' but as much more complex identities.[1] Equally, as Angela V. John has recognised, we cannot view these women as 'totally free agents, gradually and deliberately "modernising"'.[2] Karen Hunt and June Hannam have pointed out that historians of socialism have largely told the story of socialism from a masculinist point of view with little time for the gendering of the socialist movement.[3] Hunt and Hannam do not see 'socialist women' as a fixed entity but a series of contested entities. Clare Collins has also emphasised the contested nature of the role and identity of women in Labour politics at this time.[4] To understand this identity we need to consider the extent to which women activists may have 'looked at their politics through the prism of gender'.[5] With these ideas in mind, the aim of this chapter is to foreground the women activists of 1926 in south Wales; to understand their values and perspectives, the structures and constraints which they worked within and the role they played in the Lockout.

The national context is obviously of great importance. Women had been active in local government from the 1880s and by the early 1920s, women were acting as local councillors, Poor Law guardians and local magistrates (JPs). Women members specialised in matters of health, education and welfare, focused very much on small-scale reforms, such as provision of public baths, school meals, infant and maternity clinics. Although this could be depicted as a form of 'separate spheres', looked at more positively it was a locally based, practical form of socialist-feminism.[6] Many of these women were also involved in the mass movement for women's suffrage which came to fruition in 1918 with the enfranchisement of women over thirty years of age. In 1918, the new constitution of the Labour Party gave men and women the right of individual membership. The small but autonomous Women's Labour League was formally dissolved into the new Labour Party. It was clear from the start that men and women members would be treated differently and women were defined as wives and mothers first and foremost. A national women's officer and several regional officers were appointed. Annual women's conferences were held and over the next few years a vast structure of regional women's advisory councils, district committees and local women's sections came into being. According to Marion Phillips in her report to the National Conference of Labour Women, in 1925 there were 1,450 women's sections representing 200,000 women.[7] Alongside this was the growth of the Women's Co-operative Guild which by May 1926 had over 57,000 members.[8] Numbers of women involved with other left wing organisations, principally the Independent Labour Party and the Communist Party, were tiny and in any case until at least the mid-1920s many of these women were also involved with the Labour Party.

The great majority of women Labour Party members were married women who chose to be active in the local Women's Sections rather than the main party apparatus. By the late 1920s over half the Labour Party membership were women but, as both Pamela Graves and Pat Thane have written, women and the more woman-focused policies of the early socialist-feminist pioneers lost out to male dominance.[9] Nowhere is this more apparent than on the issue of birth control, where the persistent declarations of the female membership in favour of the dissemination of birth control information were routinely disregarded by the leadership who regarded it as a 'personal issue'.[10] Co-op women were also campaigning for birth control at this time. It is very likely that it was largely the same women who were involved in both organisations. Labour women were required to help run the party machine – vital at election times – and undertake fund-raising activities, but in no sense could they exercise power over party policy. A key aim for the full-time officers was to keep women members in line with the masculinist leadership. Increasingly this meant distancing them from feminist organisations which were seen as 'divisive' as they drew attention to gender difference. The party had a very clear working-class orientation and women members were expected to exercise this class bias, which in practice meant acquiescing in the male leadership. As the 1920s wore on and unemployment and consequent social distress became a serious problem, it became increasingly difficult for Labour Party women to exercise links with feminist organisations.

Within the south Wales coalfield, the lack of women's employment and the domination of the miners in local politics from the late 1890s made it difficult for women to intervene in public life. The women's column of the *Rhondda Socialist* newspaper in 1912 drew attention to the middle-class 'sympathisers' rather than real working-class women in the Women's Labour League and made apparent the disregard of women in local socialist groups and the miners' lodges.[11] Despite these obstacles women did emerge into the public domain in the mining communities in the years before the First World War. There is little evidence though for militant suffrage activity. When Margaret Haig Thomas and Annie Kenney attempted to speak at a public meeting (the original invitation from the Liberal Club was withdrawn) on women's suffrage in 1909, they were drowned out by musical instruments and pelted with herrings and tomatoes.[12] It was unfortunate that this meeting was preceded by the horsewhipping of Winston Churchill by militant suffragettes in Bristol which angered Liberal ranks. Margaret Haig (later Viscountess Rhondda) was the daughter of local coal baron, D. A. Thomas (later Viscount Rhondda) although at this time, that is before the bitter 1912 dispute, the Thomas family still had a loyal following in the town. The non-militant National Union of Women's Suffrage Societies did establish several branches within the coalfield, including the Rhondda.[13] According to Elizabeth Andrews, the first branch of the Women's Co-operative Guild was formally established in Ton Pentre in 1914, although there is evidence of Guild activity in the valleys before this date.[14] The Guild continued to make steady progress and became recognised as a very significant women's organisation in the coalfield, involved in campaigns on pithead baths, birth control, infant and maternal welfare.[15] Active membership in the 1920s appears to be somewhat smaller than Labour women, although of course many women were in both.

A small number of important local women activists emerged at the time and two in particular made an outstanding contribution. Elizabeth Andrews (née Smith), born in 1882 into a large mining family in Hirwaun, was both deeply religious (Nonconformist) and committed to socialist politics.[16] She was the leading force in the development of the Women's Co-operative Guild . In 1916, Andrews was the first woman to be elected to the executive of the Rhondda Labour Party. Rose Davies (née Rees) daughter of a tinworker, was also born in 1882, in the Aberdare area. Davies became an infant school teacher and interested in feminist and socialist politics. In 1906, she joined the ILP and in 1908 helped to form a

Elizabeth Andrews.

women's branch of the ILP in Aberdare. Starting with her co-option to the Education Committee of the Aberdare Urban District Council soon after her marriage in 1908, Davies began a long career of public service. She was also co-opted on to the Maternal and Child Welfare Committee and developed a particular interest in children with special needs. Unlike Andrews, who was married and childless, Davies had five children and managed to perform a prolific regime of public duties. Appalling rates of infant mortality led Rose Davies and others on the local UDC to establish an infant welfare clinic in 1915 which, according to Anthony Mor-O'Brien, made Aberdare a leading town in infant welfare.[17]

From the end of the First World War, local government in the coalfield was dominated by the Labour Party. Women were also making important gains. In Abertillery in 1920, Labour women were represented on the council housing, pensions and food committees and also the Trades Council and the Guardians.[18] Abertillery appears to have been a lively place for active women around this time as there was also a Women Citizens' Association in the town. These women carried on the independent feminist activity of the pre-war women's movement. In December 1924, leading feminist Eleanor Rathbone spoke to the group at a public meeting on family endowment.[19] There is no evidence that miners' wives were involved in the Women's Citizens' Association. After an initial defeat, Rose Davies became a Labour Councillor in 1920 and went on to become an alderman and the first woman County Councillor in south Wales in 1925.[20] She continued to campaign for projects such as maternity homes, nursery schools and play centres for children.[21] Davies and Andrews both sat on the Board of Health's Welsh Consultative Council which was established in 1919 to report on health services in Wales and make recommendations for improvements.[22] Eliza Williams from Gelli was also elected to the Rhondda UDC in 1920.[23] Other women activists included Mrs E. Evans and Mrs D. Smith who were co-opted onto the Maternal and Infant Welfare Committee of the RUDC. The Maternal and Child Welfare Act of 1918 allowed for two co-opted members from women's organisations, but this was not approved of by County Medical Officers in south Wales.[24] Fannie Thomas, headmistress of Ffaldau Girls' School

in Pontycymer and much respected member of the community
became the first woman member of Ogmore and Garw UDC
and later first woman leader of the Council. Women were also
elected to Boards of Guardians such as Catherine Jenkins in
Pontypridd in 1925. We should not lose sight of the fact that to a
large extent these were exceptional women and most men,
even active socialists, resented the idea of women's active participation in politics. After the 1918 Electoral Reform Act, when
only women over thirty had been enfranchised, miner's wife
Winifred Griffiths gave a speech on women's rights and the
need for an equal franchise in an unnamed 'mining village'
close to Bettws (near Bridgend) where she was living. The
Labour Party audience gave her a 'rather cold reception. The
all-male audience obviously had some doubts about even
women over thirty being allowed to vote. They did not seem at
all enthusiastic about demanding any more freedom for their
women folk.'[25]

In 1919, Elizabeth Andrews gave evidence before the
Sankey Commission on the lives of miners' wives in south
Wales on behalf of the SWMF. In 1919, she became full-time
Women's Organiser for the Labour Party in Wales, working
under the direction of National Women's Organiser, Marion
Phillips. This post took her to all areas of the country and
involved translating Labour Party literature aimed at women
into Welsh.

Apart from some activity around the campaign for pithead
baths, the Women's Labour League had failed to flourish in
mining areas before 1914 but the newly constituted Labour
Party drew in women with astonishing success, starting with a
Labour Women's Conference in Pontypridd in 1918.[26] By
1920, there is evidence in the Rhondda of Labour Party
Women's Sections in Maerdy, Ferndale, Tylorstown, Porth,
Tonypandy, Ystrad, Ton Pentre, Cwmparc and Treherbert.[27]
In 1920–1, Rose Davies helped to establish Women's Sections
in the new parliamentary constituency of Aberdare.[28] Weekly
meetings were held, with outside speakers, study and sewing
sessions. The success of Labour women at this time can be
attributed to the fact that women responded to the call for a
movement based on both Labour loyalty and the collective
identity of women.[29] As Lowri Newman has written, Labour

women in Wales adopted a maternalist brand of politics that did not pose any challenge to the gender basis of society, but did create a movement that was aimed at highlighting the plight of working-class wives and mothers and making life easier for them.[30] In addition to this practical, woman-centred reformist politics there was a recognition that women needed supportive educational programmes to bring them into public life and a belief that the movement involved a wider cultural life as well as formal political meetings. Labour dances, children's outings and other social gatherings played an important role in bringing the 'Labour family' and the wider community together.

District committees were also in existence and an East Glamorgan Labour Women's Advisory Council which had a representative from both Rhondda East and Rhondda West.[31] Minutes from the East Glamorgan Labour Women's Advisory Council for September 1925 show that there were 1,138 members in the region (including Cardiff), organised into 38 sections.[32] Surprisingly, only 708 of these members actually took *Labour Woman*. There were 11 Women's Sections which did not take any copies at all. The poverty of Labour Party women members is likely to have been a major factor in the low take-up of the women's paper. It could also have been the case that some male Labour activists enrolled wives who had little time to participate in politics. The Council was very keen to organise education conferences for women. Leading women activists promoted the idea that, as women were new to citizenship, many felt uninformed and therefore needed to be educated about current affairs in order to raise their self-confidence.

The Communist Party (CP), although small numerically was very active in the coalfield towns. Formally the party was committed to sexual equality, but in practice it was highly gendered. The Party's emphasis on industrial policy and work in the miners' lodges necessarily excluded women, arguably making it even more masculinist than the Labour Party or the ILP. When leading party activist Isabel Brown spoke at a party meeting in Ystradgynlais she was shocked to discover that the woman comrade who had given her tea before the meeting could not attend branch meetings as she was the only woman and 'it would cause a scandal in the village'.[33] Idris Cox, a leading party member and resident of Maesteg in the early 1920s, told me that, although women could join the party, 'they could not participate to the same extent as the men, as the main struggle was over wages and conditions of work, which they had no part in'.[34] Consequently, Cox indicated that the 'main activity' of Communist party women was to 'organise socials and bazaars.' It seems to be the case that there were relatively few Communist women and those who did join were largely the wives of male members. Communist women were active in local Labour Party Women's Sections and Women's Co-operative Guilds. The Labour Conference in Liverpool in 1925 resolved to expel Communists from the Labour Party. This was difficult to implement in south Wales as the Communists were so firmly embedded in local Labour structures and the Lockout diverted attention elsewhere. There is evidence that in 1927 and even beyond, Communist women were still active in local Labour Party women's sections in the valleys.[35] Communist women were not formally excluded from the Women's Co-operative Guild but they were banned from holding office. Communists in the upper Rhondda valley, which was particularly progressive, appear to have been especially interested in birth control. In 1923, the Maerdy, Tylorstown and Ferndale Party branches invited birth control campaigner Stella Browne for a lecture tour.[36] She came for a week and spoke to large, separate audiences of men and women.[37] It is likely that many of those attending were not party members. This event does not seem to have been tied in with the party's general orientation towards women in the coalfield at this time.

WOMEN AND THE LOCKOUT

In the spring of 1926, as the industrial crisis unfolded and the coalfield was in a state of heightened tension, every effort was made by socialist women to support the miners and promote solidarity between men and women. Elizabeth Andrews took the lead in addressing meetings and writing the women's page for the *Colliery Workers' Magazine*, official organ of the SWMF. The East Glamorgan Women's Advisory Council met in March

1926. [38] Rose Davies addressed the conference on a broad range of issues including equal suffrage, secondary education, unmarried mothers and peace and the looming prospect of industrial conflict. It was this latter topic which appears to have focused the discussion. The recent activities of the Women's Guild of Empire (WGE) led by Mrs Flora Drummond were of particular concern. Previously a militant suffragette and close confidante of Emmeline Pankhurst, Drummond was closely involved in the spectacular 'Votes for Women' processions which took place before the First World War.[39] In 1916–17 Drummond, often referred to as 'the General' on account of her military dress and bearing, played an active role in the Pankhursts' 'industrial campaign' which was opposed to strike action at a time of war on patriotic grounds. Drummond took the campaign to south Wales where, according to the *Western Mail* which approved of her activities, she had some success.[40] In the post-war years, Drummond (together with Elsie Bowerman) set up the WGE chiefly as a vehicle for women to express disapproval of strikes as a means of settling industrial disputes. In January 1926, the WGE was active in the south Wales coalfield and Andrews was forced to admit that the organisation had succeeded in gaining some support for a mass rally in London on 17 April. She urged that every effort should be made to stop this movement; 'they betray their men in their fight for a decent existence . . . It is up to us to do all we can to save these women from themselves.'[41] *Labour Woman* also urged women not to get involved with the WGE: 'Miners' Wives . . . Be cautious! Give it a cold shoulder! . . . Keep solidly by the Trade Union of your menfolk, and Remember you are Workers *not* Blacklegs!'[42] The Communist *Workers' Weekly* also denounced the WGE event as largely consisting of 'shop-keepers, parsons' wives, squires' daughters and colliery managers' women folk' who wouldn't dare to march through working-class areas.[43]

The *Times* reported that over 20,000 women attended the WGE rally in London, including a contingent from south Wales 'led by women from Swansea and Cardiff, some of whom were in national dress'.[44] Details of miners' wives at the event are frustratingly scarce but according to the *Aberdare Leader*, 75 women attended from Ynysybwl behind their own banner. The report also reveals that £42 was raised by the Ynysybwl women towards the cost of staging the event and that they were led by Mrs R. A. Lewis Cartrel.[45] Abertridwr and Senghennydd were also known to have sent 'about eight' women.[46] The colourful procession, obviously designed to conjure up the spirit of pre-war suffrage marches, was over a mile long and complete with Scottish pipers and women on horseback acting as leaders and outriders, and was subjected to heckling and disruption from local Communists but managed to arrive intact at the Albert Hall. The highly-staged rally which followed pressed for secret ballots, district settlements and arbitration and negotiation as opposed to strikes for settling industrial disputes. The event culminated in a resolution to this effect which was supported by, amongst others, what the *Times* refers to as 'the wife of a South Wales miner'. The *Caerphilly Journal* named Mrs Trembath of Abertridwr as the miner's wife who spoke along with two other working women in support of the resolution proposed by Mrs Bowerman.[47] Predictably, Andrews was scathing about the rally, arguing that the numbers involved were exaggerated and commenting 'What a farce! Women on horseback leading! They must be the miners' wives, who, after sending their husbands to work, can spend their mornings riding in Rotten Row, Hyde Park.'[48] She named the woman who spoke as a 'South Wales miner's wife' as Mrs Henry Dubbs and accused her of joining the demonstration for a cheap outing to London.

In an explicit attempt to counter the 'mischevious' activities of the Women's Guild of Empire and make an all-out effort to promote unity, Elizabeth Andrews, in conjunction with the SWMF, organised a series of mass meetings for miners' wives. The idea for these meeting was first raised at the East Glamorgan Labour Women's Advisory Council on 6 March.[49] Between 12 April and 13 May, Andrews addressed twenty meetings attended by over 10,000 women.[50] The *British Worker*, official strike bulletin of the TUC, stated that on 10 May, 2,000 women attended an open air women's rally in Tonypandy and another in 500 in Gelli. A meeting was also held in Mountain Ash in which Mrs Andrews was keen to contradict the reported figure of 20–30,000 women attending the London rally, arguing instead that only 3,490 turned out for this event.[51] The overriding theme of these meetings and the women's page of the *Colliery Workers Magazine* over the months and weeks of the Lockout was solidarity. The struggle was depicted in class terms as a 'fight for bread' in which it was the duty of mothers to protect home life and fight for their children to grow up without want.[52] The 'idle rich' capitalists were portrayed as blood-sucking vampires seeking to 'divide and rule' to maximise their own interests.[53] It was the capitalists, not the workers, who were destroying families by trying to pitch miners' wives against their husbands.[54] Elizabeth Andrews took it for granted that political deference to men was necessary as men would be better informed than women. She urged miners to 'have patience, and spare a little time to explain this problem to them'.[55] Women were expected to express complete confidence in the leadership despite the fact that they had had no say in the formulation of MFGB policy. The only long-term solution, women were told, was the nationalisation of mines and ultimately a more just, socialist society based on principles of equality and true fellowship between men and women. The offensive against the WGE appears to have been effective as little more is heard of it in south Wales during the Lockout, although Drummond did address the Senghennydd and Abertridwr branches in July. The meeting in Senghennydd was given heavy police protection. Mrs Drummond and her supporters were subjected to boos, hisses and missiles from 'the crowd of between 500 and 600 people, mostly women' on entering and leaving the meeting. Police reinforcements had to be rushed in from Caerphilly and Treharris to stop a full-scale riot.[56]

Labour women were very busy in local government during the Lockout. Eliza Williams, as a member of the Education Committee on RUDC, sat on the Central Canteen Committee and helped oversee the arrangements for school feeding, which involved liaising with teachers, volunteers, local suppliers and so on. It was a difficult task, as committee members were duty-bound to try and keep expenditure down by ensuring that only children in dire need were fed, but in an area dominated by the coal industry a great many of the children could be described as 'necessitous'. Milk for expectant and nursing mothers was also an important issue for Labour women councillors during this time. The Maternity and Child Welfare Clinic of RUDC included Councillors Mrs Annie Price and Mrs Eliza Williams plus co-opted members Mrs Evans and Mrs Smith. On 11 May, the committee voted in favour of supplying free milk for necessitous nursing mothers and children under school age at specially established emergency feeding centres.[57] Indeed, this proposal was an extension of a scheme already in operation. But when the council sought sanction from the Ministry of Health, via the Welsh Board of Health, for the extra expenditure involved in funding these centres it was refused.[58] There is no doubt that mothers and babies were in real need.[59] When the first free distribution of milk was made to nursing and expectant mothers in Maerdy, it was accompanied by what the local press called 'disgraceful scenes'.[60] It was said to be 'doubtful' whether a second distribution could take place without police protection. The committee wrangled with the Ministry for the entire length of the dispute, pressing for a deputation and enlisting the help of local MPs for the cause. As we have seen, the central concern of central government was to contain expenditure. The Ministry of Health (via the Welsh Board of Health) therefore pursued the line that 'the Council are at present supplying milk under their scheme to children who should be in receipt of relief from the (Poor Law) Guardians'.[61] In an obvious attempt by central government to quieten the demands for free milk for mothers and infants in need, Minister of Health Neville Chamberlain abolished the Welsh Consultative Council, thus ensuring that women representatives Rose Davies and Elizabeth Andrews no longer had direct access to the Ministry of Health.[62]

Women were also to be seen outside the town halls protesting. It was reported that on 5 June 2,000 people in Blaenavon confined the relieving officer to his office for several hours after he refused to pay out relief unless husbands signed receipts.[63] It seems likely, given the nature of the protest, that most of these 2,000 'people' were in fact women. On 2 September, the *South Wales Echo* reported that about 60 miners' wives marched from Llanhilleth to Griffithstown workhouse where the Pontypool Guardians were in session, demanding admittance which was refused. The paper reported on the 'remarkable spectacle' which then ensued of 'two relieving officers being chased by a mob of angry women'. The largest single protest of the Lockout appears to be the mass demonstration of 7 July against reductions in relief scales in the Pontypridd Poor Law Union which were forced upon the authority by central government. This demonstration, which claimed to represent 30,000 Rhondda miners, consisted of several separate contingents from different areas which converged at Ynysangharad Park, Pontypridd, by this time numbering about 5,000.[64] The mid-Rhondda contingent which assembled at Pandy Square, Tonypandy, was headed by women who marched through Penygraig and Dinas. A deputation of Mr Davies from Pontypridd and Mrs Evans from Penygraig presented the case to the RUDC.[65]

During the dispute, most of the energies of local Labour Women were devoted to relief work. As has already been described, nationally Labour women collected funds in all kinds of imaginative ways, which were then channelled to the mining areas through the Women's Committee for the Relief of Miners' Wives and Children (WCRMWC).[66] Grants were sent to the regional Women's Advisory Councils which were then distributed to local committees. In effect, these were reconstituted Women's Sections. Labour women identified families in need and assisted wherever they could with food tickets, clothing and maternity grants. In many areas, special committees were established to deal specifically with maternity cases. Many Women's Sections had special fund raising activities to fund local boot repair depots. This work was greatly appreciated by the communities concerned. They also did much fund-raising, including concerts and competitions, organised sewing circles to patch and remake used clothing, arranged for the temporary fostering of very needy children and helped out in the soup kitchens. In Maerdy, there was signs of friction between the Labour women and the Distress Committee. Crates and bundles of clothing and sometimes boots arrived regularly from sympathisers in the Labour movement, channelled via the Women's Committee, usually amounting to about 40 crates or bundles a week. They were sent to Mrs Porter as local representative for the WCMWC. The Distress Committee was alarmed by Mrs Porter's apparent authority to act independently. Consequently Lewis Lloyd, chairman, was deputed to see Mrs Porter. 'with the intention of transferring all parcels to this committee' and writing to the agencies, 'informing them that if any parcels or goods are available for distribution they should be sent to the Distress Committee'.[67] Two weeks later it was noted that a deputation had visited Mrs Porter who agreed to co-operate with the Distress Committee.[68] This incident is worth recalling as it perhaps indicates (in addition to the sheer level of need in the town) that the Distress Committee, which was usually dominant in local matters relating to relief in the town, was uneasy about the ability of the Labour Party women to receive and make grants to local women. The fact that it was prepared to squabble with the women over bundles of used clothes could be taken as an indication that it felt that power was ebbing from the committee, which was very male-dominated, to the women on account of their work for the WCRMWC, which was part of a national scheme which the Distress Committee had no control over.[69] The fact that Mrs Porter backed down and agreed to the Distress Committee's request can be read as indicating that the women had been put in their place and male dominance reasserted.

The pages of *Labour Woman* make it clear how preoccupied Labour women around the country were in the struggle to provide continuous support for the families of the miners. The National Conference of Labour Women, which was due to take place in October in Huddersfield, was first postponed then abandoned entirely:

> It is better to go on devoting our energies entirely and wholeheartedly to getting the miners through their troubles and we are sure that you will agree with this decision . . . this does not mean any slackening of the bonds between us . . . the trouble in the mining areas has bound us together in a real sisterhood and the care of the miners' children has come to be one of the first thoughts of all of us.[70]

Whilst it appears that Labour women nationally were focusing almost entirely on relief work, within the wider coalfield region there are signs that in some areas women were still keen to continue with more traditional political activity, perhaps even more so than in 'normal' times. Women's sections still held regular meetings with speakers in addition to their work for the WCRMWC. The Cambrian Lodge (mid-Rhondda) minutes reveal that 15 local Labour Party women were competing to be delegated to the (later abandoned) Huddersfield Labour Women's Conference. In addition they were ready with a resolution on birth control, although this was later overturned by the Rhondda Borough Labour Party, perhaps indicating that Rhondda Labour women were more radical than men on this issue.[71] *Labour Woman* in July reported that the Aberavon divison had organised a successful series of meetings for women's week in which Miss Ishbel MacDonald (daughter of Ramsay MacDonald) and Mrs Andrews spoke to over 4,000 women and men. The Monmouth-shire Labour Party women's regional conference in Caldicot in September had an audience of 500 for a morning session on local government (this would have dealt with the crisis of local government due to the Lockout) and 800 for the after-noon speakers, again Mrs Andrews and Ishbel MacDonald, this time listed as speaking on family endowment.[72] The conference of the East Glamorgan Labour women, however, scheduled for September, was cancelled.

Trying to reach out to the experiences of individual women is a frustrating business as there is little personal information to go on. Regrettably, opportunities for oral testimony have been lost. Rose Davies, alderman, county councillor, JP, governor of various schools and member of many public bodies was the woman who was the most engaged with the local state. She was also a leading Labour Party activist and member of the ILP. Davies, together with Elizabeth Andrews, undoubtedly had very high standing in the community as a leader of women. Some indication of this is given by the fact that Davies spoke at the mass meeting of miners early in October following the miners' national delegate conference. She was the only woman to speak, undoubtedly called upon to give the 'women's point of view' and to speak in favour of soli-darity with the men. The fact that a meeting of south Wales miners had a woman speaker at all was something of an advance and must surely have arisen due to the outstanding relief work which women were performing. Beyond this, we have very little detail of Davies's activities during the Lockout.

The only memoir left by a woman in the mining community at this time is Elizabeth Andrews's *A Woman's Work is Never Done*. The period of the Lockout is not dealt with in any depth and focuses mainly on the relief work of the WCRMWC. It certainly seems to be the case that many women from the mining community really developed as speakers, activists and leaders of their communities during the Lockout. Andrews mentions three women in particular as being 'miners' wives and good speakers': Mrs Beatrice Green of Abertillery, Mrs Johanna James of Tonypandy and Mrs Herman of Pentre.[73] Regrettably, we know very little about either Mrs James or Mrs Herman. Clearly a very active woman, Mrs Herman stood in September 1925 in the election for Vice-President of the East Glamorgan Labour Women's Advisory Council, proposed by Penygraig and Ystrad delegates. She came second out of four candidates. Mrs Herman reported on the state of destitution in her home town of Treorchy to *Labour Woman*.[74] We also know that she spoke at the Labour women's mass rally for the miners held in London in early July.[75] It is possible that these women participated in the large meeting at Kingsway Hall in June organised by the Women's Section of the National Union of General Workers, chaired by Margaret Bondfield, in which Sybil Thorndike and five miners' wives spoke. Mrs Herman and Mrs James may also have helped with the women speakers who accompanied touring miners' choirs. According to Marion Phillips, these women 'undoubtedly made a profound impression when they spoke of the lives of the people in the coalfields from personal experience, and appreciably increased the collections wherever they went'.[76]

We know a little more about Beatrice Green due to her writings for *Labour Woman* and the obituaries which flowed from her premature death in 1927. Claimed by Lowri Newman as representative of the many nameless women activists of this period, she can also be claimed as an outstanding woman activist of the Lockout who, until recently has been overlooked.[77] Born Beatrice Dykes in 1895 in Abertillery, Monmouthshire, her father was a tin worker who became a miner when she was five. Her introduction to public life came through the Ebenezer Baptist Church, where she played a very active role in the Sunday School. After a County school

Beatrice Green.

education she became a teacher. She was said to have a 'charming personality and brilliant gifts'.[78] Although very obviously talented in her profession, she was forced by the marriage bar then in operation to give up teaching upon her marriage to a miner in 1916. Green developed an interest in public work and by the early 1920s she was deeply involved with supporting the local district hospital and the women's section of the Abertillery Labour Party. As Lowri Newman notes, in common with other Labour women in South Wales at this time, she did not call for a radical transformation of gender roles in society.[79] She did, however, believe that women should gain control over those areas of life which most concerned them and to this end they should engage in public work on the same terms as men. By 1926, Green was the mother of two sons but this does not seem to have prevented her from fully engaging as an activist, including being President of the Monmouthshire Labour Women's Advisory Council. She threw herself into work for the WCRMWC. As part of this work, Green helped to form a Maternity Relief

Committee in Abertillery which focused specifically on women in confinement, channelling funds from the WCRMWC to ensure that these women had enough food, milk, blankets and clothing for the period just before and after the birth. Green was also involved with the fostering scheme which the WCRMWC organised to provide very needy children with temporary homes. In July, Beatrice Green and Elizabeth Andrews accompanied a group of 50 miners' children from Rhondda, Merthyr, Dowlais and Abertillery to London to be looked after by foster families for the duration of the Lockout.[80]

Green was also a talented public speaker and writer. The July edition of *Labour Woman* contains an interview with Green, in which she vividly describes life in Abertillery including details of the Poor Relief system and what it was like to be a mother of a large family without a waged income coming in. Moving accounts such as these, which were not overly sentimental but carefully composed to provide meaningful insights, meant that Green could really convey the reality of the Lockout to those outside the mining areas.

It is not surprising then that Green was asked to speak at rallies in London and was invited to participate in a MFGB delegation to the Soviet Union. The nineteen-strong delegation, which included six women representing miners' wives in different coalfields, was designed to cement the bond between the British miners and Soviet workers following the donations sent by Russian trade unionists to the miners for relief in the Lockout. It was a lengthy trip, from 27 August to 16 October during which the British women visited workplaces, clubs, hospitals, schools and explored many aspects of Soviet life. Travelling by train and mostly sleeping in their compartment, the women delegates toured the country extensively, including Muslim areas where women traditionally wore the veil. According to Marion Phillips this trip was 'a crowning happiness in her life' during which she blossomed as a speaker, writer and activist and made firm bonds with the other women delegates.[81] Green sent in two long articles to *Labour Woman* recounting these experiences.[82] Although not declaring herself a Communist, Green was clearly impressed with the Soviet system, and wrote that women had achieved equality. She was not entirely uncritical of the Soviet Union, but viewed from a modern perspective these articles seem somewhat naive.

It is clear that the Lockout politicised large numbers of women in south Wales. This resulted in increased political involvement in both the Labour Party and the Communist Party. Communist Party archives show that Communist Party membership in South Wales doubled during the Lockout to over 1,500, of which over 200 were women, in 41 branches.[83] According to Idris Cox, both Maerdy and Maesteg party branches had about 30 women members at this time.[84] Sales of the CP women's paper, *The Woman Worker*, had increased and party women found the WCG fertile ground to conduct propaganda work.[85] Communist Party women and men at this time did whatever they could to support the Lockout and maintain working-class solidarity. They were very vocal in opposition to Flora Drummond's Women's Guild of Empire, understanding well that without the support of the women, the Lockout would collapse. According to a contemporary account from Idris Cox, the Party was the most stalwart supporter of the communal kitchens in Maesteg.[86] It campaigned against relief cuts and was an important force in the picketing to prevent the drift back to work, details of which are given below. Although the period preceding the Lockout was characterised by sectarian strife between Labour Party and Communist women, there is no evidence of this in the Lockout, when political differences seem to have been set aside in the urgency of the moment.

Details of individual Communist Party women in south Wales during the Lockout are scarce, but we do have testimony, recorded in 1977, of grass-roots activist Lil Price, who illustrates well the women who were caught up in the party momentum of 1926.[87] Price was born in 1906, the daughter of a Cardiff dock worker. After leaving elementary school, employment opportunities proved intermittent. Price came to Bedwas in a period of unemployment to help in a sister's confinement and stayed on. She married a miner in August 1926, joining the party soon after. Her husband was not in the CP; according to Price, it was the influence of one of her brothers which prompted her to join the party. She was active in both the Young Communist League and the main party branch, but did not wish to be associated with any kind of women's section. Price recalled that there were two other women attending meetings of the Bedwas CP. Very much an independent spirit, she told me that many of the wives of party members were 'a bit scared' of the CP but then added 'it didn't bloody worry me'. She described the party meetings in the local workman's hall as 'fabulous'. To pay for the hall, Price would use her rent money of ten shillings, which she would have to recoup from those attending. This energetic young woman threw herself into party activity, acting as treasurer to one of the committees, joining the co-operative movement and helping in the local communal kitchen. She was also active in demonstrations against blacklegs and selling the party newspaper. Unlike many women who joined the CP in 1926, she remained a party activist and was jailed in the early 1930s for riotous behaviour and assault. By this time she was a mother. In the interview she was happy to recall the political involvement of her younger days: 'I was up to my neck in it, I loved every minute.'

WOMEN AND PICKETING

From August, the first cracks began to appear and a small number of miners drifted back to work. Individual communities were still very solid, but it was often the men who came in from outside who were the first to cave in, or unsupported single men who had no family to fall back on. Local businesses failed and sources of credit dried up. Gradually the carnival atmosphere of the early summer gave way to a grimmer mood as families struggled to keep going. In September, the trickle back to work accelerated and, by October, the valleys were in open warfare as those still loyal to the Lockout attempted to stem the tide back to the pits. In an effort to control the situation, police reinforcements came from outside the coalfield, which increased the antagonism local communities felt towards the authorities.[88] Rose Davies and other prominent members of the community complained at the brutal behaviour of the police towards pickets.[89] As Hywel Francis and Dai Smith have noted, there were countless minor events involving the police and eighteen major disturbances resulting in hundreds of prosecutions, all as a result of pickets trying to prevent blacklegs from working.[90] It was often the case, usually in the smaller settlements, that the defendants were well known to the pickets. Many of those charged were highly respected members of the community, but nevertheless heavy penalties were invariably imposed, including custodial sentences.

Many of the disturbances and the prosecutions which followed involved women.[91] This is not altogether surprising; as Angela V. John has observed, there is a long tradition in south Wales of mining women participating in popular disturbances, including resisting rent collection, court bailiffs and evictions as well as demonstrating against blacklegs.[92] In mining communities, it was usually the women who upheld community values and in this 'alternative' coalfield society solidarity with the men in the Lockout was regarded as a crucial part of community morality. On 24 September, *The South Wales Daily News* reported recent events in August in Ogmore Vale when large numbers of miners and their wives were alleged to have assembled in the street and, after a bugle call, demonstrated against colliery officials on their way to work.[93] The trial at Bridgend Court involved 20 defendants, 12 of whom were women, charged with unlawful assembly and intimidation. Fourteen women were charged with unlawful assembly following an incident at Cwmaman on 3 November.[94] There are numerous other examples of prosecutions against women and reports of women in riotous demonstrations. Most of the press reports refer to large crowds of both men and women, booing and shouting at blacklegs and throwing missiles, usually stones. The *Merthyr Express* for 16 October reported that a substantial number of miners had returned to work in New Tredegar and that the men 'were subjected to a considerable amount of booing by large crowds, mostly composed of women.' In an interview recorded in 1973, Mrs J. Evans talked about the activities of her mother, Mrs Tudor, who she says was linked with the Communist Party: 'all Maerdy was up in arms about it . . . people were pelting the doors and everything and going to the windows and making faces at them and all, through the windows. My mother was even doing that.' [95] William Morley lived in the village of Onllwyn. He described what happened when two 'scabs' started to go by train to work in the Nantewlaeth Colliery some distance away:

> They didn't walk through the village, always people waiting for them so avoided it and went with police out a back way . . . weren't prepared to come through the village because the women, particularly the women, would be waiting for them, and there was always a few up at the school there, some women would be there shouting and acting and so on.[96]

Francis and Smith suggest that older women were most prominent in these prosecutions, but evidence from the contemporary press indicates a spread of ages. Eight women were charged with intimidation, unlawful assembly and attempting to cause disaffection amongst the civilian population resulting from incidents in September at Nantewlaeth where eight or nine men were being transported to work under police escort. In one of these incidents, a crowd of about 500 threw sticks, stones and other missiles at the lorry, causing the windscreen to be smashed. The press report describes many of the women defendants as being 'quite young'. The judge said he was 'sorry to have to prosecute these women, but it was equally the duty of both sexes to regard the law'.[97] In another disturbance at Cwmcarn, five women were amongst those charged with riotous assembly following an alleged attack on safety men which involved a hostile crowd of about 200 booing and shouting. The women's ages were given as 20, 58, 34 and 43 and 32, all married women from Cwmcarn. In addition, two other women aged 57 and 32 were witnessed by a policeman to have thrown clods at officials.[98] Following disturbances involving an estimated 1,500–2,000 people at Ton Pentre on 24 August, seven female defendants came up before the Glamorgan Assizes in Swansea in December on various charges of riotous assembly, assault and intimidation. In a trial covering more than five days, one of the women charged kept her baby with her in court and nursed it when necessary, providing a vivid contrast between the context of her appearance in court charged with aggressive behaviour and the nurturing role she was performing for her baby.[99]

The most well-known example of women in these protests is

that of Elvira Bailey of Treorchy who threw a stone at a policeman, injuring him in the hand on 21 October, when working miners were stoned by a hostile crowd. In sentencing her to two months in prison, the judge declared that 'I find that the women have been taking too prominent a part in these disturbances and I must impose a penalty that will be a deterrent to others.'[100] What is not so well known is that local women gathered a petition to the Home Secretary for Elvira Bailey. Mrs Bailey, although described as 'elderly' in press reports, had four children still living with her, the youngest of whom was nine. The local miners' lodge, Abergorki, handled the case which does not appear to have been successful.[101] Although most mining communities were solidly behind the strike until the very closing stages, there were places where support was less than 100 per cent. It was rare though to find an example of anyone speaking against the strike in public. In the only example I have been able to find of a woman openly opposing the strike, Beatrice Barnes of Ton Pentre declared 'I am no follower of Cook' during demonstrations against her husband returning to work at Maindy Colliery. As a result of demonstrations against miner Barnes, eleven men and nine women were prosecuted for various charges of unlawful assembly, intimidation and assault.[102] I asked Lilian Lawrence if anyone in her community carried on working in the Lockout:

> Oh yes . . . my Uncle Bill carried on working in Nelson . . . my mother and aunt threw stones at the windows in the house. There was quite a lot of that went on . . . they didn't believe in going on strike . . . there would be demonstrations against, they'd paint their windows, put paint on their doors.
> *Who were you saying smashed the windows?*
> My mother! (laughs)
> *She went and smashed the windows of her own brother's house?*
> Yes, yes, I always remember that . . . he said he needed the money, he couldn't live without the money. They hadn't long moved into this house and they were struggling. They only had two children and my mother's argument was that she had four children to look after.
> *Did she break anybody else's windows?*
> Oh yes, the ones that was scabs, yes. There was quite a lot of them in Nelson.[103]

Some of the women's demonstrations against blacklegs involved the practice of 'white shirting' which had its roots in pre-industrial public shaming rituals, particularly the *ceffyl pren*. Although originally used to humiliate or scold 'unruly' women, by the nineteenth century public shaming rituals in Wales were being used by women in a more political context, including against scab or anti-union labour.[104] 'White shirting' had many variations, but it usually involved grabbing a scab, pasting him with whitewash, forcing him to wear a white shirt and strapping him in a wheelbarrow. He was then paraded about accompanied by 'rough music', a mock serenade on a concertina or an accordion. This ordeal often ended with a ducking in the river. In this ritualised display of community solidarity, popular justice was dispensed against those who transgressed established social norms.[105] There are numerous reports of 'white shirting' incidents during the Lockout. There are several accounts of the incident at Pencoed on 12 August, where an early breakaway movement at the Meiros Colliery, near Pencoed, in August resulted in a number of miners returning to work under a police escort. One elderly miner declined the police escort and insisted on using his bicycle. At a road junction he was confronted by a crowd of about 300 men and women. According to the memoirs of a policeman present:

> A number of women in front of the crowd advanced in line towards him, with hands joined across the road followed by the crowd. They rushed forward at him and he collided with one of the women and fell off his bicycle ... A woman he knew, shouted at him: 'We'll stop you, you bloody blackleg.' This woman produced a white shirt and with them still holding him, tried to pull it over his head. There was a struggle in which the shirt was ripped. Failing to get it over his head, it was tied tightly round his neck by means of the two sleeves. He continued to resist. He was struck on the back of his head and kicked on the buttocks and hind parts. He was forced to march before the mob for a distance of 300–400 yards ... he was trembling with fear and on the point of collapse.[106]

This account comes from a retired policeman whose memoirs are highly coloured by virulent anti-communism and anti-unionism, but there are press reports of this incident which are essentially the same except for the emotive content.[107] The incident resulted in charges of unlawful assembly and intimidation against four women and three men at Bridgend Police Court. When the women were asked to think about what they had done Mrs Coombes, who had put the shirt on the miner said, with a baby in her arms, 'he is a scamp, he doesn't think about the starving women and children'.[108]

After another incident, also on 12 August, at Heol-y-cyw six women were charged with unlawful assembly and intimidation. All but one were commited for trial. The women were said to have acted 'entirely on their own' in placing a white shirt upon miner William Gregory (outspoken opponent of the SWMF, see chapter 6) on his way to Bryneath Colliery. According to the *South Wales Daily News*, Gregory was conveyed in a wheelbarrow to his home in Coity accompanied by a concertina.[109] The white shirt used in these demonstrations symbolised women's clothing and hence the 'feminising' of the blackleg, as a key aim was to undermine the masculinity of the strike-breaker. In the committal, counsel said that 'the greatest indignity that could be cast on a collier was to attempt to place him in a white shirt when there was an industrial stoppage proceeding'.[110] The women were bound over to keep the peace for twelve months.[111] In these communities striking was associated with heroic manhood and to scab was to let down your workmates and your community.

Rosemary Jones has written that from the nineteenth century, these ritualised street protests became dominated by women and can be viewed as an expression of women's relative lack of power.[112] 'Separate spheres' ideology meant that women, especially in mining areas, had been marginalised in the public domain by increasingly strict gender divisions and notions of domesticity which placed them outside the world of work and politics. As we have seen, there were a few outstanding women political activists in south Wales by the 1920s, but these women were still very marginal to the central foci of power in coalfield society. Merfyn Payne was a leading union activist in Pencoed in the 1920s. When interviewed in 1975, he was asked about the 'whiteshirting' incident recalled above and said it was 'just a game with the women' and in any case the scab 'wasn't more than fifteen ounces upstairs'.[113] By reacting so dismissively, he both undermined the character of the scab and marginalised the role of the women who were

outside of and therefore beyond the control of the formal
structure of the miners' lodge. What Payne described as 'just a
game' with the women was serious enough for them to be
prosecuted. According to Francis and Smith, these women's
protests were effective in at least temporarily stemming the
tide back to work and also resulted in the arrival of new
detachments of police from outside the area.[114] These demonstrations, in which women were assertive and dominating (and
also violent) display meanings beyond simple expressions of
community solidarity and identification with the miners'
cause. As expressions, albeit weak, of women's political power,
they represented not just a moral stance but were in effect
contesting the masculinist basis of political power in the
coalfield.

6

DEFEAT, AFTERMATH AND LEGACY

The last few weeks of the Lockout in south Wales were characterised by increasing desperation, violence, police repression and searing poverty. As labour historians have noted, after the collapse of the General Strike the defeat of the miners was inevitable. Large stocks of coal were in hand and from July coal began to be imported from the USA and Europe. The miners were not well placed to exert pressure on the employers. Nationally, there was a significant drift back to work from August, particularly in areas such as Nottinghamshire which did not have the strong community cohesion of south Wales, where there was an incredible determination to fight on and the belief that by remaining united they could win. Except for one or two isolated areas, there were only occasional individual cases of miners returning to work. Such was the 'alternative culture' in most of the south Wales coalfield that it was 'social suicide' to return to work.[1] Blacklegging was seen as a wrong against the whole community. Nevertheless the tide turned against the miners. The local economy was in ruins with councils and businesses in massive debt. Aberdare grocer Thomas Lewis was declared bankrupt after admitting he owed £633 due to extending credit to locked-out miners. Many other grocers faced the same fate if they continued to extend credit. The effects of the dispute spread to all sections of society. Avis Williams was thirteen at the time of the Lockout. Her father owned property in Porth where they lived. Property was extremely cheap in the mining areas in the 1920s. Although they lived better than mining families, they did not live an affluent lifestyle. During the Lockout their income from rent disappeared. She told me about a conversation she overheard between her mother and one of their tenants:

> *Mother/Landlady* It is awful hard times.
> *Tenant* What have you got to grumble about when you own all these houses?
> *Mother/Landlady* My husband can't take a slate off your house to feed his children if you don't pay the rent.[2]

In Merthyr more than one in three of the population was on poor relief in late October, as opposed to a national average of just over one in twenty.[3] The Ministry of Health called for further cuts in relief.[4] In Pontypool, outdoor relief was terminated entirely although a small amount was allowed following intervention from the Ministry of Health.[5] Community cohesion was severely strained as groups such as ratepayers began to be more outspoken in their demands for tighter controls on spending to offset the soaring cost of poor relief.[6] Various clothes and boot schemes were in operation, but even so ragged children were an increasing sight on the streets. The warm summer weather and the carnival atmosphere had gone. During October, there was a trickle back to work which produced open warfare in the valleys, the most serious incidents being in the Afan valley.[7] Large numbers of police had to be brought in from outside the region to protect miners who wanted to return to work. As we have seen, both men and women took part in picketing.

Even as late as early November, only a small percentage of south Wales miners were at work, but the numbers rose sharply in mid-November.[8] Nationally the numbers at work were much higher and it was clear that all was lost. On 19 November, the MFGB conceded defeat and called for the opening of district negotiations with no prior conditions. After many years of national agreements that was a huge defeat in itself. The following week, the flow of returning miners turned into a flood as men scrambled back to work in a frantic effort to return to their old positions. When the executive council of the SWMF met the Monmouthshire and South Wales Coal Owners' Association on 30 November, they had no choice but capitulate and order an immediate resumption of work. The south Wales miners remained solid until it was clear that at the national level it was hopeless, and even then some lodges refused to accept the settlement. Government figures show that at the end of the dispute there were still less than 38,000 south Wales miners at work out of a workforce of 250,000. [9]As Gilbert has pointed out, this shows both the power and the limits of localism. Within their own local society the miners had won, but this was not enough.[10] It was the national context, over which they had no power, which defeated them.The terms of the settlement were devastating: utter and complete defeat. The miners faced the humiliation of savage wage cuts and the imposition of an eight-hour day. In addition, miners' wages continued to fall, so that by 1930 they were below 1914 levels.[11] The settlement in south Wales was the most severe of all the district settlements.

Arthur Horner hit an upbeat note when he wrote that the seven-month Lockout enabled hundreds and thousands of miners across the country to enjoy the summer sunshine instead of being incarcerated in the earth and, in addition, such was the appalling mortality in mining that there were about seven hundred men alive who would otherwise have died through pit accidents, plus many thousands who escaped injury.[12] There is very little else that can be said about the aftermath of the Lockout that is remotely cheerful. Employers used the longer working day to reduce the labour force whilst maintaining the same level of production.[13] In March 1927, the *Colliery Workers Magazine* estimated that there were 60–70,000 fewer miners working than before the dispute. Conditions varied from district to district. Some pits never reopened. Coal seams in the eastern part of the coalfield in Monmouthshire were largely worked out even before the Lockout. The more prosperous anthracite area on the other hand did rather better in the return to work. Lodge officials and activists were victimised.[14] Blacklists were kept by colliery managers. Oral respondents Mary Lowrie in Trealaw and Lizzie Davies in Maerdy both told me that their fathers never worked again.[15] Mary Lowrie went on to say that 'none of the older ones went back'. Mavis Llewellyn lived with three miners, her father and two uncles, neither of whom worked again.[16] Her uncle Fred went on to become a Communist councillor and leading unemployed activist in the 1930s. The SWMF tried to ensure that only union members were employed, as directed by the lodge, and that older miners were given priority in the return to work. These attempts at some sort of control by the Fed were disregarded by coalowners who clearly held all the cards. As a result, the seniority rule was ignored; older miners failed to be offered work and blacklegs were kept on, although on the new rates, not the fifteen shillings a day they had previously been paid.[17] A letter from the Abergorki Lodge to colliery officials in February 1927 states that 'strangers' had started work, whilst 41 men in the lodge who had been working on 30 April 1926 were still not working.[18] Cwmdu Colliery protested against the actions of the colliery manager in bringing in workmen to the pit 'while so many old workmen are unemployed'. [19] Similar work was being carried out by union lodges throughout the coalfield. The desperate state of the 60,000 unemployed miners in south Wales can be seen in the hunger march of November 1927, when 270 Welsh miners marched to London to protest against the recommended cuts in benefit under the Blanesborough Report.[20] Although the march had no official backing from either the TUC or the MFGB, due to the bitter sectarian atmosphere following the collapse of the General Strike and later the Lockout, the men were given a warm welcome and hospitality en route and whilst in London from rank-and-file labour activists. The march concluded with a rally in pouring rain in Trafalgar Square, at which the men sang 'Land of my Fathers' and A. J. Cook defiantly told supporters 'we are not going to beg for the right to live. We are going to demand it.'[21]

The mood of despair and demoralisation led to a disastrous decline in membership of the SWMF which lost 70,000 members during the dispute and continued to fall.[22] It was down to 136,250 in January 1927 but declined further to 59,858 by December 1928.[23] In addition, lodge officials were treated with contempt by colliery managers. The posting of union notices on colliery premises and other 'privileges' previously accorded to the Fed was banned.[24] Bert Coombes recalls how the dispute committee of his lodge in 'Treclewyd' (which was actually Resolven in the Vale of Neath) went to the colliery office to argue the case for the 400 old hands who had not been reinstated: 'he [the colliery manager] did not allow them to step inside the office out of the rain, would not allow them to sign on as willing to work'.[25] Coombes was offered his old job back but found that he had to work with blacklegs. The colliery manager refused to allow any union presence on the site, so a cabin had to be erected outside the colliery premises so that the Fed dues could be paid.[26] In addition to non-unionism, the Fed also faced another problem; for the first time since 1898 a rival union sprang up, under the leadership of William Gregory (previously mentioned in chapter 5). The South Wales Industrial Union was established on a 'no-strike, non-political' basis in the new, modernised Taff-Merthyr Colliery at Trelewis in December 1926, with full management approval and protection.[27] By April 1927, the new union had four full-time organisers, ran two cars and claimed 35,000 members. Francis and Smith argue that the true membership figure varied between 2000 and 6000.[28] The SWMF faced a long struggle to eliminate the 'scab' union; this was only finally accomplished in 1938, although the decisive battle was in 1935 with the 'stay-down strikes'.

In the aftermath of defeat, the SWMF was a mere shadow of its former self. Funding for the Central Labour College was axed and the *Colliery Workers Magazine* was discontinued. Like many miners' institutes, Senghennydd was on the verge of bankruptcy; its income had fallen from £30 a week to £9 and it had incurred a £2,000 mortgage.[29] The Miners' Welfare Fund, which supported scholarships for miners' children, recreation facilities, convalescent placements and medical aid societies, also suffered a decline in funding in 1926, which must have had serious consequences for the beneficiaries.[30] The Fund wrote to the RUDC in February 1927 stating that a large number of applications for grants had been received and that it was not possible to allocate any funds to any of the Councils' schemes until January 1928 at the earliest.[31] It also drew attention to the fact that many local welfare associations had 'incurred liabilities very much in excess of the funds at their disposal'. Most miners' canteens were closed by late December as many male voluntary helpers returned to work and borrowed utensils and equipment were returned. Whilst many miners were back at work, others were left in limbo as relief agencies refused to recognise the end of the dispute until 23 December, leaving miners without work destitute. Institute libraries declined as there was little money for books or periodicals. The Treharris Workmen's Fund of £268 had been accumulated for the creation of a technical college in Merthyr, but it had to be diverted to the relief of local distress instead.[32] Broken or lost games equipment such as billiard tables could not be replaced.[33] More seriously, there were 900 cases of riot and unlawful assembly in south Wales in 1926, many of which dragged on well into 1927.[34] J. Morgan and Albert Jenkins appeared before the Nixon's Workmen's Hall and Institute committee and appealed for help towards the expenses of Cwmaman workmen at the assizes. The committee were unable to provide any funds but offered the use of the theatre for a benefit concert.[35] It is likely that this sort of reaction was experienced elsewhere. It is clear though that whatever their financial position and despite widespread demoralisation, mining communities held in the highest regard those men and women who had been arrested and imprisoned during the Lockout. Such was the case with the nine men and two women who were formally presented with inscribed gold cigarette cases for the men and necklets and gold pendants for the women in Fochriw's Carmel Congregational Chapel in December, 1926, after their release from prison.[36] They had acquired the status of heroes of the class struggle.[37]

School feeding on a large scale was discontinued fairly soon after the return to work. The RUDC resolved to discontinue school feeding on 17 December, with the proviso that the matter would be taken up again in cases where unemployment benefit had not been paid to families in which the workmen had not resumed work.[38] This was clearly a contentious issue, as many families remained in desperate need. The SWMF pressed for the feeding of necessitous children to be continued, as did the Rhondda Teachers' Association, but after eight months of voluntary assistance in the canteens they asked for other arrangements to be made on account of the serious interference with school work that this entailed. The RUDC was sympathetic, but aware that large-scale feeding was a financial burden which the council was unable to bear. The date for the discontinuation of school feeding was put back to 30 December, with the council pressing the guardians to 'resume their full responsibilities'.[39] To this end, the RUDC sent a deputation to the Pontypridd Poor Law Union asking for the scale of relief to be increased from two shillings to three shillings per child; this was refused owing to the 'financial situation'.[40] In fact, the Poor Law Union had no choice in the matter as the Ministry of Health consistently refused to sanction such requests. The council again debated the issue in

January 1927 and passed a resolution to feed necessitous schoolchildren in cases where no unemployment benefit or relief from the Guardians was being paid.[41] The Board of Education (Medical Branch) made it clear that although they 'would not approve feeding on a scale similar to that which existed during the general stoppage', they would regard the feeding of up to a thousand children who were unable to benefit from education due to lack of food much more leniently.[42] By March 1927, 3,740 cases of severe hardship had been identified. School attendance officers were instructed to 'make close investigations into every case reported by head teachers' and to make parents aware that if they accept school feeding relief would be cut correspondingly.[43] Thus by reducing the number of recipients the RUDC continued limited school feeding.[44] As the industrial depression deepened and distress became prolonged, hard-pressed local authorities throughout the coalfield contrived to find ways to continue to feed necessitous children and provide them with milk.[45]

By the end of the dispute, the scale of spending on extra relief was enormous. It was estimated that about two and a half million pounds had been spent on extra relief during the Lockout.[46] This was greatly in excess of the corresponding figure for the 1921 Lockout. In the Poor Law Union of Pontypridd (which included about half the Rhondda population) 93,966 people were dependent on poor relief out of a population of 315,650.[47] This level of spending had produced a debt of £470,000. Approximately £10,000 a week was being spent on relief as against £6,000 for the corresponding period the previous year.[48] The figures for Merthyr were similar. By early December, Merthyr Guardians owed £362,000.[49] Figures for workhouse accommodation remained constant; all extra spending was on out-relief as miners (apart from a small number of destitute medically unfit single men) refused to accept institutional relief, rendering the offer of indoor relief, in effect the withdrawal of relief.[50] The government instructed that funds paid out in relief should be regarded as a loan, but in practice many Labour-controlled Boards of Guardians did not make repayment of poor relief a condition of receiving it.[51] Local authorities were in dire straits and were caught between the Ministry of Health's draconian directives for reducing expenditure and increasing resistance from ratepayers to the hugely inflated rate demands which far exceeded rates in non-mining areas. In March 1927, the RUDC applied to the Ministry of Health for a further loan. It was made clear that financial assistance would only be forth-coming 'on the understanding that the council would undertake to cut down their expenditure in all departments, and for that purpose appoint a small committee to further revise, reduce and control expenditure in future'.[52] Labour activists called for the 'Goschen' loans to be written off and for a public acceptance that the cost of the dispute should be regarded as a national rather than a local responsibility, but this plea went unheeded by central government.

Although most local authorities eventually attempted to conform to government spending directives, a few were fairly blatant in their disregard for them and this was particularly so in the Bedwellty Union, situated in western Monmouthshire and comprising six districts with a total population of 140,000. Even before the Lockout, the northern districts were in dire straits due to the closure of the iron and steel works and the exhaustion of local coal seams. Extra relief could be granted if a medical note was supplied. In the poverty-stricken Nantyglo and Blaina districts, 4924 claimants (out of a total of 7,600) received extra relief on this basis over the latter half of the Lockout.[53] In many cases, 'milk and eggs' were prescribed whilst other medical notes just stipulated 'nourishment'. The Bedwellty Union also gave out extra relief at Christmas. This attempt to run the Bedwellty Union with a human face resulted in massive debt, amounting to over a million pounds by January 1927.[54] It was alleged that not all of the Bedwellty spending was on humanitarian causes. The *Colliery Guardian* argued that the cost of administration in Bedwellty was twice as much as in the Merthyr Union and this was attributed to the abuse of medical notes and to the large number of relieving officers and assistants appointed, many of whom had family connections with guardians or were Labour activists.[55] Siân Williams argues that spending in Bedwellty was higher than other south Wales councils but 'not excessively so'.[56] Due to increasing difficulty in collecting rates, the council came to rely heavily on government loans which they had no hope of repaying.[57] The council were also very influenced by the Poplarist movement of the 1920s, whereby a small number of left-wing councils overspent as a means of pressing the case for central rather than local government to shoulder the burden of the unemployed. So in this sense the failure to avoid massive debt was a political decision. The Tredegar Iron and Steel Company protested against the Bedwellty Guardians, increased spending on outside relief, the cost of which would largely fall on them. They complained that an additional 68 relieving staff had been employed.[58] Bedwellty was precisely the sort of authority which Neville Chamberlain had in mind when he introduced the Board of Guardians (Default) Bill in the House of Commons in the autumn of 1926. The Act, as it subsequently became, empowered the Ministry of Health to remove guardians who had allegedly been too generous in their distribution of poor relief and to place control in the hands of government-appointed commissioners.[59] It was only ever used against three unions, including Bedwellty, where it struck in January 1927.[60] Spending on relief was seriously reduced, although interestingly even the government-appointed commissioners did not succeed in making a significant reduction in the overall level of debt.[61]

After the end of the dispute, it was argued by the Labour Party and left-wing commentators that the miners had been 'starved back to work'. This argument was countered by the view that the payment of relief to the families of locked-out miners had in effect enabled the Lockout to continue much longer than it would have otherwise done and this was the view taken by the Ministry of Health. An internal report concluded that the 'considerable degree of success . . . which attended the attempt to finance the industrial dispute from the poor rate makes it quite certain that as time goes on the experiment will be repeated'.[62] It was regarded as 'remarkable' that only in one or two isolated areas had there been a serious failure to pay the very high rates that this involved. Ultimately, therefore, the coalmining communities were themselves willing to underwrite the cost of supporting locked-out miners and their families. The government formed the view that a 'stiffer administration was possible which, while remaining humane and reasonable, would have resulted in a shortening of the struggle'.[63] This would have involved 'some reduction in relief ... without inflicting undue hardship'. The constant references in the mining communities to the 'plight of the single men' had made it clear that married miners were being supported from the relief paid to wives and children. This was considered unacceptable as it meant public funding for the dispute. The government were convinced that public support had ebbed away from the miners by the third month of the Lockout.[64] They were also gratified by the fact that a complete collapse of the financial basis of the Poor Law system had been averted.[65] These judgements were obviously rather hasty as within three years the Poor Law system had been swept away and the Poor Law Unions merged into new local authorities, which in Labour-controlled areas were determined to operate the Poor Law in a much more humane manner. It is undoubtedly the case that it was the suffering of the miners that had contributed to the new thinking on poor relief. It was unfortunately the case, however, that debts inherited from 1926 were still outstanding and had to be transferred to the new bodies, thus very much restricting what could be done.

Turning now to gender, there is no evidence that the increased fellowship between men and women that was recorded in earlier chapters was maintained after the Lockout. The very particular circumstances that existed from May to December 1926 produced a shift in cultural practices that allowed women to begin to break down the rigid sexual divisions within the public domain in mining communities. Men no longer endured backbreaking toil underground and women were spared the domestic drudgery that was involved in servicing miners at work. The heart of this change was in the soup kitchens and others activities around the miners' institutes and welfare halls. Men and women were forced to collaborate closely and publicly to run soup kitchens for sheer survival. In addition, women were a forceful presence in picketing. By January 1927, the Lockout had ended, the soup kitchens were disbanded and communal eating abandoned and so the material basis for increased companionship between men and women was fatally undermined. Miners' wives, daughters and mothers had to resume the routine of cooking, cleaning, washing and coping with coal dust which left them with little time for anything else. For those men who were not able to resume work, there is no evidence that they were more willing than before to identify with domestic work. Unemployed miners were deprived of the work which was the major signifier of masculine status. To identify with 'feminine' domestic work was potentially dangerous as it could undermine their masculinity still further and hence was to be avoided. Time was therefore spent on the usual masculine pursuits, such as allotments and fishing. Crucially important was the male bonding that took place in the pub and in the recreational pursuits in the miners' welfare hall, where unemployed men found mutual support. Women participated in upholding patriarchal values in order to bolster up the morale of their unemployed husbands.[66]

During 1927 and 1928, there were occasional letters to *The Miner* from miners' wives indicating discontent with the MFGB leadership. These letters were critical of both the politics and culture of the labour movement.[67] As far as they can be identified, none of the women were associated with the south Wales coalfield. The feeling that miners' wives were not being taken seriously was the context for the debate about women's sections of the MFGB at this time. Women's sections were formed in some mining localities, particularly Nottingham, where women voiced their opposition to 'Spencerism'.[68] As Gier-Viskovatoff and Porter have indicated, there is no evidence that women's sections of the MFGB had any official recognition or influence within the Federation at this time.[69] Nor is there any evidence of any women's sections of the Fed being formed in south Wales. It appears to be the case that women activists in the south Wales coalfield were very busy in Labour Party women's sections, Women's Co-operative Guild branches or other labour movement organisations such as the Communist Party and saw no need to form women's sections of the SWMF. Indeed, in such a near mono-industrial culture in many towns and villages, the local Labour Party women's section was, in effect, already a group of miners' wives so it was not necessary to form a new group.

After collecting a grand total of almost a third of a million pounds, the work of the Women's Committee for the Relief of

Miners' Wives and Children was wound up soon after the return to work.[70] Almost all of the fostered children returned to their homes and in many cases lasting bonds of friendship were forged, so that whole families were 'adopted' by foster parents and continued to provide food parcels and other support long after the children had returned home. In a few cases, older children reached the age of 14 and found work in their adopted locality and never returned. After the frantic period of the Lockout when many routine activities were put aside for relief work, Labour women in south Wales settled down to their usual round of activities focusing primarily on health, housing and welfare based on a particular maternalist brand of socialist-feminist politics. As Lowri Newman has shown, these women activists forged an identity as 'Labour women' that was informed by both class and gender.[71] By the late 1920s, local Labour Party organisations woke up to the fact that the women's sections were a force to be reckoned with.[72] It was shown in the previous chapter that the most outstanding example of a grass-roots woman activist in the south Wales coalfield during the Lockout was Beatrice Green from Abertillery, a miner's daughter and a miner's wife whose life was transformed in 1926. During 1927, Green continued to be a rising star among Labour women. From January to October, she wrote a series of lengthy, informative and articulate articles on various aspects of childcare for *Labour Woman*. She also wrote for a French socialist paper. In September, she presided over a conference of almost eight hundred women held by the Monmouthshire Labour Women's Advisory Council. According to Marion Phillips she was 'the very centre of its inspiration'.[73] Sadly, Beatrice Green's life was cut short by ulcerative colitis. She died at the age of 32 on 19 October 1927, leaving two young sons. An ambulance in Abertillery was named after her in recognition of the role she had played in promoting health services in the town. In a moving tribute, Marion Phillips wrote that had she lived Green would have gone on to hold 'more and more important positions of leadership in the Labour Movement'.[74] Lowri Newman has written that Green's leadership qualities 'in all probability would have ensured her a place in Parliament'.[75] In fact, impressive though she was as a speaker, writer and organiser, had she lived Green was unlikely ever to have made it to Parliament. This is evident from the example of Rose Davies from Aberdare, whose record of public service in south Wales was second to none. During the 1920s, she served as a councillor, alderman, county councillor, JP and on various public bodies such as the Welsh Consultative Council for the Board of Health and held important offices within the labour movement. Davies was an ideal candidate for Parliament but the only opportunity she was ever given was the hopeless seat of Honiton in Devon in 1929, where she secured a derisory 2.6 per cent of the vote.[76] Given that by 1939 south Wales had eighteen Labour MPs, thirteen of whom were sponsored by the SWMF, it is astonishing that someone of the calibre of Rose Davies was not selected for a safe Labour seat. The explanation lies in the deeply-rooted gender divisions within south Walian society at this time which still marked out high office as a preserve of men. In this regard, the experience of the Lockout had made no lasting change.

The Communist Party failed to maintain new women members from mining areas who were recruited during the momentum of the Lockout. The Ninth Congress of the CPGB in October 1927 reported a serious falling off in women members.[77] The party women's paper, the *Woman Worker* (from February 1927 *Working Woman*) lacked influence and support. Increasingly, party propaganda directed towards women focused on anti-war issues and the contrast between life for women in Britain and the Soviet Union. This compared unfavourably with Labour women's more practical grass-roots campaigns. There were however, many Communist women activists working within the Labour Party, particularly in the Rhondda and in a few local women's sections, such as Maesteg and Caerau, Communist women had a dominating influence.[78] These groups were resistant to the 1925 Labour Conference decision to expel Communists, which was only really tackled in Wales in 1927. Following the marked deterioration in Communist Party-Labour Party relations after the Lockout, it became much more difficult for CP women to work within the Labour Party. When Ferndale Miners' Lodge voted to support a Communist, Mrs Smith, against the Labour candidate, Mrs Jacobs, for the Rhondda Council elections in 1927, there was a storm of protest from leading Labour activists in the Lodge.[79] In her autobiography, Elizabeth Andrews, the Labour woman's organiser for south Wales at this time, is clearly hostile to Communist women on account of 'their attacks, which were often very personal.'[80] By 1928, when the Communist Party launched into its disastrous ultra-left 'Third Period', relations between Labour and Communist women appeared to have broken down completely. Relations did improve during the 1930s, however, when women were prominent in the struggles of the unemployed against the Means Test (see below) and the 'stay-down' strikes against company unionism; much of this work was broadly-based across party divides.

There is little sign of activity by the Women's Guild of Empire (which had gained some support in the mining communities of south Wales in 1926 for its opposition to strikes) in the period following the Lockout. The Guild held an event in Cardiff in October 1927 which included visits to the City Hall and National Museum and a rally reported to be attended by 500 Guild members.[81] The Guild leader, Flora Drummond gave a report on her recent tour of Canada and appealed for mothers to let their children emigrate to Canada 'where the advantages and opportunities for energetic people were far greater than here'. She offered support in the form of letters of introduction and practical help on arrival. Regrettably, there is no indication of how many of those present had connections with mining or whether Drummond's appeal produced any willing recruits. Drummond was a pallbearer at Emmeline Pankhurst's funeral in 1928, continued to be controller of the WGE at its London head-quarters throughout the 1930s and was also active in the feminist movement, but there is no indication of any serious WGE involvement in the south Wales coalfield after the Lockout.[82] It is very likely that women in the Welsh valleys who were in some way connected with the WGE in 1926 were also connected with men who supported the breakaway 'scab' union, the South Wales Miners Industrial Union, as there is clearly a common outlook between the two organisations. In Ynysybwl, for example, there may have been a connection between WGE activity, the early breakaway movement from the Lockout and the unusually active supporters of the

Conservative Party in the village. Little work has been done, however, to establish these connections, so at present we can only speculate on these possible links.

THE AGONY CONTINUES

The crisis in the coal industry deepened and with the onset of a general depression in 1929. The industry slumped into a deep trough with 1932 recorded as the lowest point when unemployment in the south Wales coalfield reached 53 per cent.[83] The halcyon days of south Wales coal were over and, being basically a near mono-industrial society, the region was plunged into an economic abyss from which there could be no short-term recovery. The Pilgrim Trust investigation into long-term unemployment reported on the 'steady trail of human wreckage' in south Wales.[84] Unemployment in the Rhondda in 1936 was seventy times higher than that of Deptford in south-east London.[85] The town of Merthyr appeared to be in such terminal decline in the 1930s, that there were serious proposals to relocate it at a coastal site.[86] The 'heads of the valleys' communities connected with a defunct iron trade and exhausted coalmines were worst hit. In Blaina and Abertillery, unemployment was running at around 80 per cent of the workforce. In 1927, there were 377 employed members of the Maerdy lodge and 1,366 unemployed.[87] It was particularly hard for unemployed miners, who had been regarded as 'labour aristocrats' before 1914 to be degraded to such a level. As Dai Smith has pointed out, it was not just a question of idle men, lack of bread and poor housing but 'the terrible feeling of not being wanted'.[88] The previously assertive miners were now silent and cowed; persistent problems such as underpayment of wages could not be tackled as employers were likely to sack any miner who complained that his wage packet had been calculated wrongly. Government did little to alleviate the problem of unemployment in south Wales. Government training centres for the unemployed and a feeble policy of 'industrial transference' were a minimal response to the crisis. It was not until 1936 that south Wales was designated a 'special area' and more effort was made to channel other industry into the coalfield, such as the establishment of the Treforest Trading Estate in 1938.

Alongside the decidedly tardy actions of government with regard to long-term unemployment in south Wales, the voluntary sector needs to be considered. Having established a large network of boot-repair workshops and sewing circles during the Lockout, the Quakers felt strongly that their work in south Wales should continue. Having secured the blessing of miners' leaders, Emma Noble, together with her husband William and friends such as A. Lindsay, Master of Balliol College, Oxford, launched a permanent social and educational centre in the Rhondda, modeled on the settlements established in slum areas of English cities before the First World War.[89] The Nobles moved into Maes-yr-Haf ('summer meadow'), a large detached house in its own grounds in Trealaw, near Tonypandy in April 1927 and made it their permanent home. For the rest of the inter-war period Maes-yr-Haf worked with the unemployed, organising evening classes, teaching manual skills and acting as a focus for relief work. Other Quaker educational settlements were established; Merthyr Tydfil (1930), Risca (1931), Bargoed and Rhymney (1933), Pontypool (1934), Dowlais (1935), Aberdare (1936) and Pontypridd (1937).[90] A large range of activities was pursued, including weaving, furniture-making, shoe-repairing, poultry farming and beekeeping. Efforts were made to lift the spirits of women as well as unemployed men. The Quakers acted on the principles of 'self help' and avoidance of religious dogma. Less visible was the mission to counteract the influence of Marxism and the 'moral decay' of the long-term unemployed who were losing the incentive to work. This was well understood by the Communist Party and the National Unemployed Workers Movement, who saw such charitable efforts as diversionary and no real solution to the crisis which had been a product of irresponsible and unchecked capitalism. Oral evidence, however, was very positive regarding the Quakers in the Rhondda. Nine interviews were conducted in Trealaw where the folk memory of the Quakers is still strong. For instance Mary Lowrie told me how she learnt to repair shoes, make quilts, and make coats from unpicking and reusing old material, 'I was always with Maes-yr-Haf learning different things'.[91]

As the depression deepened, the plight of south Wales, as

Britain's worst-hit region, became known nationally and internationally. Well publicised visits and appeals by the Prince of Wales and other society figures helped to bring relief funds into the stricken regions of south Wales. The SWMF insisted that all relief funds be channelled through the democratic processes of the local miners' lodges. As we have seen, in most mining communities the lodge was the leading force and often acted in a controlling or adjudicating manner. Outside donors sought to undermine these well-accepted procedures on account of the often dominant left-wing forces within the lodge In the case of Maerdy the Distress Committee, which had practically run the town during the General Strike and Lockout, was fatally undermined in 1928, when a secret agreement, facilitated through the Lord Mayor of London's relief organisation, arranged for funds to be channelled from the town of Rugby to a new non-elected body from which the Distress Committee was specifically excluded. [92] The previous unity of the town was undermined as the non-mining representatives on the Distress Committee, such as teachers, priests and shopkeepers, transferred to the new committee, leaving the Distress Committee bankrupt. The Fed, in its much weakened state, was unable to counter such manoeuvres. These interventions were mirrored in other communities where 'twinning' or adoption arrangements were established with more prosperous towns, which brought in much-needed relief funds but sometimes with the heavy hand of paternalism and at the expense of undermining community control.[93]

Although greatly weakened, the labour movement continued to stand up for the miners and their families. The south Wales miners were represented on all the national hunger marches of the 1930s and in 1934 the Welsh contingents included a women's section.[94] In south Wales, the Public Accounts Committees, which took over from the old Poor Law Guardians in 1929, continued the tradition of treating the poor relatively generously compared to other local authorities. Worried about escalating costs and wanting to standardise the situation, the government introduced the Unemployment Act 1934, the second part of which was an attempt to create a uniform system. In south Wales, this would mean a much harsher implementation of the Means Test of 1931, particularly with regard to making one family member in work responsible for unemployed family members. Opposition to the proposals was universal. The mass protests culminated in a demonstration of 300,000 on 3 February 1935, the greatest demonstration Wales has ever known.[95] Women were especially noticeable in these protests and were responsible for storming and ransacking the Merthyr Unemployed Assistance Board (UAB) office on 4 February. As Gwyn A. Williams wrote, 'it was the women who carried this broken society on their backs'.[96] The following day, the government announced the postponement of the new regulations. Aware that a general election was imminent, the government had been forced to back down. Although a modified version of the original bill was eventually implemented, it was still a great victory and, coming after the defeats of 1921 and 1926, it had huge symbolic importance for the people of south Wales.

In the years before 1914 when 'coal was king', migrants were attracted to the south Wales coalfield from rural Wales and western England. After 1921, when the industry began to falter the trend was reversed. What began as a trickle of emigration in the early 1920s became a flood in 1926. According to Eli Ginzberg, in the four years following the General Strike there was a net loss from migration of 100,000.[97] It was a trend which was to continue. It has been estimated that about half a million people left Wales in the interwar years, mostly to settle in England, but many also went overseas.[98] The Parliamentary Labour Party Report of 1928 explicitly points in this direction:

> Steps must be taken to effect transference of population from the areas which are hopelessly derelict to other places. This may very well commence with the single able bodied men and juveniles, but must ultimately (unless there is some unexpected development of industry) extend to the whole population. We suggest that various forms of administrative action be taken immediately to give encouragement to such emigration.[99]

After the end of the Lockout, James Evans, Chief Inspector for Wales at the Ministry of Health, addressed the Pontypridd Board of Guardians and specifically encouraged young men in the area to emigrate as there was 'no expectation of so many young men being absorbed in the coal industry in the future as had been in the past'.[100] As we have seen, it was already the case that there was very little work for women in the mining community and this forced many families to send their daughters into domestic service in other areas of Britain. This trend continued after 1926 and from this date many girls went to government training centres for three months before being sent away. The only form of training on offer for girls was domestic service. Maria Williams from Maerdy is perhaps a typical example of this. She was sent into domestic service in 1927 at the age of seventeen, after three months at a government training centre in Pontypridd where she was taught cooking, housework and sewing. She then took up a post in Sutton, Surrey where, as she told Hywel Francis in 1973, she did not get much to eat and 'I didn't feel part of the family at

Girls in service late 1920s and their manager.
Lizzie Davies is on the far right.

all. I felt I was the servant you know and I was there to do my work and that was that.'[101] The image below shows Lizzie Davies and fellow workers in service in London in the late 1920s, which she described as 'very hard work'.[102]

Migration patterns were varied. Sometimes whole families migrated together, although this was considered too risky for most. There are many cases of groups of young men or women migrating together so that they could look after each other. The most usual pattern was for a young man or woman to go first and then secure employment for other family members. By whatever method, it was undoubtedly the case that young men left the valleys in large numbers during and after the Lockout, often on foot as they had no other means. In his memoir of Mountain Ash, Bernard Baldwin wrote that after the Lockout many miners began to search different areas of England for work, some walking over 200 miles to London.[103] In August 1928, the *Sunday Worker* reported on the 'hundreds of men' from the south Wales coalfield stranded in London, 'jobless, penniless, far from home, quite often without relief of any kind' and dependent on street collections for their next meal.[104] Lizzie Davies told me that two of her brothers left after the Lockout, one to become a nurse in Maidstone, Kent and the other a builder in London: 'they had to, they never came back'.[105] For some though the ties of home were too strong. Glyn Williams from Glyncorrwg was eighteen in 1926. He said in an interview in 1974 that many of his friends were leaving for London in the summer of 1926 and he intended to walk to London with them. When he told his mother of his intentions she cried and he thought about his four younger siblings and the fact that there would be no potential wage-earner in the house (his father had silicosis) and he did not go.[106] He later found work in Glynneath where he lodged for a brief period before coming back to Glyncorrwg when he found local work as a haulier.

Cast adrift from the close-knit bonds of family and neighbourhood in coalfield society where 'everyone knew everyone else', many migrants felt incredible loneliness in the anonymity of the big city. Some were clearly bewildered by this new way of life, like the miner who wrote from London: 'I am sitting in Hyde Park. There are thousands of people all round me and not a single one has spoken to me.'[107] Although a few south Wales miners migrated to other, more prosperous coalfields in the Midlands, most migrants became unskilled workers in the 'new' consumer industries of prosperous interwar Britain.

There were, however, about two thousand miners (often with families) who migrated to the Kent coalfield, which rapidly expanded from 1925 and became a refuge for many militants who had been victimised in the Lockout. It was the only coalfield in Britain to grow during this period. Although a small coalfield with only four pits, over a quarter of the east Kent miners were migrants from south Wales.[108] Albert Newton told the story of Gerry Quick who walked from Merthyr Tydfil. After seven months of the Lockout and four weeks on the road he hobbled up to the Betteshanger pit, hungry and exhausted. After four days of rest and recovery and thanks to the generosity of fellow Welsh miners he was able to start work.[109] Although lured by the prospect of full-time work and above average wages, many Kent migrants had to endure considerable prejudice from local residents. In a local oral history study of the Kent coalfield, respondents referred to hostility to miners' families in local shops and reluctance to rent accommodation to miners.[110] It was the women who bore the brunt of this discrimination, which led many families to return to their previous homes, preferring the prospect of unemployment and poverty in a mining community to bleak and isolated lives in Kent. As Eli Ginzberg put it, 'many felt it was better to go hungry among friends than to be lonely among strangers'.[111]

The reality of life in south Wales for the long-term unemployed was grim.[112] Every week, very fine calculations were necessary in order to get by, so difficult choices had to be made between competing demands for very limited resources. After a few months, when household items or clothing needed to be replaced, there was often no other option but to cut back on food. Allotments could make a big difference to the nutrition of an unemployed family, but in the narrow, steep-sided valleys of the mining communities of south Wales, land for allotment plots was not always available. Housing conditions were still very poor as poverty-stricken councils could not secure funds for new building and landlords were unlikely to make improvements or even repairs on houses in rent arrears. Even when more accommodation became available due to out-migration, poor families could not take up these opportunities as they could not afford the increased rent involved in moving from a house share (an 'apartment') to a sole tenancy. Studies show that the role of the housewife in an unemployed family was absolutely crucial in keeping the family afloat, but even the most careful and resourceful housewife would not be able to cope if her husband drank or gambled. Fortunately, this sad scenario was not typical and in most unemployed families there was a fierce determination to uphold standards and therefore social standing whenever possible. The Pilgrim Trust study was impressed with what they saw in south Wales, 'in Crook and in the Rhondda, house after house was well kept and well managed, while in Liverpool house after house was dreary and ill-equipped'.[113]

Low wages meant that men on short time were often actually worse off than men who were wholly unemployed, something which Steven Thompson argues has not been recognised previously.[114] This was understood however by oral respondents such as Lilian Roberts, who told me that when men were on short time they could not claim dole, which often meant they only brought home about two pounds a week to support a large family.[115] It was recognised that miners who had two or more children were better off on the dole than working.[116] Working miners also faced the problem of debt, as rent arrears from the Lockout were deducted from pay and took many years to pay off, thus eroding the incentive to work still further. It is not surprising that older miners with dependent children reconciled themselves to a life without work. The Pilgrim Trust reported that many older unemployed miners were 'probably now as happy as or happier than they had ever been'.[117] It should also be borne in mind that by 1936, when this study was undertaken, consistently falling prices meant that unemployed families were marginally better off than in the 1920s. Evidence shows that the period immediately after the Lockout was much harder. Arthur Horner wrote that after the Lockout the offices of the MFGB in London were inundated with requests for help by destitute miners.[118] Labour MP George Hall raised the question of distress in Aberdare in parliament in November 1926, asking the Minister of Health to take immediate steps in the form of provision of increased relief, boots and clothing. The Minister's reply made no offer of extra funds and merely referred to the level of debt in the local authority, already amounting to £297,000.[119] The Labour Party Committee of Enquiry into Distress in South Wales in early 1927 found alarming signs of poor nutrition among children and mothers. In the Rhondda, infant mortality rose sharply in the year after the Lockout.[120] Girls in particular were singled out. In Abertillery, the weight of girls in all age groups was falling and, in Abergwynfi, the investigators were 'shocked at the condition and clothing of the girls'.[121] There is little doubt that mass unemployment and poverty had a detrimental effect on health. The discrepancies which existed between mortality rates in south Wales with the national averages worsened during the Depression. Still births and neo-natal deaths, for example, which are regarded as key indicators and closely linked to the well-being of the community generally, were 'consistently and often considerably higher than the England and Wales aggregate'.[122] Neo-natal mortality rates increased most in the areas of highest unemployment and poverty. Children were also lighter and shorter in these areas.

The gendered impact of the Depression is also apparent, with women suffering disproportionately compared to men. Many oral respondents told me that their mothers had very hard lives. Gladys Davies spoke for many when she said, 'my mother had a terrible hard life, always working'.[123] It is well documented that women went hungry in order to provide for other family members. As Eli Ginzberg noted, 'mothers deprived themselves so that children could eat'.[124] It was common practice for men and boys to be fed first. As Gladys Davies said, 'any meat we had . . . it was cut for the men . . . if we had stew (laughs) you'd have to catch the meat going through it'.[125] After the men, mothers fed their children, often leaving little for themselves. In the Pilgrim Trust study the women in the survey were found to be eating 356 calories less than their daily dietary requirements.[126] It is not surprising, therefore, to find that in several different respects death rates for women in south Wales were worsened by the Depression. For example, both maternal mortality and deaths from tuberculosis among women rose at this time.[127] As the evidence above shows, girls were often of low weight and poorly clad, indicating that mothers expected daughters to follow in their footsteps and be prepared for self-denial.

RECENT PERSPECTIVES

This disastrous period in Welsh history came to an end with the outbreak of war in 1939 and only then was the blight of mass unemployment lifted. Light industrial work for women, which had been slowly increasing before the war, largely through the government training schemes, became a flood, with six munitions factories opening in south Wales including the Royal Ordnance Factories at Bridgend and Glascoed, together employing 35,000 women by 1943.[128] This work was, however, largely seen as 'for the duration' rather than providing an opportunity for a major restructuring of the gender order. The miners had a 'good war' and by 1945 they were held in high esteem by a grateful nation. Nationalisation of the mines followed swiftly with only token resistance from mineowners described by Francis and Smith as 'morally and politically bankrupt'.[129] By the 1950s, the older generation of miners who had lived through 1926 was fading into the past and with it the most trenchant attitudes of class hatred and bitterness. Rising real income and initial enthusiasm for nationalisation also helped to create a period of relative industrial harmony. This came to an abrupt end with the miners' strikes of 1972 and 1974, when new uncertainty about the future of Britain's energy sources and favourable public opinion led the miners to victories which were seen as the final revenge for the humiliation of 1926 and the other defeats of the inter-war years. By 1984 the climate had changed completely and the miners were defeated in an epic struggle from March 1984 to March 1985 to prevent mass pit closures between National Union of Mineworkers (NUM) leader Arthur Scargill and Prime Minister Margaret Thatcher.

A significant feature of the 1984–5 dispute was the movement Women Against Pit Closures. Starting in Barnsley and based in the Yorkshire coalfield, the movement developed a huge momentum very quickly building local support groups and organising well-attended national rallies of Women Against Pit Closures.[130] Although based around the idea of support for the miners, the women were also vocal in raising their own issues within the mining community. In practical terms, this largely centred on the question of addressing sexist attitudes and practices both inside the home and in the wider community. Coming as it did hard on the heels of the dynamic women's liberation movement of the 1970s and early 1980s, this new movement was dubbed 'working-class women's liberation'.[131] In south Wales there was almost a revival of the spirit of the 1926 Lockout, creating a wave of support for the miners across the whole community. As in many previous disputes, the south Wales miners were the most solid of all the coalfields. There were many other echoes of 1926, such as the free school meals provided by local councils for miners' children. Within this broad framework of support and solidarity, a network of women's groups sprang up across the valleys, so that by the middle of May every mining village or town had a 'community' or women's support group.[132] Although women did participate in some picketing activities, such as the mass womens' pickets of the Port Talbot steelworks, it was not a common occurrence. There was male opposition to women pickets and in any case picketing local pits was barely necessary and secondary picketing was declared illegal, so women's support work in south Wales, as everywhere, was quickly based around fund-raising and food supply. The support group in Maerdy, a very small community, raised 700 food parcels a week for miners' families.[133] There were also mixed support groups. The Neath, Dulais and Swansea Miners' Support group was a mixed group with women in the leadership. It fed a thousand families, raised £350,000 and had its own newspaper and striking miners' choir.[134] Although food parcels were the dominant form of assistance, there were some soup kitchens in south Wales. In Abertillery, for instance, the women's support group organised a makeshift kitchen in the miners' institute and from a small Baby Belling cooker, a boiler and a large electric frying pan, they produced 120–50 hot meals a day for local miners.[135]

How did the women's support work in 1984–5 differ from that of 1926? Were there any similarities in gender relations between 1926 and 1984–5? In some ways, the position of women in south Wales's coalfield society was similar to what it had been in 1926 in that mining was still a male monopoly and women were still outside NUM politics and debates. By 1984, the coal industry was still the largest single employer, but it had shrunk dramatically and employment in the service sector and in mechanical and electrical engineering had grown in importance. In essence, however, there were still a large number of miners' wives and other female kin who did not work and were dependent on the miners' wage. The women who participated in the support groups in 1984–5 were essentially performing the same roles as in 1926. In some ways, the different character of women's participation in 1984–5 has been overplayed. This can partly be attributed to a process of 'collective forgetting' of the roles women played in 1926.[136] As we have seen in earlier chapters, women in 1926 took part in picketing, hounded 'scabs', sometimes in a fairly violent manner and travelled outside the coalfield for public speaking in aid of relief work. The large-scale communal eating in 1926 meant that men and women engaged together in genuine fellowship running the soup kitchens. In 1984–5, although men participated in the community support groups, there were many women's support groups with men providing only marginal assistance, so gender divisions were still very evident. As far as masculinity is concerned, strike-breaking men in 1984–5 were regarded in exactly the same way as those in 1926. Striking miners acquired heroic status whilst those who broke the strike were 'lesser men . . . weak workers who were unprepared to support the NUM or their fellow workers'.[137]

What was different about the 1984–5 strike was that women had a consciousness *as women* and wanted to be taken more seriously as equal partners rather than passive helpers. 'Pearl' in the Abertillery group explained that she got bored with fund-raising:

> we wanted a bit more responsibility, a bit more excitement . . . we wanted to do something more important. We made our way, slowly and quietly, politically, but now we decided that we needed more contact with the men and the things they were doing. Stone the

crows we had a hell of a battle on our hands at first . . . it took ages and
ages to be accepted, but once we were, the men didn't do anything else
without consulting us first, and telling us of their plans. It was a terrific
feeling. At last we were their equals, even if it was just in times of
trouble.[138]

Although there was clearly a feminist consciousness among
women in south Wales, it appears to be much more muted
than the strident feminism shown by the Yorkshire women. As
in 1926, there was a great emphasis on community action,
even if that meant downplaying the specific needs of women.
In both disputes, women were fighting for the survival of their
communities.[139] A class perspective was still seen as absolutely
vital and overriding any issues of gender. And even though the
women of south Wales 'discovered' themselves as women, this
did not mean that they felt any affinity with the women's liberation movement, which they viewed with suspicion or even
overt hostility and in this respect they were identical with the
women of 1926 who had no connections with organised feminism. The 'common socialist culture' of the Rhondda in the
period before 1939 referred to by Chris Williams was still
evident, however diluted by the rise of a consumer society.[140] It
is still true however, that the 1984–5 dispute did prove inspira-
tional and life-changing for many women.[141] For example, the
context of the miners' strike was an important element for the
foundation of the DOVE workshop in the Dulais valley in 1987
which has been very successful in widening opportunities for
education and training for women in an area where women
have been very restricted by traditional gender stereotyping.[142]

After the 1984–5, strike women also moved into public roles
and made demands on their husbands for more equality at
home: 'I could never go back to my knitting and the kitchen
sink now.'[143] We should be careful though of attributing these
changes to the dispute, as much of the relevant 'celebratory'
literature does. Only a minority of miners' wives were actively
involved and it is likely that some of those whose lives were
transformed were already in transition as a result of wider
social forces and were looking for a mechanism to enact that
change. A study of the Yorkshire, Nottinghamshire and
Derbyshire coalfield is also cautious in this respect, arguing
that 'many of the larger claims made for the impact of the

strike on gender roles and relations cannot be validated'.[144] It is also noteworthy that although many men, including Arthur Scargill, supported the demand of Women Against Pit Closures for women to be granted associate membership of the NUM, this demand was ultimately unsuccessful.[145] It seems to be the case that whilst many mining women developed a feminist consciousness, their expectations for change amongst their men were not fulfilled. In this respect, there is perhaps another important similarity between 1926 and 1984–5 in that neither resulted in long-lasting changes to the gender order in the mining community.

After the miners were defeated in 1985, there was a large-scale programme of pit closures, so by the late 1980s there were only five deep coal mines left in south Wales. What was left of the industry was privatised in 1995. By this time, only Tower Colliery, a workers' buy-out near Hirwaun ran on co-operative lines, was left. In January 2008, this last remaining deep coal mine in Wales closed.[146] Today the former coalfield is referred to as a 'post coal community'.[147] How are individual and public memories of the 1926 General Strike and Miners' Lockout represented in today's society?[148] What are the reflections of oral respondents who were the 'children of 1926' on south Wales in the new century? Ferdynand Zweig, writing in 1948, remarked that 'whenever you start a conversation with a miner, he invariably begins by telling you about the Coal Strike in 1926. The Coal Strike is vividly impressed on their minds, like an event which happened only yesterday'.[149] The great Welsh poet poet Idris Davies famously wrote, 'we shall remember 1926 until our blood is dry'.[150] This cry from the heart was still resonating in oral evidence collected from the 1970s onwards. There were people still paying off debts from the Lockout as late as 1973.[151] Interviewees stood firm on the belief that the miners had no choice – that they were right to do what they did. They had little to say beyond these simple affirmations. They were equally supportive of the stand which the miners took in 1984–5. Old age had not dimmed their class-conscious outlook. The women of 1926 were largely remembered as victims and not for their role in picketing, which has been described above. Feelings against those who returned to work (including those associated with the 'scab' union) ran very high for many years. The Gregory family, mentioned earlier, were regarded as professional 'scabs'. According to Alun Burge, when one of the Gregory men was brought to his home in Cwmfelinfach from the pit with appendicitis in 1932 the Fed refused to allow its car to be used to take him to hospital and Gregory subsequently died. Feeling in the community was such that crowds sang jovial songs outside his house on the day of the funeral. Scabs could be expected to be banned from pubs and publicly abused in the street. As we have seen, this was basically a moral rather than a political stance. Scabs were regarded as offenders against the community. Lilian Lawrence told me that her mother broke the windows of her brother's house in Porth when he returned to work and she never spoke to him again for the rest of her life.[152] According to Gladys Davies, who was brought up in Pontycymer, a small community in the Garw valley, 'you always had this feeling of fear, that some men would go and beat up the scabs . . . because it was very hard for men to be out of work without anything and then these men going in . . . they were never accepted, after that'.[153] Gladys (and her sister-in-law who was almost 80 and sat in on the interview) went on to tell me the names of the two scabs and where they lived and this was 78 years after the Lockout. Sadly – but realistically – these very elderly people with amazing memories will not be with us for very much longer. In the community generally, there is no longer any specific public memory of the Lockout. It has submerged into a more general memory of inter-war depression, desolation and poverty.

The historical value of the former coalfield is now its greatest asset. A reality TV show, *Coal House*, based on the daily life of three south Wales miners' families in 1927, was broadcast in 2007.[154] Although undoubtedly informative, there is no question that the main intention of the programme-makers is to provide entertainment. The misery and degradation of the families of 1927 is being acted out by the bewildered participants and massaged for the viewers into quite a jolly time. The Rhondda Cynon Taff and other former coalfield councils that promote 'mining tourism' and heritage sites such as the Rhondda Heritage Park in Porth and the Blaenavon Big Pit depict the days of 'king coal', the conditions underground and the daily toil of miners and their families. Although considerable effort has been made to ensure that these sites are historically accurate and informative, the need to ensure broad appeal means that inevitably the industrial conflicts and politics of the inter-war years are played down. In particular, such tourist sites make almost no mention of the General Strike and Lockout, almost certainly the most significant industrial dispute of the twentieth century, as this would be seen as 'divisive' and 'looking backwards'. In this sense, public authorities and heritage sites are consciously shaping the 'dominant memory' of south Wales in the inter-war years to specifically exclude class conflict as it no longer fits in with the image that they wish to promote. Nowadays, the former coalfield promotes itself as 'Greater Cardiff' and is immeasurably more prosperous than in the 1920s, although social problems such as poverty, drug abuse, high teenage pregnancy and teenage suicide rates and high levels of incapacity benefit among older men are evidence of the lasting legacy of the social desolation associated with the decline of the coal industry. This image is one that local councils are struggling to overcome. Oral respondents told me of their sadness at what the Rhondda had become compared to its heyday. Lillian Lawrence told me that she met a man on a train whilst on holiday who told her, 'the Rhondda is a rough place now, I wouldn't go there'. She said, 'that nearly broke my heart'.[155] It was also noticeable that respondents were stridently opposed to the overt materialism of today's society. Jean Ellis from Pontycymer told me, 'nobody seems to be satisfied today, they want more, more, more'.[156] Elsie Pritchard, also from Pontycymer, said, 'young people today . . . they don't think of what they can do without, only what they can do with'.[157] Gwen Ratcliffe from Trealaw, whose mother was widowed early with eight children, was bewildered by the fashion for torn and ragged jeans which for her was a sign of the poverty of the past; 'today when they cut their jeans it's fashion, it's not making sense'.[158] Jill John, who was interviewed in the early 1990s, recalled, 'I do remember the joy if you could get a custard cream biscuit. We have so much of everything now that we don't realise what its like to have a very rare treat of a custard cream biscuit or a tin of fruit.'[159] The privations of the Lockout

and the era that it was part of made an indelible imprint on
these women which will never be eradicated, no matter how
much councils promote the idea of a prosperous 'Greater
Cardiff'.

7

LAST WORD

This book tells a remarkable story of resistance. The General Strike and Miners' Lockout which followed was arguably the most significant labour dispute in twentieth-century Britain. The miners were the only group of workers who presented a serious challenge to the 1920s neo-conservative economic policy of wage cuts and deflation in order to return Britain to the economic 'normality' of the pre-war gold standard. These deflationary policies added misery to the miners and their families who were already undergoing painful adjustment to the long-term terminal decline of the coal industry in the face of overwhelming foreign competition. The price for their defiance was a stoppage of seven months which drove down living standards in the coalfields to bare existence. Britain of the 1930s has often been referred to as the 'hungry thirties', yet for those on poor relief in the 1920s life was far harder, as the 1930s unemployed benefited from price falls rendering their paltry benefits more valuable in real terms. There can be no doubt of the courageous heroism of the women and men of 1926. This was echoed by the poet Idris Davies who ended his epic poem, *The Angry Summer: A Poem of 1926*, with the words 'Toiler and toiler, side by side / Whose faith and courage shall be told / In blaze of scarlet and of gold'.[1] This book has moved beyond this simple story of heroism to provide a detailed account of life during the Lockout in the south Wales coalfield, focusing on men and women as gendered subjects. As such we have encountered men and women as complex identities in an exceptional period of fluidity and dynamism.

For seven months in 1926 the objective circumstances of people's lives in the south Wales coalfield had a different framework. The General Strike and Miners' Lockout had set them against their employers in a situation of brutal class confrontation and, as a result, the feeling of separation from mainstream society grew stronger and the mining community drew into itself, thus intensifying the characteristics of an 'alternative society'. Within this context the material basis of the sexual division of labour was undermined. In a society of marked gender segregation and male dominance, the Lockout produced unexpected opportunities for change. Men could no longer depend on heavy manual labour, male bonding at the coalface and 'breadwinning' to ensure their masculine status, and mining women were no longer tied to the very heavy domestic burden of caring for the miner in work. With the pressing economic reality of drastically reduced income and time on their hands, the men and women of 1926 in south Wales set about creating a remarkable number of miners' kitchens. Communal eating was also a feature of children's lives in 1926 as a similar network of children's canteens was established. Within these new public spaces women found a role and a new identity. In producing meals en masse day after day to feed needy miners and children, the workers of the soup kitchens found a new companionship which cut across the usual gender divide. Men and women worked together as never before and were satisfied in the knowledge that together they were making a real difference to people's lives. Despite the absence of a family wage, masculine status and identity for men was maintained though male bonding in union activity, competitive sports and various forms of food and fuel sourcing. This newfound fellowship between men and women often encroached on other areas of the community where women were able to assert themselves much more forcefully in miners' institutes and welfare halls, particularly in the numerous sporting and cultural activities during the Lockout. Ultimately though, running the home and making sure that everyone was fed and clothed, however hard this was, was still women's responsibility. Not all women were able to participate in the potentially liberating aspects of the Lockout which chiefly benefited single women, older women and mothers with school-age children. For mothers of babies and young children, still tied to their homes, living on poor relief and not able to participate in communal eating, life was invariably harder during the Lockout, as we have seen in the moving testimony provided by Marion Phillips.

In spite of this, there is no doubt that overall the Lockout brought unexpected opportunities to raise the status of women in the community, to assert equality with men and to break down some of the more oppressive aspects of men's behaviour towards women. There was the potential for women to make real challenges to the power of men. The fact that women did not collectively take more advantage of these possibilities and engage seriously with gender politics is largely due to the power of class solidarity. The miners were fighting a defensive action against severe cuts to their living standards. The women knew that at this time of naked class warfare that it was essential for women to defend their men, but in so doing they bolstered patriarchal practices which undermined women and maintained the notorious inequality of coalfield society. Solidarity for the cause meant everything to both men and women and could not be separated from male dominance and traditional gender identities. This is a story about gender. It also demonstrates the overwhelming power of class in 1920s Britain, both in the way in which the miners and their families were bound by class and in the power of collective action. The miners of south Wales held out longer and were more united than any other coalfield, but this was not enough. After seven long months they were forced to concede that on a national level all was lost. The miners were defeated and returned to work (if they could) near destitute, ragged and demoralised. Communal eating was wound up and there is no evidence that the limited gains by women were maintained as women actively sought to preserve male identity and status at a time when pit owners and the government were undermining it.

In uncovering the social and cultural aspects of the Lockout this book has brought to life the lived experience of 1920s south Wales coalfield society and in particular those momentous seven months. Although the emphasis has been on gender, this has always been firmly rooted in the mining community. We have seen how families adopted strategies to survive in a cash-starved society by helping each other out, growing their own food, foraging in the countryside, as well as establishing cost-effective patterns of communal eating. The women and men of 1926 were determined whenever possible to cope with their distress in a dignified and democratic manner without any taint of the stigma of poor relief. The amazing display of cultural life in 1926 was evident in the wonderful flowering of jazz bands, carnivals, concerts and mass sporting events. For young people who participated in these activities, this was a happy time despite the material deprivation. In the world of politics, women have been visible as political players with activists such as Beatrice Green coming to prominence through the experience of the Lockout. As we have seen, the extensive network of Labour Party Women's Sections was pivotal in channelling relief funds from other areas of the country to destitute families, particularly for women in confinement. The aftermath of the dispute is also very significant for its mass victimisation of union activists, large-scale emigration, the long and agonising death of the coal industry and the associated social problems of long-term unemployment and poverty.

This book has been greatly enhanced by the use of personal testimony. Indeed, it is the thread of individual human voices running through it that makes it such an exciting and moving story. This analysis of the women and men of 1926 shifts the subject from the confines of traditional labour history to the more fruitful territory of gender history. Both masculine and feminine identities have been analysed at a particular moment of crisis in British history, giving a new dimension to this very significant event. It is now a matter of urgency that further efforts are made to recover testimony from other events in inter-war British social history. In Wales, for example, there were very important 'sit down strikes' and UAB protests in the 1930s which deserve full-scale oral history projects before it is too late. Also more work needs to be done to further our understanding of masculinity in the coalfield, particularly the 'hidden masculinities' of the disabled miner and the homo-sexual miner. This study has examined the south Wales coalfield in depth in 1926; as the largest and most militant coalfield at the time it was an obvious choice, but other coal-fields in 1926 also need attention by gender historians. The Nottinghamshire coalfield, for example, has a very different history from the point of view both of union activity and of wives in paid employment. It is hoped, therefore that this book will be a beginning rather than an end.

NOTES

INTRODUCTION

[1]   Christopher Farman, *The General Strike, May, 1926* (St Albans: Panther, 1974), p. 56.

[2]   John Foster, 'Prologue: What Kind of Crisis? What Kind of Ruling Class?', in John McIlroy, Alan Campbell and Keith Gildart, *Industrial Politics and the 1926 Mining Lockout: The Struggle for Dignity* (Cardiff: University of Wales Press, 2004), p. 21. The paperback edition of 2009 has a new introduction.

[3]   John Foster, 'British Imperialism and the Labour Aristocracy', in Jeffrey Skelley, *The General Strike 1926* (London: Lawrence and Wishart, 1976), p. 3.

[4]   James Hinton, *Labour and Socialism: A History of the British Labour Movement 1867–1974* (Brighton: Wheatsheaf, 1983), p. 126.

[5]   Farman, *The General Strike*, p. 46.

[6]   For details see Emile Burns (ed.), *General Strike, May 1926: Trades Councils in Action* (London: Labour Research Department, 1926; new edition London: Lawrence and Wishart, 1975).

[7]   Skelley, *The General Strike 1926*, has a regional survey which includes responses from the rank and file.

[8]   Gordon Phillips, *The General Strike: The Politics of Industrial Conflict* (London: Weidenfeld and Nicolson, 1976), p. 251.

[9]   Patrick Renshaw, *The General Strike* (London: Methuen, 1975), p. 233.

[10] See, for example, James Klugmann, 'Marxism, Reformism and the General Strike', in Skelley, *The General Strike 1926*; Duncan Hallas and Chris Harman, *Days of Hope: The General Strike of 1926* (London: Socialist Workers Party, 1981); Robin Page Arnot, *The General Strike, May 1926: Its Origin and History* (Wakefield: Labour Research Department, 1975).

[11] Some of the major texts: Skelley, *The General Strike 1926*; Renshaw, *The General Strike*; Phillips, *The General Strike*; Margaret Morris, *The General Strike* (Harmondsworth: Penguin, 1976); Farman, *The General Strike, May 1926*.

[12] Keith Laybourn, *The General Strike, 1926* (Yorkshire: Huddersfield Polytechnic, 1990), pp. 2–3.

[13] Sarah Boston, *Women Workers and the Trade Unions* (London: Davis-Poynter, 1980), pp. 174–6; Sheila Lewenhak, *Women and Trade Unions: An Outline History of Women in the British Trade Union Movement* (London: E. Benn, 1977), pp. 192–3.

[14] Ian Haywood, ' "Never Again?" Ellen Wilkinson's *Clash* and the Feminization of the General Strike', in *Literature and History*, 8/2 (Autumn 1999), 34–43; Maroula Joannou, 'Reclaiming the Romance: Ellen Wilkinson's *Clash* and the Cultural Legacy of Socialist-Feminism', in David Margolies and Maroula Joannou (eds), *Heart of the Heartless World: Essays in Cultural Resistance in Memory of Margot Heinemann* (London: Pluto Press, 1995).

[15] Ellen Wilkinson, *Clash* (1929) (London: Virago, 1989).

[16] Anne Perkins, *A Very British Strike 3–12th May 1926* (Basingstoke: Macmillan, 2006).

[17] Perkins, *A Very British Strike*, pp. 177–8.

[18] Perkins, *A Very British Strike*, p. 178.

[19]   Gerard Noel, *The Great Lock-out of 1926* (London: Constable, 1976).

[20]   McIlroy, Campbell and Gildart, *Industrial Politics and the Mining Lockout.*

[21]   K. G. J. C. Knowles, *Strikes: a Study in Industrial Conflict: with special reference to the British Experience between 1911 and 1947* Oxford: University of Oxford, 1952), gives south Wales as the most militant coalfield during 1911–1945, p. 197.

[22]   Jaclyn J. Gier-Viskovatoff, an American historian, encountered similar problems in the mid-1980s when she proposed to write a PhD on women in mining communities in Britain. She was told by her thesis committee and 'most of the British Labour historians I had consulted . . . that such a project was doomed to failure for lack of available sources'. Jaclyn J. Gier-Viskovatoff and Abigail Porter, 'Women of the British Coalfields on Strike in 1926 and 1984: Documenting Lives Using Oral History and Photography', *Frontiers: Journal of Women's Studies*, 19/2, 1998, p. 221.

[23]   Hywel Francis, 'The Secret World of the South Wales Miner: The Relevance of Oral History', in Dai Smith (ed.), *A People and a Proletariat, Essays in the History of Wales 1780–1980* (London: Pluto Press, 1980), p. 167.

[24]   Dai Smith, 'The Future of Coalfield History in South Wales', *Morgannwg: Journal of the Glamorgan History Society*, XIX, 1975, p. 63.

[25]   Published 1980, London: Lawrence & Wishart; republished 1998, Cardiff: University of Wales Press.

[26]   Mark Davies (ed.), *The Valleys Autobiography: A People's History of the Garw, Llynfi and Ogmore Valleys* (Mid Glamorgan: Valley and Vale, 1992). I have also made use of the many photographical collections available for south Wales in this period.

[27]   Average age in 1926 was 11. All except one came from the Rhondda or the Garw valley. These locations were chosen for their contrasting political traditions. Although I intended to interview both men and women it proved very difficult to locate suitable elderly men. Therefore all but one of the respondents were women. This material will be deposited at the South Wales Miners' Library in Swansea when present research purposes are completed. I also had access to material from five interviews conducted in south Wales by myself in 1977 for an earlier research project on communist women in Britain. Biographical notes on oral respondents interviewed for this study are in that Appendix.

[28]   Smith, 'Future of Coalfield History', p. 62.

[29]   Some of the more important texts are: Paul Thompson, *The Voice of the Past: Oral History* (Oxford: Oxford University Press, 2000); Alistair Thomson, *Anzac Memories: Living with the Legend* (Oxford: Oxford University Press, 1994); Penny Summerfield, *Reconstructing Women's Wartime Lives: Discourse and Subjectivity in Oral History* (Manchester: Manchester University Press, 1998); Robert Perks and Alistair Thomson (eds), *The Oral History Reader* (London: Routledge, 1998).

[30]   Alessandro Portelli, 'The Peculiarities of Oral History', *History Workshop Journal*, 12, 1981.

[31]   Steven Thompson '"That beautiful summer of severe austerity": Health, Diet and the Working-Class Domestic Economy in South Wales in 1926', *Welsh History Review*, 21/3 (2003), 558.

[32]   A version of this description of the coalfield was first produced for the article 'The Politics of Food: Gender, Family, Community and Collective Feeding in South Wales in the General Strike and Miners' Lockout of 1926', *Twentieth Century British History*, 18/1 (2007).

[33]   Chris Williams gives 1920 as the peak for employment in the south Wales coal industry at 271,516 in *Capitalism, Community and Conflict: The South Wales Coalfield 1898–1947* (Cardiff: University of Wales Press, 1998), p. 21.

[34]   David Gilbert, *Class, Community and Collective Action: Social Change in Two British Coalfields 1850–1926* (Oxford: Clarendon Press, 1992), pp. 54–66.

[35] Hilary Marquand, *The Second Industrial Survey of Wales*, vol. 3 (Cardiff: University Press Board), pp. 62–4.

[36] I am grateful to Neil Evans and Steven Thompson for help on some aspects of this paragraph.

[37] Gilbert, *Class, Community and Collective Action*, p. 130. See also Stuart MacIntyre, *Little Moscows: Communism and Working class Militancy in Inter War Britain* (London: Croom Helm, 1980), pp. 176–7.

[38] Gilbert, *Class, Community and Collective Action*, p. 67.

[39] Wyn Price, *Aspects of the Urban History of the Garw Valley c.1870–1914*, PhD thesis (Cardiff: University of Wales, 2001), p. 191.

[40] Chris Williams, *Democratic Rhondda: Politics and Society 1885–1951* (Cardiff: University of Wales Press, 1996), p. 22.

[41] Gilbert, *Class, Community and Collective Action*, pp. 88–90.

[42] Steven Thompson, *Unemployment, Poverty and Health in Interwar South Wales* (Cardiff: University of Wales Press, 2006), pp. 167–9.

[43] Williams, *Democratic Rhondda*, p. 24; Price, *Aspects of Urban History of the Garw Valley*, p. 377.

[44] Dai Smith, 'Tonypandy 1910: Definitions of Community', *Past and Present*, 87 (1980), 179.

[45] Hywel Francis and Dai Smith, *The Fed: A History of the South Wales Miners in the Twentieth Century* (London: Lawrence and Wishart, 1980), p. 34.

[46] Lizzie Davies, interview, 25 August 2004, Maerdy. Lizzie requested that I use the Welsh spelling of *Maerdy* (as opposed to the English *Mardy*) which I have done.

[47] The miners' institutes were social organisations set up by the miners themselves and technically separate from the lodges, which were branches of the SWMF. In practice it was often the same men who ran the institute as well as the lodge. Miners' libraries were part of the institutes. Sometimes an institute had a welfare hall, but these were mainly later developments. I am grateful to Siân Williams (SWML) for clarifying this for me.

[48] Smith, 'Tonypandy', 183.

[49] Gilbert, *Class, Community and Collective Action*, p. 63.

[50] Francis and Smith, *The Fed*. For example see pp. 16, 54–5, 59. Also Francis, 'South Wales', in Skelley, *The General Strike*, p. 249.

[51] Williams, *Capitalism, Community and Conflict*, p. 5.

[52] Mike Lieven has written that the Conservatives, Liberals and Independents held about 30 per cent of the votes and seats on the Rhondda Urban District Council throughout the 1920s, in 'A New History of the South Wales Coalfield?', *Llafur*, 8/3 (2002), p. 95. It is easy to assume that the high degree of social homogeneity in the south Wales produced complete political homogeneity, but this was not the case.

[53] Sheila Rowbotham's early works are: *Women, Resistance and Revolution: A History of Women and Revolution in the Modern World* (London: Allen Lane, 1972); *Hidden From History: 300 Years of Women's Oppression and the Fight Against it* (London: Pluto, 1977).

[54] See, for example, Michael Roper and John Tosh, *Manful Assertions: Masculinities in Britain Since 1800* (London: Routledge, 1991); John Tosh, 'Hegemonic masculinity and the history of gender', in Stefan Dudink et al., *Masculinities in Politics and War: Gendering Modern History* (Manchester: Manchester University Press, 2004).

[55] The leading work on this is Joan Scott, *Gender and the Politics of History* (New York: Columbia, 1991).

[56] Some of the most significant works are: Deirdre Beddoe, *Out of the Shadows: A History of Women in Twentieth-Century Wales* (Cardiff: University of Wales Press, 2000);

Angela John, 'A Miner Struggle? Women's Protests in Welsh Mining History', *Llafur*, 4/1 (1984); Angela V. John (ed.), *Our Mothers' Land: Chapters in Welsh Women's History, 1800–1939* (Cardiff: University of Wales Press, 1991; see particularly article on Welsh women's suffrage by Kay Cook and Neil Evans); Rosemary Crook, 'Tidy Women: Women in the Rhondda between the Wars', *Oral History*, 10/2, 1982.

[57]   Paul O'Leary, 'Masculine Histories: Gender and the Social History of Modern Wales', *Welsh History Review*, 22/2 (2004), 256–60. See also Stefan Berger and Neil Evans, 'Two Faces of King Coal: The impact of Historiographical Traditions on Comparative History in the Ruhr and South Wales', in S. Berger, A. Croll and N. Laporte, *Towards a Comparative History of Coalfield Societies* (Aldershot: Ashgate, 2005), p. 39. Dick Greary's 'The Myth of the Radical Miner' in the same volume is also informative.

[58]   For international perspectives on women's history, gender history and mining strikes, see Priscilla Long, 'The women of the Colorado Fuel and Iron strike, 1913–14', in Ruth Milkman (ed.), *Women, Work and Protest: A Century of US Women's Labour History* (London: Routledge and Kegan Paul, 1985); Bruce Scates, 'Mobilising Manhood: Gender and the Great Strike in Australia and Aotearoa/New Zealand', *Gender and History*, 9/2, 1997.

[59]   Please note that throughout the book the term 'miners' wives' is used as a shorthand term to refer to women in mining communities including mothers, unmarried daughters, aunts and sisters.

CHAPTER 2

[1]   Susan Kingsley Kent, *Making Peace:The Reconstruction of Gender in Interwar Britain* (Princeton: Princeton University Press, 1993); Sue Bruley, *Women in Britain Since 1900* (Basingstoke: Macmillan, 1999), chapter 3.

[2]   Deirdre Beddoe, *Back to Home and Duty: Women Between the Wars* (London: Pandora, 1989), p. 94.

[3]   Judy Giles, *Women, Identity and Private Life in Britain 1900–1950* (London: Macmillan, 1995), p. 24.

[4]   Giles, *Women, Identity and Private Life*, p. 24.

[5]   Adrian Bingham, *Debating Gender: Approaches to Femininity and Masculinity in the Popular National Daily Press in Interwar Britain*, D.Phil. (Oxford, 2002), p. 254; published as *Gender, Modernity and the Popular Press in Interwar Britain* (Oxford: Oxford University Press, 2004).

[6]   Diana Gittins, *Fair Sex: Family Size and Structure, 1900–1939* (London: Hutchinson, 1982), p. 182.

[7]   John Benson, *The Working Class in Britain 1850–1939* (London: I. B. Tauris, 2003), pp. 101–2; Ruth Hall, *Dear Dr Stopes: Sex in the 1920s* (Harmondsworth: Penguin, 1978) contains many letters from men asking for advice (see, for example, p. 167).

[8]   Published as Margery Spring Rice, *Working Class Wives: Their Health and Conditions* (Harmondsworth: Penguin, 1939).

[9]   Giles, *Women, Identity and Private Life*, p. 130.

[10]   Valerie G. Hall, 'Contrasting Female Identities: Women in Coal Mining Communities in Northumberland, England, 1900–1939', *Journal of Women's History*, Summer, 2001, 110.

[11]   Walter H. Davies, *Blithe Ones* (Port Talbot: Alun Books, 1979), p. 74.

[12]   Interview with Lilian Roberts, 27 October 2004, Trealaw.

[13]   Interview with Martha Jones, 27 October, 2004, Trealaw.

[14]   Interview with Nancy Lewis, 25 November 2004, Pantygog.
[15]   Interview with Blod Davies, 27–8 October 2004, Trealaw; interview with Sally Poulton, 10 December 2004, Trealaw.
[16]   Interview with Ethel Roberts, 24 November 2004, Pontneddfechan. Originally from Cymgwrach. This was the only respondent (gained through personal contact) who was not brought up in either the Rhondda or the Garw valleys.
[17]   Interview with 'Lil', 6 August 2004, Pontycymer.
[18]   Interview with Lilian Lawrence, 27 October 2004, Trealaw.
[19]   Interview with Gwyneth Evans, 25 November 2004, Pontycymer.
[20]   Interview with Elsie Pritchard, 4 August 2004, Pontycymer.
[21]   Interview with Jean Ellis, 6 August 2004, Pontycymer.
[22]   Interview with Lizzie Davies, 25 August 2004, Maerdy.
[23]   Bill Jones and Chris Williams, *B. L. Coombes* (Cardiff: University of Wales Press, 1999), pp. 19, 53.
[24]   B. L. Coombes, *These Poor Hands: The Autobiography of a Miner Working in South Wales* (London: Gollancz, 1939), p. 35.
[25]   Hywel Francis and Dai Smith, *The Fed: A History of the South Wales Miners in the Twentieth Century* (London: Lawrence and Wishart, 1980), p. 2.
[26]   Wyn Price, *Aspects of Urban History of the Garw Valley c.1870–1914*, PhD thesis, (Cardiff: University of Wales, 2001), p. 412.
[27]   Chris Williams, *Capitalism, Community and Conflict: The South Wales Coalfield 1898–1947* (Cardiff: University of Wales Press, 1998), pp. 63–9.
[28]   Barrie Naylor, *Quakers in the Rhondda 1926–1986* (Chepstow: Maes-yr-haf Educational Trust, 1986), p. 15.
[29]   Price, *Aspects of Urban History*, p. 179.
[30]   Dot Jones, 'Counting the Cost of Coal: Women's Lives in the Rhondda, 1881–1911', in Angela V. John, *Our Mothers' Land: Chapters in Welsh Women's History, 1830–1939* (Cardiff: University of Wales Press, 1991), p. 121.
[31]   Stuart MacIntyre, *Little Moscows: Communism and Working Class Militancy in Interwar Britain* (London: Croom Helm, 1980), p. 33; Michael Lieven, *Senghennydd: The Universal Pit Village 1890–1930* (Llandysul: Gomer, 1994), p. 139.
[32]   Naylor, *Quakers in the Rhondda*, pp. 15–16.
[33]   Mark Davies (ed.), *The Valleys Autobiography: A People's History of the Garw, Llynfi and Ogmore Valleys* (Mid Glamorgan: Valley and Vale, 1992), p. 46.
[34]   Grafton Radcliffe, *Back to Blaengarw* (Mid Glamorgan: Valleys Autobiography Project, 1994), p. 8.
[35]   Ferdynand Zweig, *Men in Pits* (London: Gollancz, 1948), p. 99.
[36]   Interview, 4 August 2004, Pontycymer.
[37]   Edith Davies, *The Innocent Years: The Story of My Childhood in Ynysybwl* (Creigiau: T. Lewis, 1995), p. xii.
[38]   Alun Morgan, 'Bedlinog: Glimpses of a Pre-war Society', *Glamorgan Historian*, 11, 1975, 144.
[39]   Walter H. Davies, *The Right Place – The Right Time (Memories of Boyhood Days in a Welsh Mining Community)* Llandybie: Llyfrau'r Dryw, 1972), pp. 168–9.
[40]   Rosemary Crook, 'Tidy Women': Women in the Rhondda Between the Wars', *Oral History Journal*, 10/2 (1982), p. 42.
[41]   Davies, *Blithe Ones*, p. 70.
[42]   Lieven, *Senghennydd*, p. 167. It was felt to be beyond the remit of this chapter to provide a detailed account of sexual relations in the south Wales mining communities at this time. Michel Lieven's account is recommended for this purpose.
[43]   Zweig, *Men in Pits*, p. 4. According to Griselda Carr, evidence produced for the (Samuel) Royal Commision in 1925 showed that for an average group of 2,000 miners over a coalface working life of about 20 years 40 would be killed, 180 seri-

ously injured. More than a quarter would experience work-related accidents. Griselda Carr, *Pit Women: Coal Communities in Northern England in the Early Twentieth Century* (London: Merlin, 2001), p. 8.

44   Interview, 10 December 2004, Trealaw.

45   Grafton Radcliffe, *Back to Blaengarw*, p. 11.

46   Zweig, *Men in Pits*, p. 103.

47   Coombes, *These Poor Hands*, p. 222.

48   Davies, *Blithe Ones*, p. 36.

49   Interview, 27 October 2004, Trealaw.

50   Carol White and Siân.R. Williams, *Struggle or Starve* (Dinas Powys: Honno, 1998), p. 15.

51   Interview with Nancy Wood, 27 October 2004, Trealaw.

52   Interview, 25 August 2004, Maerdy.

53   Interview with Phyllis Lewis, 10 December 2004, Porth.

54   Interview, 27 October 2004, Trealaw.

55   Interview, 10 December 2004, Trealaw.

56   This love of children by miners and their wives is said to pervade all mining communities; see, for example, Carr, *Pit Women*, p. 78.

57   Interview, 10 December 2004, Porth.

58   Interview with Gladys Davies, 4 August 2004, Bridgend. There is a photograph of Gladys's father, William Price, in chapter 4.

59   Deirdre Beddoe, *Out of the Shadows: A History of Women in Twentieth-Century Wales* (Cardiff: University of Wales Press, 2000), p. 78.

60   Williams, *Capitalism, Community and Conflict*, p. 64.

61   Interview, 25 November 2004, Pantygog.

62   Interview with Gwen Radcliffe, 27 October 2004, Trealaw.

63   David Barnes, *Black Mountains: The Recollections of a Welsh Miner* (Talybont: Y Lolfa, 2002), p. 67.

64   Interview, 6 August 2004, Pontycymer.

65   Interview with Phyllis Lewis, 10 December 2004, Porth; interview with Helena Charles, 14 October 2004, Blaengarw.

66   Beddoe, *Out of the Shadows*, pp. 83–4.

67   *Rhondda Urban District Council Minutes, Finance Committee*, 3 May 1926, p. 29. Glamorgan Record Office.

68   Interview with Mrs Beatrice Davies and Mr D. Davies, 28 July 1977, Ystrad. There is an interview with Mrs Davies in the South Wales Miners' Library, Swansea University, and she also appeared in the film 'Women of the Rhondda', made by 11th Hour, 1971.

69   Beddoe, *Out of the Shadows*, p. 93.

70   Davies, *Innocent Years*, p. 85

71   *Coal Industry Commission*, 2, *Reports and Minutes of Evidence, 1919*, Cmd 360.

72   Interview, 4 August 2004, Bridgend.

73   Davies, *Innocent Years*, p. 32.

74   Interview with 'Sarah', 7 February 2005, Sutton, Surrey. Originally from Dinas.

75   Interview with Sally Poulton, 10 December 2004, Trealaw.

76   Interview with Mrs W. R. Jones, 4 July 1973, South Wales Miners' Library, University of Wales at Swansea.

77   Rosemary Crook, '"Tidy Women": Women in the Rhondda between the Wars', *Oral History Journal*, 10/2 (1982), p. 43.

78   Angela John, 'A Miner Struggle? Women's Protests in Welsh Mining History', *Llafur*, 4/1 (1984), p. 74. .

79   Williams, *Capitalism, Community and Conflict*, p. 68. See also Mari Williams, *A*

Forgotten Army: Female Munition Workers of South Wales 1939–1945 (Cardiff: University of Wales Press, 2002), p. 21; White and Williams, *Struggle or Starve*, p. 21.

[80] Naylor, *Quakers in the Rhondda*, p. 15.

[81] Interview with Phyllis Lewis, 10 December 2004, Porth.

[82] Radcliffe, *Back to Blaengarw*, p. 31.

[83] Davies, *Innocent Years*, p. xii.

[84] Crook, 'Tidy Women', p. 40.

[85] Interview with Ethel Roberts, 24 November 2004, Pontneddfechen. Originally from Cwmgwrach.

[86] Pamela Graves, *Labour Women: Women in British Working Class Politics 1918–1939* (Cambridge: Cambridge University Press, 1994).

[87] Interview with Beatrice Davies, 28 July 1977, Ystrad.

[88] Interview, 4 August 2004, Bridgend.

[89] Interview, 27 October 2004, Trealaw.

[90] Interview, 27–8 October 2004, Trealaw.

[91] Interview with Sally Poulton, 10 December 2004, Trealaw.

[92] Davies, *Blithe Ones*, p. 20.

[93] Coombes, *These Poor Hands*, p. 21.

[94] Crook, 'Tidy Women', 1982.

[95] Angela V. John, 'A Miner Struggle? Women's Protests in Welsh Mining History, *Llafur*, 4/1 (1984).

[96] *Colliery Workers Magazine*, March 1926.

[97] Winifred Griffiths, *One Woman's Story* (Rhondda: Ron Jones Publication, 1980), p. 77. No date, but likely to have been 1918–19.

[98] Interview, 25 November 2004, Pantygog.

[99] Interview, 14 October 2004, Blaengarw.

[100] Interview, 6 August 2004, Pontycymer.

[101] Davies, *The Innocent Years*, p. 79.

[102] Interview with Lizzie Davies, 25 August 2004, Maerdy; interview with Ethel Roberts, 24 November 2004, Pontneddfechan; interview with Helena Charles, 14 October 2004, Blaengarw.

[103] Interview with Gwyneth Evans, 25 November 2004, Pontycymer.

[104] Interview with Phyllis Lewis, 10 December 2004, Porth.

[105] Radcliffe, *Back to Blaengarw*, p. 16.

[106] *Glamorgan Gazette* (Bridgend edition), 23 July 1926.

[107] Interview, 25 November 2004, Pantygog.

[108] Davies, *The Valleys Autobiography*, p. 70.

[109] Interview, 25 November 2004, Pontycymer.

[110] Interview, 7 February 2005, Sutton, Surrey.

[111] Davies, *The Valleys Autobiography*, p. 67.

[112] W. H. Davies, *The Right Place*, p. 91.

[113] W. H. Davies, *The Right Place*, p. 102.

[114] Lewis Jones, extract from *Cwmardy* , taken from M. Stephens (ed.), *Rhondda Anthology* (Bridgend: Seren Books, 1993), p. 40. Jones was a miner and Communist activist. *Cwmardy* was set in mid-Rhondda. For whole text, see Lewis Jones, *Cwmardy: The Story of a Welsh Mining Valley* (London: Lawrence and Wishart, 1937). The story continues with *We Live* (London: Lawrence and Wishart, 1939).

[115] Interview, 4 August 2004, Bridgend.

[116] Interview, 7 February 2005, Sutton, Surrey.

[117] Williams, *A Forgotten Army*, pp. 33–4.

[118] Interview, 25 August 2004, Maerdy. There is a photograph of Lizzie Davies in service in chapter 6.

[119] Interview, 10 December 2004, Porth.

[120] Interview with Blod Davies, 27–8 October 2004. The hard lives of these interviewees as young women can be contrasted with the adolescent life of idle luxury described by the feminist Margaret Haig, Viscountess Rhondda, daughter of the coal magnate Lord Rhondda in *This Was My World* (London: Macmillan, 1933).

[121] Rosemary Scadden tapes, Museum of Welsh Life, Cardiff, Wales. Recorded in 1994.

[122] Interview with Gladys Davies, 4 August 2004.

[123] Williams, *A Forgotten Army*, p. 39.

[124] Williams, *A Forgotten Army*, pp. 39–40

[125] See, for example, *South Wales Echo*, 11 November 1926.

CHAPTER 3

[1] An earlier version of this chapter appeared as 'The Politics of Food: Gender, Family, Community and Collective Feeding in South Wales in the General Strike and Miners' Lockout of 1926', in *Twentieth Century British History*, 18/1, 2007, 54–77.

[2] Patricia Ryan, 'The Poor Law in 1926', in Margaret Morris, *The General Strike* (Harmondsworth: Penguin, 1976), p. 359.

[3] MH 57/94, The National Archive (TNA).

[4] MH 57/94, TNA.

[5] MH 79/297, TNA.

[6] MH 79/297, TNA.

[7] MH 79/297, TNA.

[8] Circular 703, Ministry of Health, 5.5.1926. Located as Appendix A, Relief Advisory Committee of the Pontypridd Union, 21 May 1926. Held at Glamorgan Record Office (GRO). See also Paul Jeremy, 'Life on Circular 703: The Crisis of Destitution in the South Wales Coalfield during the Lockout of 1926', *Llafur*, 2/2, 1977, 68.

[9] Carmarthen, Llandeilo-Fawr, and Pontypool were paying less than the MH maximum scale. The Carmarthen Board of Guardians also ensured that relieving officers refused relief for miners' wives without children and refused to issue needy children with boots. For details see David Davies, 'Guardians of the Needy Found Wanting, A Study of Social Division during the Industrial Crisis of 1926', in *Carmarthenshire Historian*, XIX, 1982. Davies argues that the rural boards, whose members were largely farmers, were mainly apathetic on the issue of relief. The *Colliery Workers Magazine* published a survey of poor relief in the south Wales coalfield in July 1926.

[10] 'Miners and Relief', *Colliery Workers Magazine*, July 1926.

[11] MH 79/297, TNA.

[12] Francis and Smith, *The Fed*, p. 57.

[13] Francis and Smith, *The Fed*, p. 53. This represented 87 per cent of all overseas donations.

[14] Marion Phillips, *Women and the Miners' Lockout: The Story of the Women's Committee for the Relief of the Miners' Wives and Children* (London: Labour Party Publishing Co., 1927).

[15] Phillips, *Women and the Miners' Lockout*, p. 24. The work of this committee is dealt with in more detail in chapter 4.

[16] Jeremy, 'Life on Circular 703', p. 70.

[17] Huw Williams, 'Merthyr Tydfil and the General Strike of 1926', *Merthyr Historian*, 2 (1978), 125.

[18] *South Wales Echo*, 25 May 1926.

[19] Michael Foot, *Aneurin Bevan 1897–1945* (London: Granada Publishing, 1975; first published London: MacGibbon & Kee, 1962), p. 73.

[20] *Merthyr Express*, 19 June 1926.

[21] *Colliery Guardian*, 28 May 1926.

[22] *South Wales Echo*, 11 June 1926; Williams, 'Merthyr Tydfil', p. 129.

[23] *Aberdare Leader*, 1 July 1926.

[24] Williams, 'Merthyr Tydfil', p. 129.

[25] *Rhondda Gazette*, 12 June 1926.

[26] *Merthyr Express*, 21 August 1926

[27] Foot, *Aneurin Bevan*, p. 74.

[28] *Glamorgan Gazette*, 16 July 1926.

[29] Maerdy Distress Committee Minutes, 17 May 1926, South Wales Coal Collection (henceforth SWCC).

[30] Interview with Lizzie Davies, 25 August 2004, Maerdy.

[31] Francis and Smith, *The Fed*, p. 56.

[32] Maerdy Distress Committee Minutes are extremely detailed and include information on menus and food ordered throughout the period of the Lockout, SWCC

[33] Tylorstown Relief Committee Order Book July–October 1926, SWCC.

[34] Chris Evans, *The Industrial and Social History of Seven Sisters* (Cardiff: Cymric Federation Press, 1964), p. 107.

[35] Gerard Noel, *The Great Lock-out of 1926* (London: Constable, 1976), p. 149.

[36] *Aberdare Leader*, 31 July 1926 and 21 August 1926.

[37] *Glamorgan Gazette*, 16 July 1926.

[38] Interview with Mavis Llewellyn, 23 July 1977, Nantymoel.

[39] Bedlinog Council of Action Minutes, 12 May 1926, SWCC.

[40] Maerdy Distress Committee Minutes, 22 June 1926, SWCC.

[41] *Glamorgan Gazette*, 10 September 1926.

[42] Interview with Ethel Brown, 24 November 2004, Pontneddfechan.

[43] Will Paynter, *My Generation* (London: George Allen and Unwin, 1972), p. 34.

[44] *Glamorgan Gazette*, 21 May 1926. There is also a report in the *South Wales Echo*.

[45] Francis and Smith, *The Fed*, p. 63.

[46] Various contributors, '1926 Remembered and Revealed', *Llafur*, 2/2 (1977), 20.

[47] Williams, 'Merthyr Tydfil', 132.

[48] Interview with Lizzie Davies, 25 August 2004, Maerdy.

[49] Maerdy Distress Committee, Sub-Committee 24 May 1926, SWCC

[50] Interview with Mavis Lewellyn, 23 July 1977, Nantymoel.

[51] *Glamorgan Gazette*, 10 September 1926.

[52] *Aberdare Leader*, 21 August 1926.

[53] Interview with Lilian Roberts, 27 October 2004, Trealaw.

[54] Interview with Ethel Roberts, 24 November 2004, Pontneddfechan.

[55] Interview with Ethel Roberts, 24 November 2004, Pontneddfechan.

[56] Susan E. Demont, *Tredegar and Aneurin Bevan: A Society and Its Political Articulation 1890–1929*. PhD thesis (University of Wales, 1990), p. 278.

[57] Abergorki Workmen's Hall and Institute Minutes, 24 September 1926, SWCC.

[58] North's Workmen's Institute, Minutes, 24 September 1926, SWCC.

[59] Christopher Baggs, *The Miners' Libraries of South Wales from the 1860s to 1939*, PhD thesis (University of Wales at Aberystwyth, 1995), has a discussion of women's access to the miners' libraries. In general, access appears to be either denied completely or very restricted. Women were more likely to granted library membership if the library was part of the facilities of a welfare hall, pp. 231–4. Mavis Llewellyn told me that women were not allowed access to the miners' library in Nantymoel. Interview, 23 July 1977, Nantymoel.

60 Maerdy Distress Committee Minutes, 21 September 1926 and 6 December 1926.

61 Maerdy Distress Committee Minutes, 9 November 1926.

62 See, for example, Rhondda Urban District Council, Central Canteen Committee Minutes, 11 May 1926, p. 75, GRO. Also, milk distribution was increased significantly during the Lockout. Fourteen emergency milk distribution centres were established by the RUDC in addition to the two existing ones. The number of persons supplied with free or below cost milk in 1926 was 9,711, compared to 3,205 in 1925. RUDC, Annual Report of the MO of Health for 1926, pp. 30–1, Treorchy Library. The cost of this venture meant that grants from the Ministry of Health for milk supplied via Maternity and Infant Welfare Clinics was quickly expended. RUDC applied for extra funding which was refused by the MH on the grounds that the council milk distributing centres were performing duties which were the province of the Guardians as they had a statutory duty to relieve cases of genuine destitution. Further details of this can be found in the Minutes of Maternity and Child Welfare Committee, July–December 1926, RUDC, GRO. The milk issue is viewed from the perspective of the women activists in chapter 5.

63 *Colliery Guardian*, 16 July 1926.

64 *Merthyr Express*, 22 May 1926. On 29 May the number being fed was reported as 'nearly 7,000'. After the first few weeks, numbers tailed off a little and only the most needy children were given breakfasts.

65 *Aberdare Leader*, 4 September 1926

66 *Rhondda Gazette*, 11 September 1926.

67 Patricia Ryan, 'The Poor Law in 1926', p. 372.

68 Monmouthshire County Council Annual Report of the Medical Inspection Department for the year 1926, p. 37, Gwent Record Office.

69 *Pontypridd Observer*, 12 June 1926. 'Miners and Relief', *Colliery Workers Magazine*, July 1926, 149. Chris Williams, *Democratic Rhondda: Politics and Society 1885–1951* (Cardiff: University of Wales Press, 1996), p. 145.

70 *Aberdare Leader*, 11 September 1926.

71 Annual Report of the Medical Officer of Health for 1926, RUDC, GRO. This report is held in Treorchy Library.

72 Charles Webster, 'Healthy or Hungry Thirties', *History Workshop*, 13, 1982, pp. 110–29.

73 RUDC, Annual Report of the School Medical Officer, 1926, p. xxxix.

74 Thompson, 'That beautiful summer', 2003, p. 568. Particularly significant is the fact that post neo-natal infant mortality (deaths in babies 1–12 months), which is regarded as a crucial indicator, fell in mining areas. See p. 558.

75 Interview with Gladys Davies, 4 August 2004, Bridgend.

76 Interview with Martha Jones, 27 October 2004, Trealaw.

77 Vernon Chilcott, *They Made Light of their Darkness*, Blaengarw, Mid Glamorgan, Valleys Autobiography Project, 1994, p. 58.

78 Interview with Gladys Davies, Bridgend, 4 August 2004.

79 *Merthyr Express*, 18 December 1926, has an article on school canteens which mentions labour as a factor in costing.

80 *Merthyr Express*, 5 June 1926.

81 *South Wales News*, 22 September 1926. Unfortunately, this image is too poor to reproduce.

82 *Aberdare Leader*, 11 September 1926.

83 *The Miner*, 11 June 1926 (TUC Archive, London Metropolitan University Library (henceforth LMU)).

84 *Pontypridd Observer*, 5 July 1926.

85 *Pontypridd Observer*, 24 July 1926.

[86] Support from the community was not universal. According to David Davies fund raising for communal eating in eastern Carmarthenshire and the Amman valley, which were more rural parts of the coalfield, were meagre. Here the farming community was not so supportive as in the more urban areas, 'Guardians of the Needy', *Carmarthenshire Historian*, 1982.

[87] See, for example, *Pontypridd Observer*, 26 June 1926,

[88] *South Wales Echo*, 12 August 1926.

[89] Maerdy Distress Committee Minutes, 6 September 1926, SWCC.

[90] Interview with Merfyn Payne, 18 June 1975, SWML.

[91] *Colliery Guardian*, 13 August 1926.

[92] From the Maerdy Distress Committee Minutes, it appears that communal feeding had ceased by 11 January 1927. SWCC.

[93] Francis and Smith, *The Fed*, p. 57.

[94] Interview with Will Arthur, 21 May 1973, SWML.

[95] Francis and Smith, *The Fed*, p. 57. Taken from an interview, 16 Februry 1970, SWML.

[96] Francis and Smith, *The Fed*, p. 57, n. 35. This is taken from the Lady Windsor Colliery Lodge minutes, July–December 1926. SWCC.

[97] *Merthyr Express*, 5 June 1926.

[98] John E. Morgan, *A Village Workers' Council: A Short History of the Lady Windsor Lodge* (Pontypridd: Celtic Press, 1956), p. 27.

[99] Morgan, *A Village Workers Council*, p. 29. See also Gilbert, *Class, Community*, p. 138.

[100] Morgan, *A Village Workers' Council*, 1956, p. 29.

[101] David Gilbert, *Class, Community and Collective Action: Social Change in Two British Coalfields 1850–1926* (Oxford: Clarendon Press, 1992), p. 137; Morgan, *A Village Workers' Council*, p. 29.

[102] Edith Davies, *The Innocent Years: The Story of my Childhood in Ynysybwl* (Creigiau: T. Lewis, 1995), p. 90, gives a date of 1920 for the introduction of a bus route reaching Ynysybwl.

[103] Mike Lieven, 'A "New History" of the South Wales Coalfield', *Llafur*, 8/3 (2002).

[104] *Glamorgan Gazette*, 18 June 1926.

[105] *Glamorgan Gazette* 13 August, 1926.

[106] Morgan, *A Village Workers' Council*, p. 27.

[107] *Glamorgan Gazette*, 18 July 1926.

[108] *Merthyr Express*, 18 December 1926.

[109] Rhondda Urban District Council, Annual Report of the Medical Officer of Health for 1926, p. xxxiv, GRO.

[110] RUDC, Annual Report of the Medical Officer of Health for 1926, p. xxxxviii, GRO.

[111] Monmouthshire CC, Annual Report of the Medical Inspection Department 1926, p. 38, GRO.

[112] Noel, *The Great Lock-out*, p. 149.

CHAPTER 4

[1] The most useful source is Hywel Francis and Dai Smith, *The Fed: A History of the South Wales Miners in the Twentieth Century* (London: Lawrence and Wishart, 1980). Chapter 2, on 1926, examines some of the social and cultural aspects of the dispute.

[2] Steven Thompson, '"That beautiful summer of severe austerity": Health, Diet and the Working Class Domestic Economy in South Wales in 1926', *Welsh History Review*, 21 (2003), pp. 558–9; see note 21.

[3] Arthur Horner, *Incorrigible Rebel* (London: MacGibbon & Kee, 1960), p. 90.

[4]   Mark Davies (ed.), *The Valleys Autobiography: A People's History of the Garw, Llynfi and Ogmore Valleys* (Mid Glamorgan: Valley and Vale, 1992), p. 40.

[5]   Idris Davies, *Gwalia Deserta* (London: J. M. Dent, 1938), p. 5.

[6]   Bernard Baldwin, *Mountain Ash Remembered* (Cowbridge: D. Brown, 1984), p. 109.

[7]   Idris Davies, *The Angry Summer: A Poem of 1926*, introduction and notes by Tony Conran (Cardiff: University of Wales Press, 1993), p. 58. This edition of the poem is interspersed with oral testimony.

[8]   R. J. Barker, *Christ in the Valley of Unemployment* (London: Hodder and Stoughton, 1937), p. 14.

[9]   *Aberdare Leader*, 26 June 1926.

[10]   *Glamorgan Gazette*, 16 July 1926.

[11]   *Pontypridd Observer*, 24 July 1926.

[12]   *Aberdare Leader*, 10 July 1926.

[13]   Maerdy Hall Minutes, 13 July 1926, South Wales Coal Collection (henceforth SWCC).

[14]   Winifred Griffiths, *One Woman's Story* (Rhondda: Ron James Publications, 1980), p. 102.

[15]   Huw Williams, 'Merthyr Tydfil and the General Strike', *Merthyr Historian*, 2 (1978), 131.

[16]   *Rhondda Gazette*, 23 October 1926.

[17]   *Pontypridd Observer*, 9 October 1926.

[18]   *Aberdare Leader*, 21 August 1926.

[19]   Baldwin, *Mountain Ash Remembered*, p. 108.

[20]   Abertridwr Institute Minute Book, letter from Mr C. Fluke requesting hire of the hall, 13 January 1927, SWCC.

[21]   Gareth Jones, *People, Protest and Politics: Welsh History Teaching Materials* (Swansea: Welsh Office Education Department, 1986), p. 65; source 129, Henry John, oral testimony held at South Wales Miners Library (henceforth SWML).

[22]   Tape No. 14, 'Mary K', Rosemary Scadden Tapes, Museum of Welsh Life, recorded in 1994.

[23]   Interview with 'Sarah', 8 February 2005, Sutton, Surrey.

[24]   *Aberdare Leader*, 24 July 1926.

[25]   *Aberdare Leader*, 2 October 1926.

[26]   Francis and Smith, *The Fed*, p. 58.

[27]   Davies, *Gwalia Deserta*, pp. 5–6.

[28]   Stuart Bloomfield, 'The General Strike and Lockout of 1926 in the Northern Part of the Rhymney Valley', *Environmental Studies in the Rhymney Valley* (Rhymney Valley District Council, 1982), p. 35.

[29]   Wyn Price, private manuscript. Consult author.

[30]   *Glamorgan Gazette*, 20 August 1926.

[31]   *Glamorgan Gazette*, 7 June 1926.

[32]   Nixons Workmen's Hall Minutes, 11 May, SWCC.

[33]   Interview with Gladys Davies, 4 August 2004, Bridgend.

[34]   Interview with Lilian Roberts, 27 October 2004, Trealaw.

[35]   *Glamorgan Gazette*, 18 June 1926.

[36]   Wyn Price, private manuscript. Consult author.

[37]   *Rhondda Gazette*, 19 June 1926.

[38]   *Glamorgan Gazette*, 25 June 1926.

[39]   *Bridgend Gazette* (Glamorgan edition), 28 May 1926.

[40]   'Women of the Rhondda', Eleventh Hour Films, 1971.

[41]   Aldo Bachetta and Glyn Rudd, *Porth and Rhondda Fach* (Stroud: Chalford, 1996), p. 42.

[42] Huw Williams, 'Merthyr Tydfil and the General Strike of 1926', *Merthyr Historian*, 2 (1978), 130.

[43] *Glamorgan Gazette*, 2 July 1926.

[44] *Glamorgan Gazette* (Bridgend edition), 13 September 1926.

[45] *Pontypridd Observer*, 14 August 1926.

[46] Jones, *People, Protest and Politics*, p. 65; Reg Fine, born 1908, quoted from interview, 2 July 1973, held at the SWML.

[47] Interview with Martha Jones, 27 October 2004, Trealaw

[48] Interview with Mary Lowrie 27 October 2004, Trealaw.

[49] *South Wales News*, 6 September 1926.

[50] Marion Phillips, *Women and the Miners' Lock-out: The Story of the Women's Committee for the Relief of Miners'Wives and Children* (London: Labour Publishing Co., 1927), p. 33.

[51] *Western Mail*, 18 June 1926.

[52] Phillips, *Women and the Miners' Lock-out*, p. 34.

[53] Bill Jones and Chris Williams, *B. L. Coombes* (Cardiff: University of Wales Press, 1999), p. 15.

[54] Interview with Lizzie Davies, 25 August 2004, Maerdy; interview with Mavis Llewellyn, 23 July 1977, Nantymoel.

[55] South Wales District WEA, 20th Annual Report 1926–7, p. 15; TUC Archive, London Metropolitan University (henceforth LMU).

[56] Richard Lewis, *Adult Education and the Challenge of Labour in South Wales 1906–1940* (Cardiff: University of Wales Press, 1993), p. 175.

[57] *Rhondda Gazette*, 22 May 1926.

[58] Letter from Emma Noble, 24 June 1926; correspondence relating to relief operations in the Rhondda Valley, 1926–80 (Maes-yr-Haf). Glamorgan Record Office (henceforth GRO).

[59] *Aberdare Leader*, 11 September 1926.

[60] Baldwin, *Mountain Ash Remembered*, p. 50.

[61] Interview with Blod Davies, 27 October 2004, Trealaw.

[62] I am aware that I have not exhausted the topic of miners and poor relief in the Lockout. This would be a suitable subject for further research.

[63] Monmouthshire County Council Education Committee, Annual Report of the Medical Inspection Department for the Year 1926, p. 18; GRO. At the infant welfare clinic in Cwmbran the number on the register was 239 compared to 210 in the previous year. Total attendances rose from 1,054 to 1,345 with average attendance increasing from 22.4 to 27.44 per cent.

[64] Thompson, 'That beautiful summer', p. 559.

[65] Thompson, 'That beautiful summer', p. 564.

[66] Interview with Nancy Lewis, 25 November 2004, Pantygog.

[67] Interview with Gladys Davies, 4 August 2004, Bridgend.

[68] Interview with Helena Charles, 14 October 2004, Blaegarw.

[69] Edith S. Davies, *The Innocent Years: The Story of My Childhood in Ynysbwl* (Creigiau: T. Lewis, 1995), p. 93.

[70] Interview with Jean Ellis, 6 August 2004, Pontycymer.

[71] Edwin Greening, '1926 in Aberdare', *Llafur*, 2/2 (1977), p. 35.

[72] Interview with Blod Davies, 27–8 October 2004, Trealaw. This quote illustrates the often complex nature of oral testimony. A simple transcript of this interview would not pick up that the interviewee's meaning was the opposite of what she was saying. It underlines the point that body language, facial expressions and other non-verbal communication needs to be assessed alongside the dialogue for a complete picture.

[73] *Aberdare Leader*, 25 September 1926.

[74]   The *Colliery Guardian*, 27 August 1926, provides an example in Pontnewynydd where 400–500 men were said to be engaged in digging and selling coal. Police had to intervene to prevent disorder when attempts were made to stop it.

[75]   *Colliery Guardian*, 30 July 1926

[76]   *South Wales Echo*, 15 September 1926.

[77]   *Merthyr Express*, for example, published reports of such fatalities, on 31 July and 9 October 1926. Chapter 3 contains an example of two brothers who were killed whilst gathering outcrop coal for a soup kitchen.

[78]   Interview with Fred and Avis Williams, 10 December 2004, Porth.

[79]   Interview with Mary Lowrie, 27 October 2004, Trealaw.

[80]   Interview with Ethel Roberts, 24 November 2004, Pontneddfechan.

[81]   Interview with Lilian Lawrence, 27 October 2004, Trealaw.

[82]   Interview with Lilian Lawrence, 27 October 2004, Trealaw.

[83]   D. Davies, 'Guardians of the Needy', *Carmarthenshire Historian*, 1982, 68.

[84]   Interview with Sally Poulton, 10 December 2004, Trealaw.

[85]   Interview with Gwyneth Evans, 25 November 2004, Pontycymer.

[86]   *Merthyr Express*, 4 September 1926.

[87]   Interview with Helena Charles, 14 October 2004, Blaengarw.

[88]   Interview with Betty Bowen, 27 October 2004, Trealaw.

[89]   Interview with Gladys Davies, 4 August 2004, Bridgend.

[90]   Interview with Phyllis Lewis, 10 December 2004, Porth.

[91]   It was recognised by the Ministry of Health that although miners did not have direct access to poor relief they would benefit from aid given to wives and children. This meant that generally married men were in a much better position than single men. Further details in chapter 3.

[92]   'Relief, Effect of the General Strike and Coal Dispute (1926) on the Poor Law System'; MH57/94.

[93]   Merthyr Tydfil Union Minute Book 1925–6, 26 May 1926, GRO.

[94]   Merthyr Tydfil Union, Register of Admissions 1925–6, GRO.

[95]   *South Wales Echo*, 17 September 1926.

[96]   Special Meeting RUDC, 1 September 1926, GRO.

[97]   *Aberdare Leader*, 17 July 1926.

[98]   Interview with Ethel Roberts, 24 November 2004, Pontneddfechan.

[99]   Reproduction of letter from M. Tomsky, 6 September 1926, Miners' Federation of Great Britain, Annual Report, 1926, p. 54. Statement of accounts, 15 July 1927, which follows report, shows sum paid to MFGB from Russia; TUC Archive, LMU.

[100]   Nine Mile Point Minute Book, 19 July 1926, SWCC.

[101]   MFGB Annual Congress, Report 1926, p. 238; TUC Archive, LMU.

[102]   Phillips, *Women and the Miners' Lockout*, p. 12.

[103]   Phillips, *Women and the Miners' Lockout*, p. 23.

[104]   Phillips, *Women and the Miners' Lockout*, p. 40.

[105]   Marian Goronwy-Roberts, *A Woman of Vision: A Life of Marion Phillips, MP* (Wrexham: Bridge Books, 2000), p. 150.

[106]   Phillips, *Women and the Miners' Lockout*, p. 35.

[107]   *The Times*, 29 June 1926. The NSPCC report produced a response from *The Miner* entitled 'Meanest Trick of All . . . Dropping the "P" out of NSPCC', 2 July 1926.

[108]   The Women's Committee was right to target the USA for fund-raising. *The Miner*, 9 July, reported that £72,000 had so far been donated from the USA, much of it from US mine workers.

[109]   This is apparent from the quotes included in the *Times* article, 'Children in the Coalfields', 29 June 1926.

[110] Marion Phillips, *Women and the Miners' Lockout*, p. 70.

[111] Hywel Francis, 'South Wales', in Jeffrey Skelley, *The General Strike, 1926* (London: Lawrence and Wishart, 1976), p. 248.

[112] Monmouthshire CC, Report upon Maternal and Child Welfare for the year 1926, p. 28, GRO.

[113] I am grateful to Steven Thompson for pointing this out to me, from his research at the SWCC archive. It is also possible that extra places were available for women as miners had a better quality of life when not working and would not, therefore, need to make use this facility as they would when facing all the rigours of underground working.

[114] Thompson, 'That beautiful summer', p. 559.

[115] Phillips, *Women and the Miners' Lockout*, p. 85. According to the Women's Co-operative Guild Annual Report, 26–7 May 1927, 387 miners children were adopted by Co-op members during the dispute. It would appear that this is additional to the total of 2,172 given by Phillips. It is not known how many of these were from Wales. TUC archive, LMU.

[116] *South Wales Echo*, 29 July 1926.

[117] *Merthyr Express*, 25 September 1926.

[118] Education Committee Minutes, RUDC, 5 January 1927, GRO.

[119] Barrie Naylor, *Quakers in the Rhondda* (Chepstow: Maes-yr-Haf Eductional Trust, 1986), p. 20.

[120] Letter from Emma Noble, 24 June 1926. Correspondence (Chepstow: Maes-yr-Haf Educational Trust), GRO.

[121] Naylor, *Quakers in the Rhondda*, p. 52.

[122] Interview with Blod Davies, 27–8 October 2004, Trealaw.

[123] *Rhondda Gazette*, 30 October 1926.

[124] Letter from Edith Pye, 29 June 1926. Correspondence relating to relief operation in the Rhondda Valley 1926–80 (Chepstow: Maes-yr-Haf Educational Trust), GRO.

[125] Letter from Edith Pye, 29 June 1926.

[126] John E. Morgan, *A Village Workers' Council: A Short History of the Lady Windsor Lodge* (Pontypridd: Celtic Press, 1956), p. 28.

CHAPTER 5

[1] Lynn Sinclair, *Silent, Suppressed and Passive? A Refocused History of Lanarkshire Women 1920–1939* (PhD thesis: University of Strathclyde, 2005), p. 243. The introduction contains a useful historiographical overview of this problem.

[2] Angela V. John, 'A Miner Struggle? Women's Protests in Welsh Mining History', *Llafur*, 4/1 (1984), 73.

[3] June Hannam and Karent Hunt, 'Gendering the Stories of Socialism: An Essay in Historical Criticism', in Margaret Walsh (ed.), *Working Out Gender: Perspectives from Labour History* (Aldershot, 1999), p. 114.

[4] Clare Collins, *Women and Labour Politics in Britain 1893–1932* (PhD thesis: LSE, University of London, 1991), p. 10.

[5] June Hannam and Karen Hunt, *Socialist Women: Britain 1880s to 1920s* (London, 2002), p. 31.

[6] For more details see Collins, *Women and Labour Politics*.

[7] *Labour Woman*, June 1925.

[8] Women's Co-operative Guild, 44th Annual Report, May 1926–May 1927 (TUC Archive: LMU), p. 7.

[9] Pamela Graves, *Labour Women, Women in British Working Class Politics 1918–1939* (Cambridge: Cambridge University Press, 1994), p. 1; Pat Thane, 'The Women

of the British Labour Party and Feminism, 1906–1945', in Harold Smith (ed.), *British Feminism in the Twentieth Century* (Aldershot: Edward Elgar, 1990).

[10]   Graves, *Labour Women*, pp. 81–98. Also Dora Russell, *The Tamarisk Tree: My Quest for Liberty and Love* (London: Virago, 1977), pp. 168–73.

[11]   'Matron', *Rhondda Socialist Newspaper, being the BOMB of the Rhondda Workers*, 21 December 1912. Reproduced in Chris Williams, *Capitalism, Community and Conflict: The South Wales Coalfield 1898–1947* (Cardiff: University of Wales Press, 1998), pp. 111–13.

[12]   Kay Cook and Neil Evans, 'The Petty Antics of the Bell-Ringing Boisterous Band? The Women's Suffrage Movement in Wales, 1890–1918', in Angela V. John (ed.), *Our Mothers' Land: Chapters in Welsh Women's History 1830–1939* (Cardiff: University of Wales Press, 1991), p. 169; Viscountess Rhondda, *This Was My World* (London: Macmillan, 1933), p. 122. I am grateful also to the late Ursula Masson for information on this.

[13]   Kay Cook and Neil Evans state that there were NUWSS branches in Bargoed, Pontypool, Rhondda Fach, Upper Rhondda and Ton Pentre, 'The Petty Antics', 1991, p. 171–2. Ursula Masson refers to NUWSS branches in Merthyr, Pontypridd and Rhondda; Keith Gildart, David Howell and Neville Kirk, *Dictionary of Labour Biography*, XI (Basingstoke: Palgrave, 2003), entry for Rose Davies, p. 40.

[14]   Elizabeth Andrews, *A Woman's Work is Never Done* (Ystrad: Rhondda, 1957), p. 6. See also new edition edited and introduced by Ursula Masson (Dinas Powys, 2006). Helen Thomas at Llafur Conference, 11 November 2006, Pontypridd. Helen Thomas researched this subject for an unpublished MA thesis.

[15]   In June 1926, the Rhondda Joint Co-op Women's Guilds asked the RUDC health committee to consider the question of allowing married persons to have access to birth control information in its clinics. RUDC Minutes, 1 June 1926. It was resolved to consider this matter at the September meeting but there is no evidence that it was ever taken up. The Labour majority appear to have followed the official line that this was a divisive issue which should not become a subject of Party policy. They are also very preoccupied with the Lockout at this time. The only birth control clinic to open in south Wales in these years was in Abertillery in 1925. It did not flourish and was soon closed. For details, see Margaret Douglas, 'Women, God and Birth Control: The First Hospital Birth Control Clinic, Abertillery, 1925.' *Llafur*, 6/4, 1995. Also Kate Fisher, '"Clearing up Misconceptions": The Campaign to set up Birth Control Clinics in South Wales between the Wars', *Welsh History Review*, 19/1, June 1998.

[16]   For details see Ursula Masson and Lowri Newman, entry for Elizabeth Andrews in Gildart et al., *Dictionary of Labour Biography*, XI (Basingstoke: Palgrave, 2003); Dot Jones, 'Andrews, Elizabeth (1882–1960)', *Oxford Dictionary of National Biography*, 2 (Oxford: Oxford University Press, 2004).

[17]   Anthony Mor-O'Brien, *The Autobiography of Edmund Stonelake* (Mid Glamorgan, 1981), p. 12.

[18]   *Labour Woman*, May 1920.

[19]   *South Wales Gazette*, 26 December 1924.

[20]   *Labour Woman* provided a monthly profile on a woman councillor. The 'Our Women Councillors' page in October 1920 was devoted to Rose Davies JP.

[21]   Ursula Masson, 'Rose Davies' in Gildart et al., *Dictionary*, 2003, p. 43.

[22]   Masson, 'Rose Davies', p. 43.

[23]   *Workers' Bomb*, no. 2, December 1920, refers to election of Mrs Williams to RUDC and campaign to get more women as elected and co-opted members.

[24]   Andrews, *A Woman's Work*, p. 28.

[25]   Winifred Griffiths, *One Woman's Story* (Rhondda: Ron James Publications, 1980), p. 76.

[26] For details of the campaign for pithead baths see Neil Evans and Dot Jones, 'A Blessing for the Miner's Wife: The campaign for pithead baths in the south Wales coalfield 1908–1950', *Llafur*, 6, 1994. Mrs Hartshorn was the leading activist and was backed by the local Women's Labour League in Maesteg, p. 14.

[27] *Workers' Bomb*, no. 1, November 1920, GRO. There appear to be very few issues of this publication.

[28] Masson, 'Rose Davies', p. 44.

[29] Lowri Newman, *A Distinctive Brand of Politics: Women in the South Wales Labour Party 1918–939* (M.Phil: University of Glamorgan 2003), p. 59.

[30] Newman, *A Distinctive Brand*, pp. 59, 88, 104.

[31] *Workers' Bomb*, December 1920. Report of a conference of Rhondda Labour Women's Sections.

[32] East Glamorgan Labour Women's Advisory 1925–6, Labour Party Archive, National Library of Wales.

[33] Interview with Isabel Brown, 5 January 1978, London.

[34] Telephone interview with Idris Cox, 10 January 1980.

[35] Wayne David, 'The Labour Party and the "exclusion" of the Communists; the case of the Ogmore Divisional Labour Party in the 1920s', *Llafur*, 3/4, 1983, p. 10, where the example given is that of Maesteg.

[36] Susan Bruley, *Socialism and Feminism in the Communist Party of Great Britain, 1920–1939* (PhD thesis: LSE, University of London, 1980). Also published as *Leninism, Stalinism and the Women's Movement, 1920–1939* (New York: Garland Press, 1986), pp. 112–13.

[37] Stella Browne's report on her time in Wales; 'Birth Control in Taff Vale', *New Generation*, October 1923. According to testimony from Ben Davies it appears that Browne exaggerated attendance at her lectures; see Bruley, *Socialism and Feminism*, p. 113.

[38] *Labour Woman*, April 1926, states that there were 107 delegates (representing 8,578 members), plus 150 visitors attending this conference. This is a dramatic increase on figures for the previous event, see above. It appears that either the figures are in some way inaccurate or the number of women Labour members in the eastern section of the coalfield had greatly expanded.

[39] For details see entry for Drummond in Elizabeth Crawford, *The Women's Suffrage Movement: A Reference Guide 1866–1928* (London: University College London Press, 1999), pp. 175–7.

[40] Nicoletta Gullace, *The Blood of Our Sons: Men, Women and the Renegotiation of Citizenship During the Great War* (Basingstoke: Palgrave, 2002), pp. 134–6.

[41] *Colliery Workers' Magazine* (CWM), April 1926.

[42] *Labour Woman*, April 1926.

[43] *Workers Weekly*, 9 April 1926.

[44] *The Times*, 19 April 1926, p. 10. Note that neither Swansea nor Cardiff were in the coalfield.

[45] *Aberdare Leader*, 24 April 1926.

[46] *Caerphilly Journal*, 24 April, 1926.

[47] *Caerphilly Journal*, 24 April 1926. The article states that there were branches of the WGE in Abertridwr and Senghennydd.

[48] *Colliery Workers' Magazine*, May 1926.

[49] Minutes of the East Glamorgan Labour Women's Advisory 1925–6, 6 March 1926 (Labour Party Wales Archive: National Library of Wales). This appears to be the first time that mass meetings for women were called for.

[50] *Labour Woman*, June 1926; *Swansea Labour News*, 12 June 1926.

[51] *Aberdare Leader*, 1 May 1926. Thanks to Neil Evans for drawing my attention to this.

[52] *Colliery Workers' Magazine*, 4/6, June 1926 and 4/7, July 1926.

[53] *Colliery Workers' Magazine*, 4/8, August 1926.

[54] *Colliery Workers' Magazine*, 4/5, May 1926, p. 116

[55] *Colliery Workers' Magazine*, 4/4, April 1926.

[56] Michael Lieven, *Senghennydd: The Universal Pit Village 1890–1930* (Llandysul: Gomer, 1994), p. 344; details recorded from *Caerphilly Journal*, 3 July 1926.

[57] RUDC Maternity and Child Welfare Committee, 11 May 1926, GRO

[58] RUDC Maternity and Child Welfare Clinic, 30 August 1926, GRO.

[59] Further evidence on this question from Monmouthshire is given in chapter 4.

[60] *South Wales Echo*, 25 May 1926.

[61] Quoted at RUDC Maternity and Child Welfare Committee, 13 October 1926, GRO.

[62] Masson, 'Rose Davies', p. 43.

[63] *South Wales News*, 12 June 1926.

[64] *South Wales News*, 8 July 1926; *Pontypridd Observer*, 10 July 1926.

[65] *Pontypridd Observer*, 10 July 1926. 'Mrs Evans' is likely to be the Mrs Evans of the Maternal and Child Welfare committee.

[66] For details of the Women's Committee for the Relief of Miners' Wives and Children, see Marion Phillips, *Women and the Miners' Lockout: The Story of the Women's Committee for the Relief of Miners' Wives and Children* (London: Labour Publishing Co., 1927).

[67] Maerdy Distress Committee, 31 August 1926, SWCC.

[68] Maerdy Distress Committee, 14 September 1926, SWCC.

[69] There were women's representatives on the Distress Committee, from the two local Labour Women's Sections, but these were not the most dominant influences on the committee, which were male members of the local Communist Party.

[70] *Labour Woman*, July 1926.

[71] Cambrian Lodge, 22 April and 5 May 1926, SWCC.

[72] *Labour Woman*, November 1926.

[73] Andrews, *A Woman's Work*, p. 25. In *Labour Woman*, Mrs Herman's name is spelt Hermon.

[74] Facts from the coalfields, *Labour Woman*, 1 July 1926, p. 101.

[75] *Labour Woman*, 1 August 1926.

[76] Phillips, *Women*, p. 35.

[77] Newman, *Dictionary*, pp. 76–82. I am grateful to Lowri Newman for information on Beatrice Green.

[78] Obituary, *South Wales Gazette*, 21 October 1927.

[79] Newman, *Dictionary*, p. 78.

[80] *South Wales Echo*, 29 July 1926.

[81] Marion Phillips, 'The Gift of a Beautiful Life', obituary for Beatrice Green, *Labour Woman*, November 1927.

[82] Green in *Labour Woman*, November and December, 1926, also a short piece in October. These articles include photographs.

[83] *Brief Summary of District Organisers' Reports*, Submitted to the 8th Congress of the CPGB, October 1926. Marx Memorial Library, London. This increased membership of both women and men was not retained.

[84] Idris Cox, telephone interview, 10 January 1980.

[85] *Congress Report and Resolutions*, 8th Congress of the CPGB, 1926, p. 32. Held at the Marx Memorial Library, London.

[86] Idris Cox, *Plebs*, October 1926.

[87] Interview with Lil Price, 21 July 1977, Cardiff. The details supplied in the following paragraph are all from this interview. Testimony from Lil Price is also held at the SWML.

[88]   William C. May, *Recollections of a County Policeman* (Ilfracombe, Devon, 1979), p. 137. May, who was a serving police officer working from Pontypridd at this time states that police were brought in from 'Devon, Cornwall, Plymouth, Sussex and other Police Forces in parts of the country where men on strike had resumed full work'.

[89]   *Aberdare Leader*, 11 December 1926.

[90]   Francis and Smith, *The Fed*, p. 65.

[91]   Francis and Smith give a figure of 12 major prosecutions involving women; *The Fed*, p. 65.

[92]   John, 'A Miner Struggle', esp. p. 75.

[93]   May, *Recollections*, gives an account of the disturbances at Ogmore and elsewhere from the point of view of a serving police officer, pp. 138–56.

[94]   *Aberdare Leader*, 18 December 1926.

[95]   Recording held at the SWML.

[96]   The recording is part of an NUM discussion group from the 1970s, held at the SWML.

[97]   *South Wales Echo*, 16 October 1926.

[98]   *South Wales Echo*, 5 October 1926.

[99]   *South Wales Echo*, 15 December 1926. The women defendants were Rose Keast, Agnes Lowe, May Clemas, Cissy James, Annie Howell, Elizabeth Harry and Catherine Williams. The report does not state which defendant was nursing her baby. There were also four male defendants.

[100] *South Wales News*, 3 November 1926.

[101] Letter to Mr De Burgh, 9 November 1926, Abergorki Lodge, SWCC.

[102] *South Wales Echo*, 27 September 1926.

[103] Interview with Lilian Lawrence, 27 October 2004, Trealaw.

[104] Rosemary A. Jones, 'Women, Community and Collective Action: The "Ceffyl Pren" Tradition', in Angela V. John, *Our Mothers' Land* (Cardiff: University of Wales Press, 1991), pp. 32–5. Also, see John, 'A Miner Struggle', p. 78.

[105] For details see Rosemary A. Jones, 'Women, Community and Collective Action: The "Ceffyl Pren" Tradition', in A. John, *Our Mothers' Land*.

[106] May, *Recollections*, pp. 149–50.

[107] *South Wales News*, 13 August. The 25 August issue gives more details of whiteshirting incidents at Elliotstown and Phillipstown.

[108] *Glamorgan Gazette*, 15 October 1926.

[109] *South Wales News*, 13 August 1926.

[110] *South Wales Echo*, 16 September 1926.

[111] *Glamorgan Gazette*, 10 December 1926.

[112] Jones, 'Women, Community', p. 37.

[113] Recording held at the SWML. In a similar vein, Will Paynter wrote that he knew of a 'family of blacklegs' in his home village of Trebannog, whom he described as 'invariably inferior as workmen' and suffering from 'weakness of character', *My Generation* (London: Allen and Unwin, 1972), p. 35.

[114] Francis and Smith, *The Fed*, p. 59.

CHAPTER 6

[1]   Hywel Francis, 'South Wales', in Jeffrey Skelley, *The General Strike* (London: Lawrence and Wishart, 1976), p. 233.

[2]   Interview with Avis Williams, 10 December 2004, Cymmer.

[3]   *Merthyr Express*, 23 October 1926.

[4]   *Merthyr Express*, 23 October 1926.

5   *South Wales Echo*, 14 December 1926.

6   *Glamorgan Gazette*, 1 October 1926, refers to the formation of an Ogmore Vale Rate Payers Association. *Rhondda Gazette*, 18 December 1926, refers to the formation of a Rhondda Rate Payers Association.

7   See, for example, *Colliery Guardian*, 29 October 1926, which gives a round-up of the week's disturbances.

8   According to the MFGB only 6,000 men out of 200,000 were back at work on 11 November. *Annual Volume of Proceedings for the Year 1926* (TUC archive: LMU), pp. 970–1.

9   CAB 27 333/334, TNA. Alun Burge provides an example of a lodge which refused to accept the settlement; Nine Mile Point in the Sirhowy Valley, which remained out until May 1927, 'In Search of Harry Blount: Scabbing between the wars in one south Wales community', *Llafur*, 6/3, 1994, 60.

10   David Gilbert, *Class, Community and Collective Action: Social Change in Two British Coalfields 1850–1926* (Oxford: Clarendon Press, 1992), p. 140 and p. 258.

11   James Hinton, *Labour and Socialism: A History of the British Labour Movement 1867–1974* (Brighton: Wheatsheaf, 1983), p. 140.

12   Arthur Horner, *Incorrigible Rebel* (London: MacGibbon and Kee, 1960), p. 90. Steven Thompson confirms that there was a small improvement in male death rates in south Wales during the Lockout in 'That beautiful summer', *Welsh History Review*, 21/3 (2003), 556.

13   Paul Davies, *A. J. Cook* (Manchester: Manchester University Press, 1987), p. 134.

14   Hywel Francis and Dai Smith, *The Fed: A History of the South Wales Miners in the Twentieth Century*, first published 1980, 2nd edition (Cardiff: University of Wales Press, 1998), p. 66.

15   Interview with Mary Lowrie, 27 October 2004, Trealaw; interview with Lizzie Davies, 25 August 2004, Maerdy.

16   Interview with Mavis Llewellyn, 23 July 1977, Nantymoel.

17   B. L. Coombes, *These Poor Hands: The Autobiography of a Miner Working in South Wales* (London: Victor Gollancz, 1974 (first published 1939)), pp. 188–9.

18   Abergorki Lodge, letter 26 February 1927, SWCC.

19   Cwmdu Minutes, 20 December 1926, SWCC.

20   For details see Peter Kingsford, *The Hunger Marches in Britain 1920–1940* (London: Lawrence and Wishart, 1982), pp. 81–6. The characterisation of Britain in the 1930s as 'the Hungry Thirties' has unfortunately obscured the hunger marches of the 1920s when, arguably, life for the unemployed was more difficult (see below).

21   *South Wales News*, 21 November 1927.

22   Francis and Smith, *The Fed*, p. 75.

23   Francis and Smith, *The Fed*, p. 97.

24   Susan Demont, *Tredegar and Aneurin Bevan: A Society and its Political Articulation 1890–1929* (PhD thesis: University of Wales, 1990), p. 320.

25   Coombes, *These Poor Hands*, p. 186.

26   Coombes, *These Poor Hands*, p. 189.

27   Alun Morgan, 'Bedlinog: Glimpses of a Pre-War Society', *Glamorgan Historian*, 11 (1975), pp. 146–7. See also *South Wales News*, 10 January 1927.

28   Francis and Smith, *The Fed*, p. 116.

29   Michael Lieven, *Senghennydd: The Universal Pit Village* (Llandysul: Gomer, 1994), p. 349.

30   *Colliery Workers Magazine*, January 1927.

31   Central Canteen Committee Minutes, RUDC, 14 February 1927, GRO.

32   Huw Williams, 'Merthyr Tydfil and the General Strike of 1926', *Merthyr Historian*, 1978, 2, p. 132.

[33] Eli Ginzberg, *A World Without Work* (London: Transcation, 1991 (first published in New York: Harper and Bros, as *Grass on the Slagheaps*, 1942)), p. 175.

[34] John McIlroy, 'South Wales', in John McIlroy, Alan Campbell and Keith Gildart, *Industrial Politics and the 1926 Mining Lockout: The Struggle for Dignity* (Cardiff: University of Wales Press, 2004), p. 150.

[35] Nixons Workmen's Hall and Institute Minute Book, 1 July 1927, SWCC.

[36] *South Wales News*, 24 December 1926.

[37] Idris Davies, *Gwalia Deserta* (London: J. M. Dent, 1938), p. 6.

[38] Central Canteen Committee, RUDC, 3 December 1926, GRO.

[39] Education Committee, RUDC, 28 December 1926, GRO.

[40] Meeting of the Relief Advisory Committee, Pontypridd Poor Law Union, 10 January 1927, GRO.

[41] Education Committee, RUDC, 11 January 1927, GRO.

[42] Report on a Deputation to the Board of Education, School Management Committee, RUDC, 19 January 1927. GRO.

[43] Central Canteen Committee, RUDC, 9 March 1927, GRO.

[44] This matter is also referred to by Chris Williams, *Democratic Rhondda: Politics and Society 1885–1951* (Cardiff: University of Wales Press), p. 172.

[45] Report of Labour Committee of Inquiry, *The Distress in South Wales* (Parliamentary Labour Party, 1928), p. 5, refers to necessitous children in the Abertillery, Blaina and Nantyglo areas of Monmouthshire receiving two meals a day at school (TUC, LMU); Kenneth O. Morgan, *Rebirth of a Nation: Wales 1880–1980* (Oxford: Oxford University Press, 1981), p. 292.

[46] *South Wales News*, 28 December 1926.

[47] *Colliery Guardian*, 26 November 1926.

[48] Meeting of the Board of Guardians, Pontypridd Poor Law Union, 15 December 1926, GRO.

[49] *Merthyr Express*, 11 December 1926.

[50] Patricia Ryan, 'The Poor Law in 1926', in Margaret Morris (ed.), *The General Strike* (Harmondsworth: Penguin, 1976), p. 375. This is also apparent from the minutes of both the Pontypridd and Merthyr Tydfil Poor Law Unions.

[51] Report of the Conference of Labour Members from South Wales, Cardiff, 23 December, in *South Wales News*, 28 December 1926.

[52] Special meeting, RUDC, 30 March 1927, GRO.

[53] *Merthyr Express*, 13 November 1926.

[54] *Colliery Workers Magazine*, January 1927.

[55] *Colliery Guardian*, 10 December 1926.

[56] Siân R. Williams, 'The Bedwellty Board of Guardians and the Default Act of 1927', *Llafur*, 2/4 (1979), 71. The figures which Williams provides are actually from 1924; the average cost per head per annum was £19 15s 1d in Bedwellty as against £19 3s 1d in Pontypridd and £17 12s 7d in Merthyr.

[57] Williams, 'The Bedwellty Board', p. 69.

[58] Ministry of Health MH57/117 Coal Dispute 1926, Relief of Miners' Dependants, Daily Lists, 1 October 1926. TNA.

[59] Michael Foot, *Aneurin Bevan 1897–1945* (London: Granada, 1975 (first published 1962)), p. 82.

[60] Ryan, 'The Poor Law in 1926', pp. 368–9.

[61] Williams, 'The Bedwelty Board', p. 75.

[62] MH 57/94, Relief, Effect of the General Strike and Coal Dispute (1926) on the Poor Law System, TNA.

[63] MH 79/297, Public Assistance, General Strike and Coal Strike 1921–6, TNA.

[64] MH 57/94, Relief, TNA.

[65] MH 57/94, Relief, TNA.

[66]   Ginzberg, *A World Without Work*, p. 161.

[67]   Examples are: 'Wife of a Coal Face Worker', *The Miner*, 19 February 1926; letter from 'Comrade Eva', *The Miner*, 16 July 1927; letter from Mrs Tait, from Yorkshire, *The Miner*, 26 May 1928. This issue has been addressed by Jaclyn Gier-Viskovatoff and Abigail Porter in 'Women of the British Coalfields on Strike in 1926 and 1984: Documenting Lives Using Oral History and Photography', *Frontiers: Journal of Women's Studies*, 19/2, 1998, 199–229.

[68]   See, for example, *The Miner*, 21 May 1927.

[69]   Viskovatoff and Porter, 'Women of the British Coalfields', 217.

[70]   Marion Phillips, *Women and the Miners' Lockout* (London: Labour Publishing Co., 1927), p. vii.

[71]   For more details see: Lowri Newman, *A Distinctive Brand of Politics: Women in South Wales Labour Party 1918–1939* (M.Phil. thesis, University of Glamorgan, 2003); Pat Thane, 'The Women of the British Labour Party and Feminism', in H. Smith (ed.), *British Feminism in the Twentieth Century* (Aldershot: Edward Elgar, 1990); June Hannam and Karen Hunt, *Socialist Women: Britain 1880s to 1920s* (London: Routledge, 2002).

[72]   See, for example the article in *Sunday Worker*, 26 August 1928.

[73]   Marion Phillips, 'The Gift of a Beautiful Life: In Memory of Beatrice Green', *Labour Woman*, 1 November 1927, p. 162. See also the obituary in the *South Wales Gazette*, 21 October 1927.

[74]   Phillips, *Labour Woman*, 1 November 1927.

[75]   Lowri Newman, entry for Beatrice Green, in Keith Gildart, David Howell, Neville Kirk, *Dictionary of Labour Biography*, XI (Basingstoke: Palgrave, 2003), p. 82.

[76]   Ursula Masson, entry for Rose Davies in Gildart et al., *Dictionary*, p. 45.

[77]   *Report of the 9th Congress, Communist Party of Great Britain*, October 1927, p. 24. Held at the Marx Memorial Library, London.

[78]   Wayne David, 'The Labour Party and the "Exclusion" of the Communist; the Case of the Ogmore Divisonal Labour Party in the 1920s', *Llafur*, 4/3 (1983), p. 10.

[79]   *South Wales News*, 4 April 1927.

[80]   Elizabeth Andrews, *A Woman's Work is Never Done* (Dinas Powys: Honno, 2006 (first published 1957)), p. 19.

[81]   *South Wales News*, 28 October 1927.

[82]   Entry for Flora Drummond in Elizabeth Crawford, *The Women's Suffrage Movement: A Reference Guide, 1866–1928* (London: UCL Press), pp. 176–7.

[83]   Williams, *Democratic Rhondda*, p. 25.

[84]   Pilgrim Trust, *Men Without Work: A Report* (Cambridge: Cambridge University Press, 1938), p. 155.

[85]   Pilgrim Trust, *Men Without Work*, p. 65.

[86]   Williams, 'Merthyr Tydfil and the General Strike', p. 132.

[87]   Francis and Smith, *The Fed*, p. 164.

[88]   Dai Smith, 'Wales between the Wars', in Trevor Herbert and Gareth F. Jones (eds), *Wales Between the Wars* (Cardiff: University of Wales Press, 1988), p. 2.

[89]   Correspondence relating to relief operations in the Rhondda Valley, 1926–8 (Maes-yr-Haf), GRO.

[90]   Barrie Naylor, *Quakers in the Rhondda, 1926–1986* (Chepstow: Maes-yr-haf Educational Trust, 1986), p. 40.

[91]   Interview with Mary Lowrie, 27 October, 2004.

[92]   Stuart Macintyre, *Little Moscows: Communism and Working Class Militancy in Interwar Britain* (London: Croom Helm, 1980), pp. 36–7. See also Maerdy Distress Committee Minutes, 28 January and 19 March 1929, SWCC.

[93]   Pilgrim Trust, *Men Without Work*, pp. 283–4.

[94] For details see Sue Bruley, 'A Woman's Right to Work? The Role of Women in the Unemployed Movement Between the Wars', in Sybil Oldfield (ed.), *This Working Day World: Women's Lives and Culture(s) in Britain 1914–1945* (London: Taylor and Francis, 1994).

[95] For details see Stephanie Ward, '"Sit down to starve or stand up to live": Community, Protest and the Means Test in the Rhondda Valleys, 1931–1939', *Llafur*, 9/2 (2005). Also Neil Evans, '"South Wales has been Roused as Never Before": Marching Against the Means Test, 1934–1936', in David Howell and Kenneth Morgan, *Crime, Protest and Police in Modern British Society: Essays in Memory of David I. V. Jones* (Cardiff: University of Wales Press, 1999).

[96] Gwyn A. Williams, *When Was Wales? A History of the Welsh* (Harmondsworth: Penguin, 1985), p. 262.

[97] Ginzberg, *A World Without Work*, p. 79.

[98] Williams, *When Was Wales?*, p. 253.

[99] Labour Report, *Distress in South Wales*, p. 17.

[100] *Colliery Guardian*, 31 December 1926. There was opposition in the labour movement to the government's promotion of immigration which was seen as a new form of 'transportation'. The *Sunday Worker*, 12 August 1928, reported that 10,000 British workers 'mostly unemployed miners are being recruited for harvest work in Canada'. The article paints a bleak picture of the conditions that awaited the newly arrived emigrants.

[101] Interview with Maria Williams, 1 July 1973, SWML.

[102] Interview with Lizzie Davies, 25 August 2004, Maerdy.

[103] Bernard Baldwin, *Mountain Ash Remembered* (Cowbridge: D. Brown, 1984), p. 49.

[104] *Sunday Worker*, 26 August 1928.

[105] Interview with Lizzie Davies, 25 August 2004, Maerdy.

[106] Hywel Francis, interview with Glyn Williams, 21 May 1974, SWML. Glyn Williams was later President of the National Union of Mineworkers (South Wales Area).

[107] Pilgrim Trust, *Men Without Work*, p. 276.

[108] Unpubished research material by R. Goffee at the University of Kent, quoted in Gina Harkell, 'The Migration of Mining Families to the Kent Coalfield Between the Wars', *Oral History*, 6/1, 1978, p. 111.

[109] Di Parkin, *60 Years of Struggle: A History of Betteshanger Colliery*, p. 4. I am grateful to Di Parkin for the opportunity to look at this pre-publication draft.

[110] Parkin, *60 Years of Struggle*, pp. 4–5.

[111] Ginzberg, *A World Without Work*, p. 127.

[112] My understanding of life for the unemployed, as shown in the remainder of this section, has been enhanced by the recent excellent work of Steven Thompson, *Unemployment, Poverty and Health in Interwar South Wales* (Cardiff: University of Wales Press, 2006).

[113] Pilgrim Trust, *Men Without Work*, p. 115.

[114] Thompson, *Unemployment, Poverty and Health*, p. 7.

[115] Interview with Lilian Roberts, 27 October 2004, Trealaw.

[116] Pilgrim Trust, *Men Without Work*, p. 165.

[117] Pilgrim Trust, *Men Without Work*, p. 172.

[118] Horner, *Incorrigible Rebel*, pp. 100–1.

[119] *Aberdare Leader*, 13 November 1926.

[120] Labour Report, *Distress in South Wales*, p. 13.

[121] Labour Report, *Distress in South Wales*, pp. 5, 15.

[122] Thompson, *Unemployment, Poverty and Health*, p. 224.

[123] Interview with Gladys Davies, 4 August 2004, Bridgend.

[124] Ginzberg, *A World Without Work*, p. 27.

[125] Interview with Gladys Davies, 4 August 2004, Bridgend.

[126] Pilgrim Trust, *Men Without Work*, p. 140.

[127] Thompson, *Unemployment, Poverty and Health*, pp. 210, 228–9

[128] Mari Williams, *A Forgotten Army: Female Munition Workers of South Wales 1939–1945* (Cardiff: University of Wales Press, 2002), p. 55.

[129] Francis and Smith, *The Fed*, p. 436.

[130] Jean Stead, *Never the Same Again: Women and the Miners' Strike 1984–5* (London: Women's Press 1984–5; Sheila Rowbotham, 'More Than Just a Memory: Some Political Implications of Women's Involvement in the Miners' Strike, 1984–5', *Feminist Review*, 23, 1986; Vicky Seddon (ed.), *The Cutting Edge: Women and the Pit Strike* (London: Lawrence and Wishart, 1986); Loretta Loach, 'We'll Be here Right to the End . . . And After: Women in the Miners' Strike', in Huw Beynon, *Digging Deeper: Issues in the Miners' Strike* (London: Verso, 1985); I am very grateful to Alan Campbell for initial help with this section.

[131] Beatrix Campbell, 'Proletarian Patriarchs and the Real Radicals', in Seddon, *The Cutting Edge*, p. 251. She quotes from the *Morning Star* (no date given).

[132] Hywel Francis and Gareth Rees, '"No surrender in the Valleys": The 1984–5 Miners' Strike in South Wales', *Llafur*, 5/2, 1989, 58.

[133] Welsh Campaign for Civil and Public Liberties and NUM (South Wales Area), *Striking Back* (Cardiff: Cymric Federation Press, 1985), p. 34.

[134] Thanks to Hywel Francis for information supplied to the author via e-mail on 12 September 2007.

[135] Jill Miller, *You Can't Kill the Spirit: Women in a Welsh Mining Valley* (London: Women's Press, 1986), p. 20.

[136] I am referring here to the way in which women were 'hidden from history' until the 1970s by the dominance of political, diplomatic and traditional labour history. This was part of a process of 'collective' or 'public' memory in which the lives of women were largely excluded and therefore unrecognised. See reference above on collective memory.

[137] Steffan Morgan, 'Stand By Your Man: Wives, Women and Feminism During the Miner's Strike 1984–5', *Llafur*, 9/2, 2005, p. 64.

[138] Miller, *You Can't Kill*, pp. 18–19.

[139] Steffan Morgan argues that women in south Wales in 1984–5 should not be simply defined by class or gender but instead argues for a more hybrid approach recognising that 'people construct their identities based on different, sometimes contradictory, elements and experiences', in 'Stand By Your Man'.

[140] Williams, *Democratic Rhondda*, p. 210.

[141] An example of this can be seen in 'I was always told I was thick. The strike taught me I wasn't'. *Guardian 2*, 10 May 2004, on Betty Cook.

[142] DOVE stands for Dulais Opportunities for Voluntary Enterprise. This women's co-operative enterprise has been very successful in securing European and other funding for its many initiatives. For details, see Mair Francis, *Up the Dove! The History of the DOVE Workshop in Banwen* (Neath: VIEW(DOVE), 2008).

[143] Miller, *You Can't Kill*, p. 40.

[144] David Waddington et al., *Split at the Seams? Community, Continuity and Change After the 1984–5 Coal Dispute* (Milton Keynes: Open University Press, 1991), p. 92.

[145] Seddon, *Cutting Edge*, p. 14.

[146] There are number of open cast coal mines now operating in Wales. Unlike deep coalmines the open cast mines are not popular with local communities, largely because of the environmental damage which they cause.

[147] Francis and Smith, *The Fed*, p. xxv. Writing in 2008, a large new open cast coal mine is being excavated in Ffos-y-fran, close to Merthyr Tydfil. *Guardian 2*, 9 October 2007.

[148] My thinking here has been influenced by oral history works on 'collective memory': Richard Johnson et al. (eds), *Making Histories: Studies in History-Writing and Politics* (London: Hutchinson and the Centre for Contemporary Cultural Studies, 1982); Penny Summerfield, *Reconstructing Women's Wartime Lives: Discourse and Subjectivity in Oral Histories of the Second World War* (Manchester: Manchester University Press, 1998); Alistair Thomson, *Anzac Memories: Living With the Legend* (Oxford, Oxford University Press, 1994); Alessandro Portelli, 'The Peculiarities of Oral History', *History Workshop Journal*, 12, 1981; Luisa Passerini, 'Work, Ideology and Consensus under Italian Fascism', *History Workshop Journal*, 8, 1979.

[149] Ferdynand Zeig, *Men in Pits* (London: Gollancz, 1948), p. 10.

[150] Idris Davies, *Gwalia Deserta* (London: J. M. Dent, 1938), VIII, p. 6.

[151] Interview with Octavius Morgan, 17 May 1973, SWML.

[152] Interview with Lilian Lawrence, 27 October 2004.

[153] Interview with Gladys Davies, 4 August 2004, Bridgend.

[154] *Coal House* was made by Indus Films and shown by BBC Wales in 2007.

[155] Interview with Lilian Lawrence, 27 October 2004, Trealaw.

[156] Interview with Jean Ellis, 6 August 2004, Pontycymer.

[157] Interview with Elsie Pritchard, 4 August 2004, Pontcymer.

[158] Interview with Gwen Ratcliffe, 27 October 2004, Trealaw.

[159] Interview with Jill John for 'People's History of the Garw, Ogmore and Llynfi Valleys Project' (n.d., early 1990s). Transcripts held at Bridgend Library, incomplete.

LAST WORD

[1] Idris Davies, *The Angry Summer: a Poem of 1926* (Cardiff: University of Wales Press, 1993), p. 66.

Appendix

BIOGRAPHICAL NOTES ON INTERVIEWS
CONDUCTED FOR THIS PROJECT

Biographical details are sometimes incomplete due to time and other constraints at the time of the interviews. Interviews were conducted in 2004–5 and updated where possible in 2008.

* Indicates that it was not possible to record the interview (this applies to only two interviews).

RHONDDA VALLEY

Betty Bowen
Born 1920 in Clydach Vale. Had two brothers. Welsh-speaking family. Attended chapel three times on Sunday. Father was a miner. He had his own gun and would hunt for rabbits. Mother had a farming background in north Wales. Father came from Devil's Bridge in mid-Wales. The family used to walk over the mountain to attend the Treorchy Eisteddfod which she very much enjoyed. Her mother wanted to move back to a farming community. They moved to Devil's Bridge in 1932 and her mother died the following year. It is not clear when Betty moved back to the Rhondda (interview not completed). Still living independently in Trealaw.

Rose Brown
Born 1912 in Tonypandy. Father came from Somerset. He was a miner and a keen runner. Mother's family were from north Wales. Rose was the sixth of eight children. The family kept ducks and chickens. Strong Labour supporters. Rose sang in a Co-op choir. Father was an atheist and did not go to chapel. Rose was taken to a Methodist chapel by her next-door neighbour. Left school at fourteen and sent to work as an undermaid for a titled family in Wiltshire. She did not like it and after a year she came home and her mother found her another service job in central London. She stayed there for a

year and then took another job in Scotland where she lived for three years. Rose married at aged twenty one and had children. Rose has since died.

Lizzie Davies

Born 1910 in Maerdy. Says she had a 'very happy family'. Both parents were originally from west Wales so they spoke Welsh at home. Daughter of Sam Davies, Secretary of the SWMF lodge in Maerdy and of the Distress Committee in 1926. Had four brothers. Describes her mother as a 'home bird', but she was a member of the Women's Co-operative Guild and regular chapel attender. Her mother made all her own bread, four large loaves every day and seven plates of tarts on Saturday. Father a teetotaller. Whole family attended chapel. Enjoyed school where she spoke English. Left at fourteen and stayed at home to help her mother. Lizzie also used to help out wider family members when needed, such as during confinements. She went to London to work in service, probably in 1929. Sent home five shillings a week to help out the family. Came home when war broke out. Stayed in Maerdy for the rest of her life. Remained single. Died 2006.

Blod Davies and Sally Poulton (sisters)

Sally was born in 1915, the oldest of seven children. Blod was born in 1918. Their mother had eight children in eleven years. The family lived in the grandparents' house into which their father moved on marriage. The household also included an unmarried uncle. The grandmother only spoke Welsh. She understood English but would answer in Welsh. The house only had three bedrooms, for five adults and seven children. The children had to sleep 'top to tail', boys and girls mixed. They also had a cousin live with them for long periods. Their mother focused on the laundry and housework whilst her mother concentrated on the cooking and the children. Their father came from Bristol to work as a miner and was a Catholic, but the children were not raised as Catholics. They attended Methodist chapel. This was the only time their mother went out. The maternal grandfather came from mid-Wales and they maintained close links, going to stay once a year. They also spent time in Bristol with their paternal grandparents. Sally and Blod's father died in 1927 from pneumonia. The family were very short of money, often going without shoes. All the girls went away to service after school and sent money home. Sally's first job was in London where she stayed several years and came home to marry her Welsh boyfriend. Blod also worked in London, earning one pound six shillings a month. Blod also married and had four children. Blod has since died. Sally still lives independently.

Martha Jones ('Mattie')

Born 1915. Had five sisters and an older married brother. Her father came from Williamstown. Both parents spoke Welsh, but they did not speak Welsh at home. Her mother died of bronchitis when Mattie was three years old. Her father and her oldest sister Hilda, who was then seventeen, brought her up. Her father never remarried. When her sister Hilda went to work as a cleaner, she had to go with her and wait outside the house for three hours with another sister. Her sister Enid went to grammar school, known as 'County'. Except for choir, her father did not go out in the evenings. After school, went into service for six months but her father missed her so much that two of her sisters came and brought her home. Then did an apprenticeship in needlework which her father paid for. Later married and was widowed in the war leaving her with three young children. Now living in sheltered accommodation in Trealaw.

Lilian Lawrence

Born 1919 in Porth. Had three siblings, but was brought up by her grandmother and step-grandfather because she was a delicate child. Stayed with her family for a week or fortnight at a time during the school holidays and her mum used to make the two-mile trip to see them on the train. Only spoke Welsh until she was about five or six. Her grandmother had a large family and her two younger children were still at home so they became like a brother and sister to her. Attended Baptist chapel. For most of the time her grandparents do not appear to be short of money. For instance, she had a variety of dresses for chapel and always beads, gloves and a hat as well, but there were other times when she had to accept shoes from charity.

Her grandmother was very religious. They had to say prayers before meals and at night. Her grandmother read passages from the Bible to her in bed by candlelight. Strong Labour family. Grandmother made her bread, faggots, brawn, Welsh cakes and fruit loaf. Lilian married in 1937 and had five children. Now a widow living in a nursing home.

Phyllis Lewis
Born 1910 in Porth. Father was a miner (haulier, ie worked with the underground ponies) Had two brothers and two sisters. Her father came from Penarth and was very musical. He played the piano for choirs in concerts. Mother baked at home. She would go out washing and wallpapering and took in sewing. Attended chapel three times on Sunday. Phyllis's father spent quite a long time unemployed. Money was always very tight. Phyllis was sent out to do cleaning jobs at aged about eleven and at thirteen she was sent to be a live-in maid for a local businessman at five shillings a week. She was allowed home only one half day a week. She moved to another service job in Williamtown for ten shillings a week. She gave it all to her mother who gave her back one shilling for pocket money. Aged about sixteen, she moved again for more money to a vicarage inYnyshir and from there she was married at the age of twenty-one. She liked her employers very much and continued working for them part-time after marriage. Had her first child at twenty-seven. Had a son and a daughter, but the daughter died as a cot death. Now a widow living in sheltered accommodation.

Mary Lowrie
Born 1911. Father had Irish origins and was a Catholic but Mary was not raised as a Catholic. Father worked as a miner and was in a band. Her mother made bread which they took to the bakehouse nearby. Mary had a brother but he was away from home for eight years. Mary had a lonely childhood. She left school at fourteen and stayed at home with her mother. She served in a shop for a period before marriage and this was the only paid work she ever did. Mary married at twenty one and had four sons and one daughter. She became involved in Maes-yr-Haf in the 1930s learning to make quilts, repair shoes

and do other work with leather. She worked for the WRVS and in Civil Defence during the war. In later life, she continued to do voluntary work. Interview incomplete. Mary has since died.

Gwen Radcliffe

Born 1921 in Blaenllechau. Gwen's father, a blacksmith, died aged thirty nine in 1925, leaving her mother with eight children. Gwen was the seventh daughter. She had a younger brother. The children had to sleep three in a bed, 'top to tail'. In 1926, her mother rented a shop. She did a lot of cooking for the shop such as baking ham and making ice cream in a machine. Gwen's six older sisters were all sent away to service when they reached fourteen. Gwen attended chapel. Her mother rented another shop for Gwen, so at the age of fifteen she was running her own business. Gwen ran the shop until she was twenty one but then was given six months' notice to close the business and report for war work. Gwen married in 1945 and continued to work helping her mother in her business. Later, she worked in a factory in Cardiff, the prime motive being to save to buy a house. Gwen and her husband chose not to have children. Interview incomplete. Now a widow living in sheltered accommodation.

Lilian Roberts

Born 1917 in Porth. Father was a miner (haulier). No siblings. The family took in lodgers. Grandparents lived next-door. Attended chapel on Sundays and twice in the week. Her mother was an organist in the chapel. Her grandfather was a deacon. It was not a lonely childhood as she had lots of cousins nearby and her grandparents doted on her. Her father was a keen gardener. The family kept a large allotment nearby and grew everything they could. Lilian's father also played in a band and repaired the instruments. Passed for grammar school and after matriculation at eighteen became a secretary. Stayed with the same company for twenty seven years. Lilian did not marry. She has since died.

'Sarah'

Born 1911, Dinas. The oldest of four children. The family spoke Welsh at home. Father was a miner. Worked on his knees all day operating a coal cutting machine. Parents sang harmonies together. Children went to chapel but not her parents. Her mother made her own bread and took it to the bakehouse to be baked. Mother also made Welsh cakes, tarts and fruit loaves. Sarah passed for grammar school but her parents could not afford to send her. Whilst Sarah was still at school their house was destroyed by fire so the family had to stay with grandparents. Her father then had an accident with his foot which laid him off work for a long time. After returning to work, he was killed in a mine explosion when Sarah was twenty one. Her mother then had to claim poor relief for herself and Sarah's younger sister. After leaving school at fourteen, Sarah stayed at home and gradually built up work sewing but, after her father's death, she went away to service to Eton School, as parlour maid to the matron. After two years she moved to Sutton in Surrey because she had a friend from Porth there. Sarah became a tailoress and worked until she was eighty three. She never returned to the Rhondda but kept in close touch with remaining family in Wales. Sarah had two daughters and is now a widow living in sheltered accommodation in Sutton.

Fred and Avis Williams

Fred was born in 1910. His family came from Somerset. Fred was the fourth child out of five. His father was a miner and a lay priest. Attendance at chapel was important to both families. Some time before the General Strike, Fred's father left the mines due to eye problems and he set up a drapery business with his compensation money.

Avis was born in 1913. She was the youngest of seven. Avis lived in a detached house and her mother had a maid to help her, but their lifestyle was by no means luxurious and her mother still did a lot of manual labour. Her mother baked at home.

Fred and Avis married in the early 1930s and lived in Trebannog. Fred was unemployed. They lived on the dole for seven years. Had two children. Avis had to go to the relieving

officer for a ten shilling note for food. Eventually, Fred's
father helped him to set up a business in a shop and bought
him a horse and cart. Fred liked to visit the pub. Avis died in
2007 and Fred is now in a nursing home.

Nancy Wood
Born 1920. Nancy was the last but one of eleven children. Her
younger sister came only thirteen months after her so her
eldest sister mothered her, although she was married by that
time, being twenty years older than her. Her father's family
came originally from Carmarthen. He spoke Welsh, but it was
not a Welsh-speaking household. Her father was originally a
miner but left the pit because of emphysema. Her father was
Mark Harcombe, a prominent Labour councillor for over
forty years on the RUDC and a very engaging public speaker.
He was also Secretary of the Penygraig Labour Club. Her
mother was a strong supporter of the local Labour women's
section, which used to meet in their house. Her mother also
attended Labour Women's Conferences. Attended the chapel
as a young child, but gave it up later. Her mother made her
own bread about twice a week which they took to the bakehouse to be baked. She also made tarts on Saturday afternoon.
This was the usual custom. Her mother had some help at
home as her father paid for someone to come in and help with
the washing on Mondays. Married after the war and had a
daughter. Now lives in sheltered accommodation in Trelalaw.

GARW VALLEY

Helena Charles
Born 1918 in Blaengarw. Her parents came from north Wales
to live in the Garw Valley. Her father was previously a slate
quarry worker and came to Blaengarw to work as a miner.
They came with eight children, leaving one behind with
grandparents who later died, and had more children in
Blaengarw. Helena's father died in 1920 when septicaemia set
in after he had some teeth removed. Her mother was left with
a baby, two toddlers (one of whom was Helena) and older children, some of whom were already working. As a widow,
Helena's mother was very hard-up and had to resort to going

out wallpapering to earn money. Her mother remarried in 1924. Her stepfather was a miner and a widower with one son who also came to live with them. At the age of nine, Helena was badly scalded by boiling water in an accident when her mother was doing washing. As no hospital bed was available, she had to be nursed at home. She had to have six months off school. It was very painful and she lost all her hair. The family were originally Welsh Methodists but switched to a Welsh Baptist chapel after her mother married a Welsh Bapist. Her mother baked at home and was always very busy so it was her stepfather who took the children to chapel. He also taught her to recite which she still does in chapel today. The family spoke Welsh at home. Her stepfather also acted in dramas and used the miner's institute library to borrow books. The family had several allotments which her brothers worked. Besides supplying the family with vegetables, there was enough left to give to extended family members living elsewhere. Left school at fourteen and went into service in a doctor's house in Blaengarw where she had to live in. Married after the war and had four children. Now widowed. Lives in sheltered accommodation in Blaengarw.

Gladys Davies
Born 1916 in Pantygog. Her mother was born in Pontycymer and spoke Welsh as a first language. Gladys thinks her father came from somewhere near Brecon. Gladys had five brothers. The family moved to nearby Pontycymer when Gladys was two. Father was a miner, mostly erecting pit props. Family were regular chapel-goers. Her grandmother was the caretaker of their chapel. Always visited relations after Sunday chapel. As a child, Gladys spent a lot of time out playing and exploring the nearby hills. The family were passionate about music. Her father and all her brothers sang in choirs. Gladys went to a grammar school, but left at fifteen to go into service. Worked in local jobs for the first year then went to work at Cliveden in Somerset for several years. Later worked in Cardiff. Came home during the war to look after her invalid mother. Stayed in Pontycymer after marriage. Had one daughter. Now a widow and lives in Bridgend in her own bungalow.

Jean Ellis*
Father a miner. One brother. Lived in Pontycymer. Her father kept racing pigeons in a loft at the end of the garden. The family belonged to the Church in Wales and were also strong Labour supporters. Her mother took in washing, doing twelve stiff-collared shirts for two shillings and sixpence. When Jean and her brother were old enough to earn money by doing paper rounds and other jobs, her mum gave up paid work. Attended church three times on Sunday sitting in the same family row every week. Jean went to grammar school and left school at sixteen. Worked at the cash desk of a large store. She left when her father set her up in business with a little shop. This was very unusual. She did this for several years but gave it up at the age of twenty-six when her mother became seriously ill. It was a musical family. Her father did impromptu ukelele sessions on the doorstep. Jean learnt violin and later the family purchased a second-hand piano. She got married at the age of twenty eight and then stayed at home but had no children. Interview incomplete. Now a widow living in a bungalow in Tondu.

Gwyneth Evans
Born 1917. Had a younger bother. Her mother came from Tenby and worked as a nanny before marriage. Her father came from a more rural, Welsh-speaking area of Pembrokeshire near Haverfordwest. Gwyneth thinks her father came to Pontycymer as the money in mining was better than farming. The family kept close links with her father's family and Gwyneth used to stay with them in the school holidays, making the journey by train (fare was eleven shillings). Her mother's parents came to live in the house next door. The two households integrated, which made it easier for Gwyneth's mother. Her father worked exceptionally hard and earned comparatively good wages. He also enjoyed a glass of stout once a week in the local pub. He was not active in the SWMF and went back to West Wales in both the 1921 and 1926 disputes. Her mother baked every day. The family were regular chapel-goers and Gwyneth still has a very strong faith. She was selected for grammar school at eleven, but did not go and left school at fourteen to go into service. Before this, she

attended a domestic training course lasting several months in Maesteg. Gwyneth went to work in London aged about fifteen. After developing an abscess on her hand, she came home and at eighteen married a local man, a miner. They had one son. She later worked for twenty-five years for the National Coal Board. Gwyneth has been a widow for many years and still lives in her own home in Pontycymer.

Nancy Lewis
Born 1918 in Blaengarw. Her father, who came from Herefordshire, died of pneumonia in the same year. Her mother had already been widowed once. Nancy had three brothers and two half-brothers. A sister died of consumption before Nancy was born.

Her mother came from Pontyypool. She baked her own bread and kept chickens. Nancy's mother cleaned the colliery offices for twenty-four years (these jobs always went to widows of miners or wives of disabled miners). Nancy had to go with her mother to work to help her. Both her mother and grandmother were in the Salvation Army. Nancy's mother earned ten shillings a week cleaning and she also had a widow's pension of five shillings and dependents' allowance of five shillings for Nancy. Nancy was made to stay on at school until sixteen so that her mother could continue to claim this benefit. Her mother also took in washing which she did at night by candlelight. Her mother never remarried and clearly it was a struggle financially for the family. After leaving school, Nancy cleaned for the family of one of the colliery manager's where her mother worked for which she earned half a crown (two shillings and sixpence). At the age of eighteen, she went to work in Bristol where she stayed with one of her brothers. She came back during the war and worked in a munitions factory. Nancy married a local man from Pontycymer and had two children. Now a widow living in Pantygog.

'Lil'*
Born 1915 into a mining family. Lived all her life in Pontycymer. Six children in the family, but one died in infancy. One girl stayed with grandparents as the babies came very close together. This was quite common at the time. Her

mother was an active Labour woman, attending Labour women's section meetings at the Miners' Institute. Her father was involved in the SWMF. Her father was also a regular at the local pub.

She was supposed to attend chapel but often hid with her brother to avoid it and her mother was lenient about it, suggesting perhaps that she did not mind too much. Had three children. Interview incomplete. Now a widow living in sheltered accommodation in Blaengarw.

Elsie Pritchard
Born 1912 and has lived in Pontycymer all her life. Elsie had six sisters. She had to sleep three in a bed. Her mother was from Pembrokeshire and her father from Somerset. Her father was a butcher, so there was always meat at home, but everything else was very basic. Her mother baked at home, which Elsie also did when she married. Her father made brawn and faggots, cured his own bacon and would earn extra money by slaughtering pigs. The family also kept pigs. Her father went to the pub every night. Her mother was a keen chapel attender. Elsie and her sisters also attended chapel, Sunday school and 'Band of Hope'. After school, Elsie worked in service for ten shillings a week in London. She later trained as a mental nurse and worked in Bridgend where she had to live-in. Married a local man and had one son. Now a widow living in residential care.

NEATH VALLEY

Ethel Roberts
Born 1918. Lived in Cwmgwrach, a mining community. Father was a miner. Both parents came from Mountain Ash. Father was Welsh-speaking. Mother did not speak Welsh. Had three brothers and two sisters. Whole family slept in three beds.

Mother baked on Fridays. Father was an ambulance man in the colliery and a keen gymnast. He also belonged to the Labour Party. He occasionally went to the pub. Attended the Church in Wales on Sunday with her mother and siblings, but her father never came. Also attended Band of Hope. One of her sisters attended grammar school. She lived with her grandmother who had a good pension and could afford the extra costs of grammar school education. Ethel left school at fourteen and worked in service for about four years. Worked in a munitions factory in Resolven during the war. Married a miner and had one child. Now a widow, living in her own house in Pontneddfechan.

BIBLIOGRAPHY

PRIMARY SOURCES

The National Archive
Ministry of Health papers
Cabinet papers

South Wales Coal Collection, Swansea University
Archives of Miners' Lodges
Archives of Miners' Institutes/Welfare Halls
Photographic collection

Glamorgan Record Office
Archives of Rhondda Urban District Council
Archives of Pontypridd Union
Archives of Merthyr Tydfil Union
Rose Davies Papers
Papers relating to Quakers in the Rhondda

Gwent Record Office
Monmouthshire County Council Archives

Marx Memorial Library
CPGB Conference Proceedings

National Library of Wales
Labour Party Archive

TUC Library
MFGB Conference Proceedings
Women's Co-operative Guild Archives
Workers' Education Association archives

Bridgend Library
Archive of the 'Valley and Vale' Project,

Museum of Welsh Life
Photographic collection

PRESS

Aberdare Leader	*Rhondda Gazette*
Caerphilly Journal	*Rhondda Socialist Newspaper*
Colliery Guardian	*South Wales Gazette*
Colliery Workers' Magazine	*South Wales Daily News*
Glamorgan Gazette	*South Wales Echo*
Labour Woman	*Sunday Worker*
Merthyr Express	*The Times*
The Miner	*Western Mail*
New Generation	*Woman's Leader*
Pontypridd Observer	

ORAL TESTIMONY

Interviews conducted for this study, 2004–5
Betty Bowen, interviewed 27 October 2004, Trealaw.
Rose Brown, interviewed 23 August 2004, Llwynypia.
Helena Charles, interviewed 14 October 2004, Blaengarw.
Blod Davies, interviewed 27 and 28 October 2004, Trealaw.
Gladys Davies, interviewed 4 August 2004, Bridgend. Originally from
     Pontycymer.
Lizzie Davies, interviewed 25 August 2004, Maerdy.
Jean Ellis, interviewed 6 August 2004, Pontycymer.
Gwyneth Evans, interviewed 25 November 2004, Pontycymer.
Martha Jones, interviewed 27 October 2004, Trealaw.
Lilian Lawrence, interviewed 27 October 2004, Trealaw.
Nancy Lewis, interviewed 25 November 2004, Pantygog. Originally
     from Blaengarw.
Phyllis Lewis, interviewed 10 December 2004, Cymmer.
'Lil', interviewed 6 August 2004, Pontycymer.
Mary Lowrie, interviewed 27 October 2004, Trealaw.
Sally Poulton, interviewed 10 December 2004, Trealaw.
Elsie Pritchard, interviewed 4 August 2004, Pontycymer.
Gwen Ratcliffe, interviewed 27 October, 2004, Trealaw.
Ethel Roberts, interviewed 24 November 2004, Pontneddfechen.
     Originally from Cwmgwrach.
Lilian Roberts, interviewed 27 October 2004, Trealaw.
'Sarah', interviewed 7 February 2005, Sutton, Surrey. Originally
     from Dinas.
Fred and Avis Williams, interviewed 10 December 2004, Cymmer.
Nancy Wood, interviewed 27 October 2004, Trealaw.

Interviews conducted previously by the author
Dora Cox, London (1977)
Idris Cox (telephone interview, 1980)
Mr and Mrs Davies, Ystrad Rhondda, and Lil Price, Cardiff (1977)
Mavis Llewellyn, Nantymoel, and Ben Davies, Dyffryn Cellwen (1977)

South Wales Miners' Library
Will Arthur, Robin Page Arnot, Mrs Brown, Dick Cook, Ben Davies, Nancy Davies, Mrs Trevor Davies, Edgar Evans, Mrs J. Evans, Glyn Evans, Reg Fine, W. Gregory, James Griffiths, Lucy James, Mrs Jones, Morgan L. Jones, Mrs Eddie Lloyd, Archie Miller, Mrs Miller, Octavious Morgan, William Morley, Merfyn Payne, Will Paynter, Bob Poole, Mrs Richards, Jack 'Russia' Roberts, Anne Thomas, Mel Thomas, Glyn Williams, Maria Williams.

Museum of Welsh Life
Interviews recorded by Rosemary Scadden, 1994
Ceinwen, Dorothy, May, Phyllis, Mary K., Hilda, Elizabeth

PUBLISHED PRIMARY MATERIAL

Burns, Emile (ed.), *General Strike, May 1926: Trades Councils in Action*, Labour Research Department, London, 1926 (London: Lawrence and Wishart, 1975 (new edition)).

Coal Industry Commission, vol. 2, Reports and Minutes of Evidence, 1919.

Hall, Ruth, *Dear Dr Stopes: Sex in the 1920s* (Harmondsworth: Penguin, 1978).

Phillips, Marion, *Women and the Miners' Lockout: The Story of the Women's Committee for the Relief of the Miners' Wives and Children* (London: Labour Party Publishing Co., 1927).

Pilgrim Trust, *Men Without Work: A Report* (Cambridge: Cambridge University Press, 1938).

Rice, Margery Spring, *Working Class Wives: Their Health and Conditions* (Harmondsworth: Penguin, 1939).

MEMOIRS

Andrews, Elizabeth, *A Woman's Work is Never Done* (Ystrad Rhondda: Cymric Democrat Publishing Society, 1957). See also new edition, edited and introduced by Ursula Masson (Dinas Powys: Honno, 2006).

Baldwin, Bernard, *Mountain Ash Remembered* (Cowbridge: D. Brown, 1984).

Barnes, David, *Black Mountains: The Recollections of a Welsh Miner* (Talybont: Y Lolfa, 2002).

Chilcott, Vernon, *They Made Light of their Darkness* (Blaengarw: Valleys Autobiography Project, 1994).

Coombes, B. L., *These Poor Hands: The Autobiography of a Miner Working in South Wales* (London: Gollancz, 1939).

Davies, Edith, *The Innocent Years: The Story of My Childhood in Ynysybwl* (Creigiau: T. Lewis, 1995).

Davies, Walter H., *The Right Place – The Right Time (Memories of boyhood days in a Welsh Mining Community)* (Llandybie: Llyfrau'r Dryw, 1972).

Davies, Mark (ed.), *The Valleys Autobiography: A People's History of the Garw, Llynfi and Ogmore Valleys* (Mid Glamorgan: Valley and Vale, 1992).

Griffiths, Winifred, *One Woman's Story* (Rhondda: Ron Jones Publications, 1980).

Horner, Arthur, *Incorrigible Rebel* (London: MacGibbon & Kee, 1960).

May, William C., *Recollections of a County Policeman* (Stockwell: Ilfracombe, 1979).

Paynter, Will, *My Generation* (London: George Allen and Unwin, 1972).

Radcliffe, Grafton, *Back to Blaengarw* (Mid Glamorgan: Valleys Autobiography Project, 1994).

Viscountess Rhondda, *This Was My World* (London: Macmillan, 1933).

Russell, Dora, *The Tamarisk Tree: My Quest for Liberty and Love* (London: Virago, 1977).

Wade, Mary, *To The Miner Born* (London: Oriel, 1984).

SECONDARY SOURCES

Books and chapters of books

Arnot, Robin Page, *The General Strike, May 1926: Its Origin and History* (Wakefield: Labour Research Department, 1975).

Bachetta, Aldo and Glyn Rudd, *Porth and Rhondda Fach* (Stroud: Chalfont, 1996).

Barker, R. J., *Christ in the Valley of Unemployment* (London: Hodder and Stoughton, 1937).

Beddoe, Deirdre, *Back to Home and Duty: Women Between the Wars* (London: Pandora, 1989).

Beddoe, Deirdre, *Out of the Shadows: A History of Women in Twentieth-Century Wales* (Cardiff: University of Wales Press, 2000).

Benson, John, *The Working Class in Britain 1850–1939* (London: I. B. Tauris, 2003).

❹ Bingham, Adrian, *Gender, Modernity and the Popular Press in Interwar Britain* (Oxford: Oxford University Press, 2004).

Berger, S., A. Croll and N. Laporte (eds), *Towards a Comparative History of Coalfield Societies* (Aldershot: Ashgate, 2005).

Bloomfield, Stuart, 'The General Strike and Lockout of 1926 in the Northern Part of the Rhymney Valley', in *Environmental Studies in the Rhymney Valley* (Rhymney Valley: Rhymney Valley District Council, 1982).

Boston, Sarah, *Women Workers and the Trade Unions* (London: Davis-Poynter, 1980).

Bruley, Sue, 'A Woman's Right to Work? The Role of Women in the Unemployed Movement Between the Wars', in Sybil Oldfield (ed.), *This Working Day World: Women's Lives and Culture(s) in Britain 1914–1945* (London: Taylor and Francis, 1994).

Bruley, Sue, *Women in Britain Since 1900* (Basingstoke: Macmillan, 1999).

Carr, Griselda, *Pit Women: Coal Communities in Northern England in the Early Twentieth Century* (London: Merlin, 2001).

Chinn, Carl, *They Worked All Their Lives: Women of the Urban Poor in England 1880–1939* (Manchester: Manchester University Press, 1988).

Crawford, Elizabeth, *The Women's Suffrage Movement: A Reference Guide 1866–1928* (London: Routledge, 1999).

Davies, Idris, *The Angry Summer: A Poem of 1926*, introduction and notes by Tony Conran (Cardiff: University of Wales Press, 1993).

Davies, Idris, *Gwalia Deserta* (London: J. M. Dent, 1938).

Davies, Paul, *A. J. Cook* (Manchester: Manchester University Press, 1987).

Davies, Walter H., *Blithe Ones* (Port Talbot: Alun Books, 1979).

Dennis, N., et al., *Coal is our Life: An Analysis of a Yorkshire Mining Community* (London: Tavistock, 1956).

Dudink, Stefan, et al., *Masculinities in Politics and War, Gendering Modern History* (Manchester: Manchester University Press, 2004).

Evans, Chris, *The Industrial and Social History of Seven Sisters* (Cardiff: Cymric Federation Press, 1964).

Farman, Christopher, *The General Strike, May, 1926* (St Albans: Panther, 1974).

Foot, Michael, *Aneurin Bevan 1897–1945* (London: Granada Publishing, 1975; first published by MacGibbon & Kee, 1962).

Francis, Hywel, 'The Secret World of the South Wales Miner: The Relevance of Oral History', in Dai Smith (ed.), *A People and a Proletariat: Essays in the History of Wales 1780–1980* (London: Pluto Press, 1980).

Francis, Hywel and Dai Smith, *The Fed: A History of South Wales Miners in the Twentieth Century* (London: Lawrence and Wishart, 1980; republished Cardiff: University of Wales Press, 1998).

Gallie, Menna, *Strike for a Kingdom* (London: Gollancz, 1959; republished Dinas Powys: Honno, 2003, with an introduction by Angela V. John).

Gilbert, David, *Class, Community and Collective Action: Social Change in Two British Coalfields 1850–1926* (Oxford: Clarendon Press, 1992).

Gildart, K., D. Howell and N. Kirk (eds) *Dictionary of Labour Biography*, XI (Basingstoke: Palgrave, 2003).

Giles, Judy, *Women, Identity and Private Life in Britain 1900–1950* (London: Macmillan, 1995).

Ginzberg, Eli, *A World Without Work* (London: Transcation, 1991; first published New York: Harper and Bros, 1942, under the title *Grass on the Slagheaps*).

Gittins, Diana, *Fair Sex, Family Size and Structure, 1900–1939* (London: Hutchinson, 1982).

Goronwy-Roberts, Marian, *A Woman of Vision: A Life of Marion Phillips, MP* (Wrexham: Bridge Books, 2000).

Graves, Pamela, *Labour Women: Women in British Working Class Politics 1918–1939* (Cambridge: Cambridge University Press, 1994).

Gullace, Nicoletta, *The Blood of Our Sons: Men, Women and the Renegotiation of Citizenship During the Great War* (Basingstoke: Palgrave, 2002).

Hallas, Duncan and Chris Harman, *Days of Hope: The General Strike of 1926* (London: Socialist Workers Party, 1981).

Hannam, June and Karen Hunt, *Socialist Women: Britain 1880s to 1920s* (London: Routledge, 2002).

Herbert, Trevor and Gareth E. Jones (eds), *Wales Between the Wars* (Cardiff: University of Wales Press, 1988).

Hinton, James, *Labour and Socialism: A History of the British Labour Movement 1867–1974* (Brighton: Wheatsheaf, 1983).

John, Angela V. (ed.), *Our Mothers' Land: Chapters in Welsh Women's History, 1800–1939* (Cardiff: University of Wales Press, 1991).

Joannou, Maroula, 'Reclaiming the Romance: Ellen Wilkinson's *Clash* and the Cultural Legacy of Socialist-Feminism', in *Heart of the Heartless World: Essays in Cultural Resistance in Memory of Margot Heinemann* (London: Pluto, 1995).

Jones, Bill and Chris Williams, *B. L. Coombes* (Cardiff: University of Wales Press, 1999).

Johnson, Richard (ed.), *Making Histories: Studies in History-Writing and Politics* (London: Hutchinson and the Centre for Contemporary Cultural Studies, 1982).

Jones, Gareth E., *People, Protest and Politics: Welsh History Teaching Materials* (Swansea: Welsh Office Education Department, 1986).

Jones, Gwyn, *Times Like These* (London: Gollancz, 1979).

Jones, Lewis, *Cwmardy: The Story of a Welsh Mining Valley* (London: Lawrence and Wishart, 1937).

Jones, Lewis, *We live* (London: Lawrence and Wishart, 1939).

Keen, R. G., *Old Maesteg and the Bridgend Valleys in Photographs* (Barry: Stewart Williams, 1979).

Kessler-Harris, Alice, *Gendering Labour History* (Urbana: University of Illinois, 2007).

Kingsford, Peter, *The Hunger Marches in Britain 1920–1940* (London: Lawrence and Wishart, 1982).

Kingsley Kent, Susan, *Making Peace: The Reconstruction of Gender in Interwar Britain* (Princeton: Princeton University Press, 1993).

Knowles, K. G. J. C., *Strikes: a study in industrial conflict, with special reference to the British experience between 1911 and 1947* (Oxford: University of Oxford, 1952).

Laybourn, Keith, *The General Strike, 1926* (Huddersfield: Huddersfield Polytechnic, Yorkshire, 1990).

Lewenhak, Sheila, *Women and Trade Unions: An Outline History of Women in the British Trade Union Movement* (London, 1977).

Lewis, Richard, *Leaders and Teachers: Adult Education and the Challenge of Labour in South Wales 1906–1940* (Cardiff: University of Wales Press, 1993).

Lieven, Michael, *Senghennydd: The Universal Pit Village 1890–1930* (Llandysul: Gomer, 1994).

Light, Alison, *Forever England* (London: Routledge, 1991).

Llewellyn, Richard, *How Green Was My Valley* (London: Penguin, 1951; first published 1939).

Loach, Loretta, 'We'll Be here Right to the End ... And After: Women in the Miners' Strike', in Huw Beynon (ed.), *Digging Deeper: Issues in the Miners' Strike* (London: Verso, 1985).

Marquand, Hilary, *The Second Industrial Survey of Wales*, 3 (Cardiff: University Press Board, 1937).

McIlroy, J., A. Campbell and K. Gildart (eds), *Industrial Politics and the 1926 Mining Lockout: The Struggle for Dignity* (Cardiff: University of Wales Press, 2004).

MacIntyre, Stuart, *Little Moscows: Communism and Working Class Militancy in Interwar Britain* (London: Croom Helm, 1980).

Milkman, Ruth (ed.), *Women, Work and Protest: A Century of US*

Women's Labour History (London: Routledge and Kegan Paul, 1985).

Miller, Jill, *You Can't Kill the Spirit: Women in a Welsh Mining Valley* (London: Women's Press, 1986).

Mor-O'Brien, Anthony, *The Autobiography of Edmund Stonelake* (Mid Glamorgan, 1981).

Morgan, John E., *A Village Workers' Council: A Short History of the Lady Windsor Lodge* (Pontypridd: Celtic Press, 1956).

Morgan, Kenneth O., *Rebirth of a Nation: Wales 1880–1980* (Oxford: Oxford University Press, 1981).

Morris, Margaret, *The General Strike* (Harmondsworth: Penguin, 1976).

Naylor, Barrie, *Quakers in the Rhondda 1926–1986* (Chepstow: Maes-yr-haf Educational Trust, 1986).

Noel, Gerard, *The Great Lock-out of 1926* (London: Constable, 1976).

Perks, Robert and Alistair Thomson, *The Oral History Reader* (London: Routledge, 1998).

Phillips, Gordon, *The General Strike: The Politics of Industrial Conflict* (London: Weidenfeld and Nicolson, 1976).

Perkins, Anne, *A Very British Strike 3–12th May 1926* (Basingstoke: Macmillan, 2006).

Renshaw, Patrick, *The General Strike* (London: Methuen, 1975).

Roper, Michael and John Tosh, *Manful Assertions: Masculinities in Britain Since 1800* (London: Routledge, 1991).

Rowbotham, Sheila, *Women, Resistance and Revolution: A History of Women and Revolution in the Modern World* (London: Allen Lane, 1972).

Rowbotham, Sheila, *Hidden From History: 300 years of women's oppression and the fight against it* (London: Pluto, 1973).

Rowbotham, Sheila, 'More Than Just a Memory: Some Political Implications of Women's Involvement in the Miners' Strike, 1984–5, Shiela Rowbotham interviews Jean McGrindle', *Feminist Review*, 23, 1986.

Savage, Michael, *The Dynamics of Working Class Politics: The Labour Movement in Preston 1880–1940* (Cambridge: Cambridge University Press, 1987).

Scott, Joan, *Gender and the Politics of History* (New York: Columbia, 1991).

Seddon, Vicky (ed.), *The Cutting Edge: Women and the Pit Strike* (London: Lawrence and Wishart, 1986).

Skelley, Jeffrey, *The General Strike 1926* (London: Lawrence and Wishart, 1976).

Stead, Jean, *Never the Same Again, Women and the Miners' Strike 1984–5* (London: Women's Press, 1984–5).

Stephens, M. (ed.), *Rhondda Anthology* (Bridgend: Seren Books, 1993).

Summerfield, Penny, *Reconstructing Women's Wartime Lives: Discourse and Subjectivity in Oral Histories of the Second World War* (Manchester: Manchester University Press, 1998).

Tanner, Duncan, et al. (eds), *The Labour Party in Wales 1900–2000* (Cardiff: University of Wales Press, 2000).

Tebbutt, Melanie *Women's Talk? A social history of 'gossip' in working class neighbourhoods, 1880–1960* (Aldershot: Scholar Press, 1997).

Thomson, Alistair, *Anzac Memories, Living with the Legend* (Oxford: Oxford University Press, 1994).

Thompson, Paul, *The Voice of the Past: Oral History*, 1978, third edition (Oxford: Oxford University Press, 2000).

Thane, Pat, 'The Women of the British Labour Party and Feminism, 1906–1945', in Harold Smith (ed.), *British Feminism in the Twentieth Century* (Basingstoke: Macmillan, 1990).

Thompson, Steven, *Unemployment, Poverty and Health in Interwar South Wales* (Cardiff: University of Wales Press, 2006).

Waddington, David, et al., *Split at the Seams? Community, Continuity and Change After the 1984–5 Coal Dispute* (Milton Keynes: Open University Press, 1991).

Welsh Campaign for Civil and Public Liberties and NUM (South Wales Area), *Striking Back* (Cardiff: Cymric Federation Press, 1985).

West, Guida and Rosa Blumberg, *Women in Social Protest* (Oxford: Oxford University Press, 1990).

White, Carol and Siân Rhiannon Williams, *Struggle or Starve* (Honno: Dinas Powys, 1998).

Wilkinson, Ellen, *Clash* (London: Virago, 1989; first published London 1929).

Williams, Gwyn A., *When Was Wales? A History of the Welsh* (Harmondsworth: Penguin, 1985).

Williams, Chris, *Capitalism, Community and Conflict: The South Wales Coalfield 1898–1947* (Cardiff: University of Wales Press, 1998).

Williams, Chris, *Democratic Rhondda: Politics and Society 1885–1951* (Cardiff: University of Wales Press, 1996).

Williams, Mari, *A Forgotten Army: Female Munition Workers of South Wales 1939–1945* (Cardiff: University of Wales Press, 2002).

Zweig, Ferdynand, *Men in Pits* (London: Gollancz, 1948).

Articles

Crook, Rosemary, 'Tidy women: women in the Rhondda between the wars', *Oral History*, 10/2, 1982.

David, Wayne, 'The Labour Party and the "exclusion" of the Communists; the case of the Ogmore Divisional Labour Party in the 1920s', *Llafur*, 3/4, 1983.

Davies, David, 'Guardians of the Needy Found Wanting: A Study of Social Division during the Industrial Crisis of 1926', *Carmarthenshire Historian*, XIX, 1982.

Douglas, Margaret, 'Women, God and Birth Control: The First Hospital Birth control clinic, Abertillery, 1925', *Llafur*, 6/4, 1995.

Evans, Neil, '"South Wales has been Roused as Never Before": Marching Against the Means test, 1934–1936', in D. Howell and K. Morgan (eds) *Crime, Protest and Police in Modern British Society: Essays in Memory of David I. V. Jones* (Cardiff: University of Wales Press, 1999).

Evans, Neil and Dot Jones, 'A Blessing for the Miners' Wife: The campaign for pithead baths in the south Wales coalfield 1908–1950', *Llafur*, 6, 1994.

Fisher, Kate, '"Clearing up Misconceptions": The Campaign to set up Birth Control Clinics in South Wales Between the Wars', *Welsh History Review*, 19/1, June 1998.

Francis, Hywel and Gareth Rees, '"No surrender in the Valleys": The 1984–5 Miners' Strike in South Wales', *Llafur*, 5/2, 1989.

Gier-Viskovatoff, Jaclyn J. and Abigail Porter, 'Women of the British Coalfields on Strike in 1926 and 1984: Documenting Lives Using Oral History and Photography', *Frontiers, Journal of Women's Studies*, 19/2, 1998.

Greenfield, J., et al., 'Fashioning Masculinity: *Men Only*, Consumption and the Development of Marketing in the 1930s', *Twentieth Century History*, 10/4, 1999.

Gregory, R., *The Miners and British Politics 1906–1914* (Oxford: Oxford University Press, 1968).

Hall, Valerie G., 'Contrasting Female Identities: Women in Coal Mining Communities in Northumberland, England, 1900–1939, *Journal of Women's History*, Summer, 2001.

Harkell, Gina, 'The Migration of Mining Families to the Kent Coalfield Between the Wars', *Oral History*, 6/1, 1978.

Harrison, Brian, 'Class and Gender in Modern British Labour History', *Past and Present*, 124, 1989.

Haywood, Ian, '"Never Again?" Ellen Wilkinson's *Clash* and the Feminization of the General Strike', *Literature and History*, 8/2, Autumn 1999.

Jeremy, Paul, 'Life on Circular 703: The Crisis of Destitution in the South Wales Coalfield during the Lockout of 1926', *Llafur*, 2/2, 1977.

John, Angela, 'A Miner Struggle? Women's Protests in Welsh Mining History', *Llafur*, 4/1, 1984.

Lieven, Mike, 'A New History of the South Wales Coalfield?', *Llafur*, 8/3, 2002.

Morgan, Alun, 'Bedlinog: Glimpses of a Pre-war Society', *Glamorgan Historian*, 11, 1975.

Morgan, Stefan, 'Stand By Your Man: Wives, Women and Feminism During the miner's Strike 1984–5', *Llafur*, 9/2, 2005.

O'Leary, Paul, 'Masculine Histories: Gender and the Social History of Modern Wales', *Welsh History Review*, 22/2, 2004.

Passerini, Luisa, 'Work, Ideology and Consensus under Italian Fascism', *History Workshop Journal*, 8, 1979.

Portelli, Alessandro, 'The Peculiarities of Oral History', *History Workshop Journal*, 12, 1981.

Scates, Bruce, 'Mobilising Manhood: Gender and the Great Strike in Australia and Aotearoa/New Zealand', *Gender and History*, 9/2, 1997.

Smith, Dai, 'The Future of Coalfield History in South Wales', *Morgannwg: Journal of the Glamorgan History Society*, XIX, 1975.

Smith, Dai, 'Tonypandy 1910: Definitions of Community', *Past and Present*, 87, 1980.

Thompson, Steven, '"That beautiful summer of severe austerity": Health, Diet and the Working-Class Domestic Economy in South Wales in 1926', *Welsh History Review*, 21/3, 2003.

Various contributors, '1926 Remembered and Revealed', *Llafur*, 2/2, 1977.

Walsh, Margaret (ed.), *Working Out Gender: Perspectives from Labour History* (Aldershot: Ashgate, 1999).

Ward, Stephanie, '"Sit down to starve or stand up to live": Community, Protest and the Means Test in the Rhondda valleys, 1931–1939', *Llafur*, 9/2, 2005.

Webster, Charles, 'Healthy or hungry thirties', *History Workshop*, 13, 1982.

Williams, Huw, 'Merthyr Tydfil and the General Strike of 1926', *Merthyr Historian*, 1978.

Williams, Raymond, *Border Country* (London: Hogarth Press, 1988; first published 1960).

Williams, Siân Rhiannon, 'The Bedwellty Board of Guardians and the Default Act of 1927', *Llafur*, 2/4, 1979.

Zweiniger-Bargielowska, Ina, 'Miners' Militancy: A Study of Four South Wales Collieries During the Middle of the Twentieth Century', *Welsh History Review*, 116, 1992.

Zweiniger-Bargielowska, Ina, 'South Wales Miners' Attitudes

Towards Nationalization: An Essay in Oral History', *Llafur*, 6, 1994.

Theses

Baggs, Christopher, *The Miners' Libraries of South Wales from the 1860s to 1939*, PhD, University of Wales, 1995.

Bingham, Adrian, *Debating Gender: Approaches to femininity and masculinity in the popular national daily press in interwar Britain*, DPhil, Oxford, 2002.

Bruley, Susan, *Socialism and Feminism in the Communist Party of Great Britain, 1920–1939*, PhD, London School of Economics, 1980.

Collins, Clare, *Women and Labour Politics in Britain 1893–1932*, PhD, London School of Economics, 1991.

Demont, Susan E., *Tredegar and Aneurin Bevan: A Society and Its Political Articulation 1890–1929*, PhD, University of Wales, 1990.

Newman, Lowri, *A Distinctive Brand of Politics: Women in the South Wales Labour Party 1918–1939*, MPhil, University of Glamorgan, 2003.

Price, Wyn, *Aspects of the Urban History of the Garw Valley c.1870–1914*, PhD, University of Wales, 2001.

Sinclair, Lynn, *Suppressed and Passive? A Refocused History of Lanarkshire Women, 1920–1939*, PhD, University of Strathclyde, 2005.

INDEX

INDEX